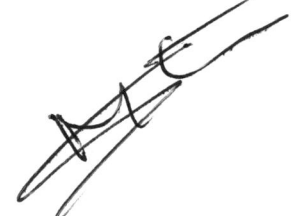

Statistics and Computer Methods in BASIC

Statistics and Computer Methods in BASIC

J. D. LEE

Senior Lecturer in Chemistry and Computing
Loughborough University of Technology

and

T. D. LEE

Cambridge

VAN NOSTRAND REINHOLD COMPANY

New York — Cincinnati — Toronto — London — Melbourne

**Published by Van Nostrand Reinhold Company Ltd.,
Molly Millars Lane, Wokingham, Berkshire, England**

*Published in 1982 by Van Nostrand Reinhold Company,
135 West 50th Street, New York, NY 10020, USA*

*Van Rostrand Reinhold Limited,
1410 Birchmount Road, Scarborough, Ontario, M1P 2E7,
Canada*

*Van Nostrand Reinhold Australia Pty. Limited,
17 Queen Street, Mitcham, Victoria 3132, Australia*

Library of Congress Cataloging in Publication Data

Lee, J. D. (John David), 1931–
  Statistics and computer methods in BASIC.

  Includes index.
  1. Statistics—Data processing. 2. Basic.
(Computer program language) I. Lee, T. D.
(Timothy D.) II. Title.
QA276.4.L43   001.64′24   81-11378
ISBN   0-442-30474-9   AACR2
ISBN   0-442-30475-7 (pbk.)

Printed and bound in Great Britain by the Alden Press, Oxford

Preface

This book is aimed at a readership who are primarily concerned with acquiring an introductory grasp of statistical procedures for inference from scientific experiments and observations which are common to all scientific disciplines studied up to and including the undergraduate level.

The first half of the book covers a number of commonly encountered elementary statistical topics, covering errors, averages and the spread of results, distributions, tests of dissimilarity (chi-squared), comparison of samples both large and small (F- and t-tests), and correlation coefficients. This is followed by four chapters dealing with some commonly encountered numerical techniques for curve fitting of straight lines and polynomials, solving equations and calculating areas. Finally, in the last chapter, some techniques for sorting data are described. The choice of what to include and what to leave out is based on many years of personal experience of the types of problems encountered by students, rather than the syllabus of any particular examining body.

The aim of this book is to cover these topics in a readable manner. Statistics and probability are essentially sophisticated subjects, and an understandable down-to-earth treatment that will satisfy the professional mathematician is well nigh impossible. We have deliberately avoided jargon such as univariate statistics, bivariate statistics and non-parametric statistics, since these tend to intimidate beginners. The techniques are introduced by means of detailed worked examples, and in a conflict between mathematical rigour and readability, we have chosen to err on the side of readability. Where appropriate, chapters include exercises; solutions giving some of the intermediate steps are given at the back of the book, rather than just giving answers.

Since we are in the middle of a computer revolution it is appropriate that a computer program is provided with each method. These may be used without any programming knowledge provided that the reader has access to an interactive computer which supports BASIC. The programs themselves are coded in an elementary subset of BASIC, which should facilitate their implementation on a wide variety of computers. No attempt is made to teach BASIC programming since this is covered in many other books. Program descriptions are provided, which require the reader to have some familiarity with the language. Considerable care has been invested in the development and testing of the computer programs. These are organised to yield numerically accurate results, and contain many error checks to make them tolerant and robust with respect to accidentally incorrectly typed or pathological data. The programs are fairly long, partly because of these features, and partly because they include extensive provisions for editing (checking and correcting) the input data. These features make the programs particularly easy to use, especially when the amount of data is substantial. Statistics programs should never be used without an understanding of the data and the statistical procedures involved, otherwise the results and conclusions may be invalid. There are too many cases of statistics being misapplied and abused. It is worth remembering the perhaps cynical, but nevertheless true comment attributed to Disraeli: 'There are three kinds of lies: lies, damned lies and statistics'.

Our most sincere thanks are due to a number of friends and colleagues whose advice and helpful criticisms have been invaluable in the preparation and checking of the manuscript. These include Professor J. N. Miller, Dr A. G. Briggs, Mr S. Sherman, Mr J. R. Buxton, Dr B. Negus, Mr M. J. Hunt and Mr J. Fernandiez. Any errors which remain are ours not theirs, and we will try to correct errors where they are shown to be such.

J. D. Lee
T. D. Lee

April 1981

Contents

Introduction

The origin of modern statistics can be traced to the mid-eighteenth century, arising from two unrelated areas of interest, namely games of chance and political science. The interest in games of chance was largely motivated by gambling, and led to the mathematical treatment of *probability* and *errors* of measurement. The political science interest arose from the need to describe and summarise numerical data on political units such as countries, provinces or towns. This now forms what is known as *descriptive statistics* in which data are represented by graphs, histograms, bar charts or pie charts, and no attempt is made to infer anything which goes beyond the original data.

There has been an enormous growth in interest in statistics during the later part of the twentieth century for two main reasons. Firstly, the amount of data which are collected, processed and disseminated has increased astronomically. Secondly, many branches of science and business have become increasingly quantitative. The data collected are generally only a sample, and it is required to make *statistical inferences* which go beyond the collected data, and refer to the whole population. There has thus been a shift from descriptive to *inductive statistics*.

It is essential that the data collected in a sample are not biased since this will invalidate any inferences made. A classic example of the failure to do this was a poll of voting intentions in the United States presidential elections in 1936. A random sample of telephone owners were questioned, ignoring the fact that many lower income families could not afford a telephone! The poll was highly biased, and the wrong result was forecast! Similar situations may occur in the collection of any sample data, and to avoid any bias the utmost care should be taken to gather data randomly. It must be remembered that no amount of fancy mathematics or statistical tests can counteract the effects of badly planned surveys or experiments. This is often stated as the GIGO principle (Garbage In Garbage Out). Since all statistical procedures take numbers in as data and produce a final number or numbers, an understanding of both the procedures and the data types is essential to avoid making useless calculations and drawing erroneous conclusions. The types of data are as follows:

(i) Random samples drawn from a large population of a single variable, for example measuring the heights of a set of men. From such data it is possible to calculate the mean, median, mode, range, variance, standard deviation, coefficient of variance and Pearson's coefficient of skewness as described in Chapter 2.

(ii) An ordered list of a single variable, for example data for the speed of a dragster car measured every second. This type of data may be used to find the area under the curve, which in this case gives the distance travelled. This is discussed in Chapter 11.

(iii) A set of observed *frequencies* for comparison with some model distribution, or less commonly with another set of observed frequencies. This is explained in Chapter 5.

(iv) Two totally independent random samples, not necessarily having the same number of values in each sample. This is equivalent to having two sets of data of type (i), for example measuring the heights of a set of men and the heights of a set of women. The two sets may be compared to see if they differ significantly—see Chapter 6.

(v) Two sets of related values, usually called x and y, where each x value corresponds to a unique y value, for example the heights and weights of a set of men. Such data are used in Chapters 7 and 9.

The book is organised into the following broad categories:

Chapters 1–7   Elementary statistics
Chapters 8–9   Curve fitting
Chapters 10–11 Numerical techniques (solving equations and areas)
Chapter 12   Sorting techniques

The chapters in this book are largely self-contained. Each begins with a summary, and ten contain one or more computer programs written in BASIC. However, there is some interdependence of chapters, and Chapter 1 (Errors) and Chapter 2 (Average and spread of results) are widely used throughout the text and should be read by those not familiar with this elementary statistical material. It is not necessary to read all of the chapters in order, with the following exceptions. Chapter 5 (Test of dissimilarity) and Chapter 6 (Comparison of two samples) both use distributions discussed in Chapter 4. Chapter 8 (Straight line fitting) uses Pearson's correlation coefficient which is fully discussed in Chapter 7. Chapter 9 (Curve fitting) uses some of the equations from Chapter 8 (Straight line fitting). This chapter also requires an understanding of matrix manipulation.

The computer programs are written in an elementary subset of BASIC which should be implemented with little or no change on a wide variety of interactive computers which support a floating point version of BASIC and permit the printing of 72 columns of output on a line. The BASIC language was chosen because it is the most widely used interactive language, and is implemented on both mainframe and microcomputers. To improve the readability of the program listings, loops have been indented as is common for ALGOL. The programs are robust with respect to incorrect or pathological data, and have been extensively tested by a large number of users on a variety of machines. Generally they provide facilities for correcting wrongly typed data, and are thought to be almost 'student proof'. The numerical methods used have been chosen with care to preserve the maximum accuracy.

The following points not covered by the ANSI Minimal BASIC standard specification may need attention by the user:

1. In these programs strings are DIMensioned in the first line of each program, e.g.

   10 DIM I$(3)

   This is intended to reserve space for a maximum of three characters in the string I$. On some computers it in fact reserves space for four strings: I$(0), I$(1), I$(2) and I$(3), each of which may contain a series of characters. On computers implementing the latter form it is better and will save space if the string declarations are removed from the DIMension statement.

2. Certain versions of BASIC including TRS-80 level II, RML 9K and Xitan disc BASIC should have the string declarations removed from the DIMension statements as above, and instead they require a CLEAR statement to reserve space for all the characters in all of the strings used.

3. The spacing of the printout produced by the programs may vary slightly from machine to machine because of slightly different implementations of TAB and , in PRINT statements.

4. Certain of the programs use an IF statement to jump out of a FOR . . . NEXT loop prematurely. This procedure works with most versions of BASIC, but some including Xitan

disc BASIC and North Star BASIC may report a stack error. To cure this the offending IF statement should be changed to read

IF . . . THEN EXIT line number

instead of IF . . . THEN line number

5. Sample runs are provided to give sample data for testing the programs. All user input is preceded by a question mark and a space.

1

Errors

Accuracy and Precision

Experimental results are always subject to errors, and in assessing the reliability of the final result the accuracy and precision should be considered. Accuracy may be expressed as how closely the experimental result agrees with the true or most probable value. In contrast, precision may be defined as how closely a set of measurements of the same quantity agree with each other. Thus accuracy expresses the correctness of a measurement whereas precision describes the reproducibility of the measurement.

These two concepts are illustrated in Table 1.1 by the results of four separate students, who each determined the density of a piece of glass three times. The true density of the glass is 2600 kg m^{-3}. The results may be summar-

ised in Table 1.2. Two measures of precision are the standard deviation and the coefficient of variation, both of which are discussed in Chapter 2.

Table 1.2

	Accurate	Inaccurate
Precise	Student 1 2590 ± 10	Student 2 2450 ± 10
Imprecise	Student 3 2610 ± 150	Student 4 2750 ± 130

Significant Figures and Rounding

An understanding of significant figures is essential in order to avoid claiming an unreasonably high or low accuracy in a *final* result. The number of significant figures in a value is the total number of digits in the value excluding leading zeros (see Table 1.3).

Table 1.1

Student	Reading 1	Reading 2	Reading 3	Average and spread
1	2580	2590	2600	2590 ± 10
2	2440	2460	2450	2450 ± 10
3	2610	2760	2460	2610 ± 150
4	2880	2620	2750	2750 ± 130

Table 1.3

Value	Number of significant figures
3.142	4
0.020	2
12.020	5
0.012 020	5

An alternative way of working out the number of significant figures is to express the value in standard (scientific) form as used on many calculators. The number of significant figures is the number of decimal places plus one (see Table 1.4).

Quantities which are measured should be recorded with only one uncertain figure. Thus if a measurement is subject to error in the third decimal place, then only three decimal figures may be claimed. Furthermore the implication of claiming a value of 3.142 (with three decimal figures), is that the true value is closer to 3.142 than either 3.141 or 3.143. Thus

Table 1.4

Value	Standard form	Decimal places	Significant figures
3.142	3.142×10^0	3	4
0.020	2.0×10^{-2}	1	2
12.020	1.2020×10^1	4	5
0.012 020	1.2020×10^{-2}	4	5

$3.1415 \leqslant$ true value < 3.1425. It is important that no rounding of intermediate answers is performed when making calculations using measured quantities, since this would introduce additional and unnecessary errors. In contrast, the final answer should always be rounded to give one uncertain figure. The purpose of rounding is to remove inaccurate digits from a final answer so that all of the digits quoted are meaningful. Thus if a three significant figure answer is required, the three digit value closest to the calculated value should be given, for example

Table 1.5

Number of significant figures	Rounded value of π
6	3.141 59
5	3.141 6
4	3.142
3	3.14
2	3.1
1	3

$\pi \simeq 3.141\ 592\ 653\ 6$ (Table 1.5). It can be seen that rounding a number amounts to truncating it to the appropriate number of digits, except when the first truncated digit is 5 or more then 1 is added to the least significant digit retained.

Classification of Errors

The types of errors which may affect an experimental result may be conveniently divided into three groups: gross accidental errors, systematic errors and random errors.

Gross Accidental Errors

These are large irregular errors which are caused by *incorrect* experimental technique or calculation. These include:

(i) weighing a damp sample rather than a dry sample;
(ii) weighing a sample which is still warm (the weight will be affected by convection currents);
(iii) using a 20 ml pipette inadvertently when requiring a 25 ml pipette;
(iv) using the wrong value for a shunt on a galvanometer;
(v) mismatching units, e.g. density in g per cc instead of kg m^{-3}, temperature in °C rather than K, or solutions whose concentrations are expressed as normal rather than molar;
(vi) transcription errors;
(vii) errors in calculation—particularly common with the use of electronic calculators.

Systematic Errors

These consistently give a result which is wrong by a fixed amount. Some examples are as follows:

(i) Instrumental errors such as the zero incorrectly adjusted, or calibration errors (particularly thermometers, pipettes, barometers, voltmeters).

(ii) Reagent errors. A sample used as a primary standard may be impure, or may have been made up to the wrong concentration of solution.

(iii) Personal errors, for example parallax if a voltmeter is always viewed in an identical way from the side, or if a burette is consistently viewed from beneath. Some experiments involve detecting a colour change (titrations or colour dyeing), and people observe colours differently.

Random Errors

If the same observer makes the same measurement repeatedly, under apparently identical conditions, it will be found that slight variations occur. These are random errors, and are caused by unknown factors changing without the observer being aware of this. Some examples of such factors are small changes in room temperature, pressure or humidity, draughts, fluctuations in the mains electricity supply, vibrations, stray magnetic fields or parallax errors arising from reading an instrument from differing angles. The slight variation in the level to which a pipette or a standard flask is filled with a solution is another source of random error.

If a sufficiently large number of measurements are taken, the average value obtained will be close to the true value since positive and negative errors are equally likely, and will on average cancel. Furthermore the distribution of random errors will be approximately *normal*. Such a distribution is shown in Fig. 1.1. An alternative name for this distribution is Gaussian.

Figure 1.1 shows that small errors occur much more frequently than large errors. Since there is an equal chance of obtaining a positive error and a negative error, the curve is symmetrical, and the mean error is zero.

The horizontal or error axis of Fig. 1.1 is calibrated in terms of σ, where σ is the standard deviation of the population of measurements. The standard deviation is a

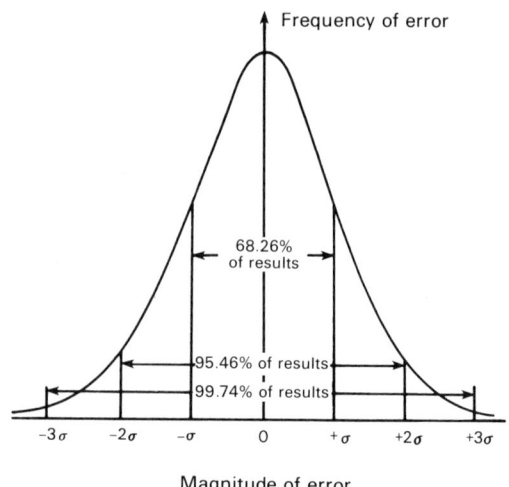

Fig. 1.1 *Normal* distribution curve.

measure of the spread of the measurements. Thus a wide spread of results yields a large standard deviation and closely grouped results give a small standard deviation. The standard deviation is estimated as

$$\text{Estimated } \sigma = \sqrt{\frac{\text{sum of errors squared}}{\text{number of measurements} - 1}}$$

This is fully described in Chapter 2.

Figure 1.1 also shows that 68.26% of the errors lie within $\pm$ one standard deviation, 95.46% of the errors lie within $\pm$ two standard deviations and 99.74% of the errors lie within $\pm$ three standard deviations for a normal distribution. The word normal has a precise mathematical meaning, and the area under a normal curve is tabulated in Appendix 4. The normal curve is used together with the standard deviation to calculate confidence limits as mentioned later.

If there are only a small number of measurements then the normal distribution is not adequate for this purpose. This problem was overcome by Student in 1908 by using the *t*-distribution when the number of measurements was small. ('Student' is a pseudonym for W. S. Gosset, *Biometrika*, 1908, **6,** 1.) The *t*-distribution tends towards the normal distribution as the number of terms becomes large, as can be seen in Appendix 6. (In this context the number of degrees of freedom is equal to the number of measurements minus one.)

How to Avoid or Reduce the Effects of Errors

Gross accidental errors are completely avoidable by care in experimental technique. Transcription of numbers should be avoided wherever possible by recording directly into the laboratory notebook. Repeating the experiment generally indicates the erroneous value.

Systematic errors cannot be detected from a single experiment, no matter how often the experiment is replicated using the same equipment and apparatus. The only way of detecting these errors is to repeat the experiment using a different set of apparatus and different reagents.

Random errors arise from causes beyond the control of the experimenter, and consequently cannot be avoided. Since these errors are just as likely to give a low reading as a high reading, their effect can be reduced by taking many readings and averaging the results. The average result will then be close to the true result provided that gross accidental errors and systematic errors are insignificant.

Ways of Quantifying Errors

Two common ways of expressing the magnitude of the errors are (i) to give the range of results, and (ii) to quote the standard deviation of the results.

Range

The range of the results is obtained by subtracting the smallest value obtained from the largest value. Frequently the result is expressed as average value $\pm \frac{1}{2}$ range. In many cases, the final result depends on readings of several quantities, each of which has an error term. The total error in the final result depends on the individual errors combined in an appropriate manner. The rules for combining errors are derived below.

Standard Deviation

The standard deviation of a set of results is harder to calculate than the range, but is more representative of the spread of results since it takes account of all of the results rather than just the upper and lower values as used for the range. It is possible to calculate 95% or 99% confidence limits (that is limits within which the true value is 95% or 99% certain to lie) from the standard deviation and either the normal distribution or the t-distribution. The way in which standard deviations and confidence limits are calculated is described in the next chapter. If the final result is based on more than one quantity then the standard deviation of the final result depends on the individual standard deviations combined in an appropriate manner. The rules for combining standard deviations are given in Chapter 2.

How to Combine Errors

Consider two terms x and y which are used to calculate the final result. The range of the x readings is $2\Delta x$, hence the value of x is quoted as $x \pm \Delta x$. Similarly the range of the y values is $2\Delta y$, hence the value of y is quoted as $y \pm \Delta y$. The way in which x and y are combined to give the final result determines the way in which the errors Δx and Δy are combined. The derivation of the four cases for addition, subtraction, multiplication and division is given below. Readers who are only interested in applying the rules should skip the derivations and move on to the summary.

Derivation of Rules for Combining Errors

(i) *Addition*   result $= x + y$

$$(x \pm \Delta x) + (y \pm \Delta y)$$

The largest possible result is

$$x+y+\Delta x+\Delta y = (x+y)+(\Delta x+\Delta y)$$

The smallest possible result is

$$x+y-\Delta x-\Delta y = (x+y)-(\Delta x+\Delta y)$$

The range of the results is thus $2(\Delta x+\Delta y)$. Hence the result should be expressed as

$$(x+y)\pm(\Delta x+\Delta y) \qquad (1)$$

(ii) *Subtraction*   result $=x-y$

$$(x\pm\Delta x)-(y\pm\Delta y)$$

The largest possible result is

$$x-y+\Delta x+\Delta y = (x-y)+(\Delta x+\Delta y)$$

The smallest possible result is

$$x-y-\Delta x-\Delta y = (x-y)-(\Delta x+\Delta y)$$

The range of the result is thus $2(\Delta x+\Delta y)$. Hence the result should be expressed as

$$(x-y)\pm(\Delta x+\Delta y) \qquad (2)$$

(iii) *Multiplication*   result $=x\cdot y$

$$(x\pm\Delta x)\cdot(y\pm\Delta y)$$
$$= xy\pm x\Delta y\pm y\Delta x\pm\Delta x\Delta y$$

The second order term $\Delta x\Delta y$ is ignored since it is very small

$$\simeq xy\pm x\Delta y\pm y\Delta x$$

The largest possible result is

$$\simeq xy+(|x\Delta y|+|y\Delta x|)$$

The smallest possible result is

$$\simeq xy-(|x\Delta y|+|y\Delta x|)$$

Hence the result should be expressed as

$$xy\pm(x\Delta y+y\Delta x) \qquad (3)$$

Rather than considering the *absolute* errors Δx and Δy it is convenient to consider the *relative* errors δx and δy, where

$$\delta x = |\Delta x/x| \quad \text{and} \quad \delta y = |\Delta y/y| \qquad (4)$$

Substituting δx and δy into Equation 3

$$= xy\pm(xy\delta y+xy\delta x)$$
$$= xy\pm xy(\delta x+\delta y) \qquad (5)$$

The relative error in the product is thus $(\delta x+\delta y)=$ the sum of the relative errors.

(iv) *Division*   result $=x/y$. To simplify the derivation, it is assumed that both x and y are positive.

$$(x\pm\Delta x)/(y\pm\Delta y)$$

The largest possible result is

$$\frac{x+\Delta x}{y-\Delta y}$$

Substituting for Δx and Δy using Equations 4,

$$\frac{x+x\delta x}{y-y\delta y} = \frac{x}{y}\left(\frac{1+\delta x}{1-\delta y}\right)$$

making the approximation that $1/(1-\delta y) \simeq 1+\delta y$ for small δy

$$\simeq \frac{x}{y}(1+\delta x)(1+\delta y)$$

$$= \frac{x}{y}(1+\delta x+\delta y+\delta x\delta y)$$

The second order term $\delta x\delta y$ is ignored since it is very small.

Largest possible result $\simeq \dfrac{x}{y}+\dfrac{x}{y}(\delta x+\delta y)$

Similarly,

Smallest possible result $\simeq \dfrac{x}{y}-\dfrac{x}{y}(\delta x+\delta y)$

Hence the result of the division can be expressed as

$$\frac{x}{y}\pm\frac{x}{y}(\delta x+\delta y) \qquad (6)$$

This result applies for all combinations of x and y both positive and negative. The relative error in the quotient is thus $(\delta x+\delta y)=$ the sum of the relative errors.

Summary of Equations for Combining Errors

If the *absolute* errors in two terms x and y are Δx and Δy and the *relative* errors are $\delta x=|\Delta x/x|$ and $\delta y=|\Delta y/y|$, then

the absolute error in $(x+y)$
is $\pm(\Delta x+\Delta y)$ (see Equation 1)
the absolute error in $(x-y)$
is $\pm(\Delta x+\Delta y)$ (see Equation 2)
the abolute error in $x \cdot y$
is $\pm(x\Delta y+y\Delta x)$ (see Equation 3)
or $\pm xy(\delta x+\delta y)$ (see Equation 5)
and the absolute error in x/y
is $\pm\dfrac{x}{y}(\delta x+\delta y)$ (see Equation 6)

These equations can easily be memorised by remembering that the *absolute* error of a sum or a difference is the sum of the *absolute* errors. The *relative* error of a product or a quotient is the sum of the *relative* errors.

Standard Error

If an experiment is repeated n times, it is likely that the final result calculated from each experiment will vary. The spread of experimental readings in one experiment is measured by the standard deviation of the readings and is discussed in Chapter 2. In an analogous manner the spread of the final results from the replicate experiments is measured by the standard error of the final results.

The first step in calculating the standard error is to evaluate the mean $\bar{R}$ of all of the n final results. The differences Δ_i between each of the final results R_i and the mean $\bar{R}$ are then evaluated. The standard error is calculated:

Standard error of final results

$$= \sqrt{\frac{\text{Sum of differences squared}}{\text{Number of terms minus one}}}$$

$$= \sqrt{\frac{\Sigma\Delta_i^2}{n-1}}$$

It can be seen that this equation is essentially the same as that given earlier for calculating standard deviations. The difference between standard errors and standard deviations is that standard errors refer to the spread of calculated values such as means, slopes or final results whereas standard deviations refer to the spread of experimentally observed results.

Confidence Limits

Having calculated a final answer, which could be a slope, a mean or any other derived quantity, it is often useful to derive a range within which the true result is 95% or 99% likely to fall. This range is called the 95% or 99% confidence limit. Confidence limits are calculated:

Confidence limits
$= \text{Answer} \pm t \cdot \text{Standard error of answer}$

The constant t is based on the confidence level chosen (95% or 99%) and the number of points measured. The t-distribution is discussed in Chapter 4, and a table of values is given in Appendix 6. Applications of confidence limits are found in Chapter 2.

Example 1—Errors Involved in Making a Standard Solution

In many branches of physical science it is necessary to prepare standard solutions, that is solutions whose concentrations are exactly known. Generally this involves dissolving an exactly known weight of solute in the solvent, and making the volume of the resultant solution up to an exactly known amount in a graduated flask. Ignoring any personal (human) errors, and errors due to impurities in the solute and solvent, the accuracy of the standard solution depends on the accuracy of the weighing and the accuracy of calibration of the graduated flask.

The National Physical Laboratory permits the tolerances shown in Table 1.6 on Class A standard weights. (NPL recognises no other grade of weights.) Two grades of graduated flasks Class A and Class B are commonly used. The tolerances for Class B flasks are given in Table 1.7. (Class A have approximately half these tolerances.) Concentration is calculated as weight/volume. In this example 4.2501 g of silver nitrate were weighed, dissolved in water and made up to 250 cm^3 of solution in a graduated flask. The concentration is 4.2501/250 g/cm$^3 = 0.017\,00$ g/cm^3. The

Table 1.6 Tolerance of Grade A Weights

Weight/g	Tolerance/g
100	0.000 5
50	0.000 25
30	0.000 15
20	0.000 1
10–0.1	0.000 05
0.05–0.01	0.000 02

Table 1.7 Tolerance of Grade B Flasks

Volume of flask/cm^3	Tolerance/cm^3
1000	0.80
250	0.30
100	0.15
25	0.06
5	0.04

weight of 4.2501 g was made up of two 2 g weights, a 0.25 g weight plus the rider. The tolerance on the weight of 4.25 is thus the sum of the tolerances of the three individual weights (ignoring any error due to the rider) =

$$0.000\ 05 + 0.000\ 05 + 0.000\ 05\ \text{g}$$
$$= 0.000\ 15\ \text{g}$$

The tolerance in a Class B 250 cm^3 graduated flask is 0.30 cm^3. The error in the concentration is calculated as shown in the summary of equations for combining errors. The relative errors in the weight and volume respectively are

$$\frac{0.000\ 15}{4.2501} = 0.000\ 035$$

and

$$\frac{0.30}{250} = 0.0012$$

The relative error of the quotient (mass/volume = concentration) is the sum of the two relative errors

$$= 0.001\ 235$$

The absolute error in the concentration is thus

$$0.001\ 235 \times 0.017\ 00 = 0.000\ 021\ 0\ \text{g/cm}^3$$

The concentration should thus be stated as 0.017 00 ± 0.000 02 g/cm^3.

The error derived in this way is the maximum possible, and usually the actual error will be smaller than this, because the individual errors may be less than their maxima, and one error may partly cancel another.

It is apparent that the relative error from the glassware exceeds that from the weights by a factor of 34, and hence the error in the weights is almost insignificant. In the laboratory, weights can be determined much more accurately than volumes.

Example 2—Errors in Volumetric Analysis

Chemists and biologists commonly carry out titrations to estimate the concentration of a solution of unknown strength. Titrations are also used to estimate the purity of a sample by preparing a solution containing an accurately known weight of sample, and performing a titration to find the weight of active ingredient actually present. Two solutions are used which will react together—a standard solution and the unknown solution. A known volume of one solution is measured with a pipette and delivered into a conical flask. The other solution is added from a burette until the equivalence point is reached, which is usually detected by a colour change in an indicator which has been added to the conical flask. Ignoring gross personal errors and indicator errors, four main errors remain:

(i) The pipette may not deliver exactly the stated volume even though filled exactly up to the calibration mark.

(ii) The burette may not deliver exactly the volume indicated by the scale due to incorrect calibration.

(iii) It is not possible to deliver less than one drop of solution from the burette. Thus the volume delivered by the burette may be up to one drop beyond the true equivalence point.

(iv) Observational errors when reading the burette.

Pipettes and burettes are available to Class A and Class B specifications. Typical tolerances are given in Table 1.8 and it should be noted that the tolerance of Class B apparatus is approximately double that for Class A.

Table 1.8   Tolerance of Pipettes and Burettes

Volume/ cm^3	Class A pipettes (cm^3)	Class B pipettes (cm^3)	Class A burettes (cm^3)	Class B burettes (cm^3)
100	±0.06	±0.12	±0.10	±0.20
50	0.04	0.08	0.06	0.10
25	0.03	0.06	0.04	0.08
10	0.02	0.04	0.02	0.04
5	0.02	0.03	0.02	0.03

Consider a titration using a 25 cm^3 Class A pipette and a 50 cm^3 Class A burette. The magnitudes of the four errors given above are:

Pipette calibration	±0.03 cm^3
Burette calibration	±0.06 cm^3
One drop	0.04 cm^3
Error in reading burette	±0.01 cm^3

Most burettes deliver between 20 and 30 drops per cm^3 hence the size of one drop is approximately 0.04 cm^3. The excess volume of solution added from the burette will vary between 0 and 0.04 cm^3. On average the excess will be 0.02 cm^3, and this should be subtracted from the amount delivered. This corrected delivered volume is subject to an error of ±0.02 cm^3, that is $\pm$ half a drop.

Most burettes are calibrated in intervals of 0.1 cm^3, which corresponds to about 2 mm in height. The burette can usually be read to the nearest 0.02 cm^3, thus the maximum error from a single reading is ±0.01 cm^3.

The equation for the titration may be written

$$\begin{array}{l} \text{Volume of} \\ \text{standard} \end{array} \times \begin{array}{l} \text{Concentration} \\ \text{of standard} \end{array}$$

$$= \begin{array}{l} \text{Volume} \\ \text{of unknown} \end{array} \times \begin{array}{l} \text{Concentration} \\ \text{of unknown} \end{array}$$

Hence

$$\begin{array}{l} \text{Concentration} \\ \text{of unknown} \end{array} = \frac{\text{Volume of standard}}{\text{Volume of unknown}}$$

$$\times \text{Concentration of standard}$$

Assuming that the standard solution was measured using the pipette, and the unknown using the burette

Volume of standard

$$= 25 \pm 0.03 \text{ cm}^3$$

Initial burette reading

$$= 0.53 \pm 0.01 \text{ cm}^3$$

Final burette reading

$$= 22.36 \pm 0.01 \text{ cm}^3$$

Difference in burette readings

$$= (23.36 \pm 0.01) - (0.53 \pm 0.01) \text{ cm}^3$$

$$= (23.36 - 0.53) \pm (0.01 + 0.01) \text{ cm}^3$$

$$= 22.83 \pm 0.02 \text{ cm}^3$$

(The errors have been combined using Equation 2.)

The observed volume from the burette is thus 22.83 ± 0.02 cm^3, but the tolerance to which the burette is calibrated is ±0.06 cm^3. The delivered volume from the burette must lie in the range

$$22.83 \pm 0.02 \pm 0.06 \text{ cm}^3$$
$$= 22.83 \pm 0.08 \text{ cm}^3$$

This volume will on average be too large by half a drop $= 0.02$ cm^3, and is also subject to an error of $\pm$ half a drop $= \pm0.02$ cm^3.

The volume of unknown used to reach the equivalence point is thus

$$(22.83 \pm 0.08) - (0.02 \pm 0.02) \text{ cm}^3$$
$$= 22.81 \pm 0.10 \text{ cm}^3$$

In working out the concentration of the unknown, the volume of standard is divided by the volume of unknown. It can be seen from Equation 6 that the relative error of a quotient is the sum of the relative errors of numerator and denominator.

Relative error of numerator

= relative error of volume of standard

= 0.03/25 = 0.0012

Relative error of denominator

= Relative error of volume of unknown

0.10/22.81 = 0.0044

Total relative error

= 0.0012 + 0.0044 = 0.0056

= 0.56%

The final answer for the concentration of the unknown is thus subject to an error of 0.56% regardless of the units used. It is worth noting that the burette introduces most of the error.

Exercises

1.1 (a) Explain what is meant by the standard error of the mean.

(b) In the two examples (i) and (ii) given below the mean of a large population is given, together with three possible values for the standard deviation.

(i) Boxes of matches are stated to contain 50 matches. The mean number per box is 51.2 matches, which standard deviation is the most reasonable: 0.5, 5.0 or 50?

(ii) The average height of adult males is 175 cm. Which standard deviation is the most reasonable: 0.7, 7.0 or 70 cm?

1.2 Calculate the density of a ball-bearing, and give the accuracy of the answer using the following data: mass = 3.8251 ± 0.001 g; diameter = 1.126 ± 0.0005 cm; volume of sphere = $\frac{4}{3}\pi r^3$.

1.3 A machine to produce bars of chocolate can be adjusted to give any average mass required, but the standard deviation is always 5 g. What average mass should the machine be set to so that fewer than

(a) 15.87%
(b) 2.27%
(c) 0.13%

of the bars have a mass less than 250 g?

2

Average and Spread of Results

Arithmetic Mean

Suppose we have a set of numbers x_1, x_2, $x_3, \ldots, x_n$ which for example correspond to the total number of GCE subjects passed by all the n pupils taking the examination in the whole country. The arithmetic mean (usually called just the mean) is denoted by the Greek symbol μ and is the sum of the number of subjects passed by each student divided by the total number of students. Thus

$$\mu = \frac{x_1 + x_2 + x_3 + \ldots + x_n}{n}$$

$$= \frac{\sum_{i=1}^{i=n} x_i}{n} \qquad (1)$$

This gives an exact result because we are using all the numbers in the population rather than taking just a sample.

Median

Another measure of the pupils' achievements is given by the median value. This is calculated by arranging the n values in either descending order (largest first) or ascending order (smallest first), and choosing the middle value, that is the $\frac{1}{2}(n+1)$th value in the ordered list. If there are an even number of values, then there is no middle value in the list and the average of the middle two values is taken. Sorting a large list of numbers into order by hand is laborious and time consuming, and for these reasons some automatic sorting process is necessary.

Various methods of sorting are described in Chapter 12, together with a computer program for calculating the median.

The median is generally much less affected by a freak value than the mean. This is illustrated by the following example.

A company has 1000 shareholders, 999 of whom have invested £10 each, and the remaining shareholder has invested £90 010. The mean value invested by each shareholder calculates as £100, but the median value is £10. Clearly in this case the median is more representative of a 'typical' shareholder.

It is found that the median tends to vary more between different samples from the same data than does the mean. The consequence of this is that the median is less reliable than the mean, hence statistical inferences are usually based on the mean rather than the median.

It is sometimes useful to compare the values for the mean and the median for a set of data. Whether these two values are nearly the same or considerably different indicates whether the data are symmetrical or skewed (lopsided) as shown in Figs. 2.1 and 2.2. A measure of how much a distribution is skewed is given by Pearson's coefficient of skewness later in the chapter.

Mode

A third measure of the pupils' achievements is given by the modal value. The mode is defined as the most frequently occurring value. The relation between the mean, median and mode is shown in Fig. 2.3.

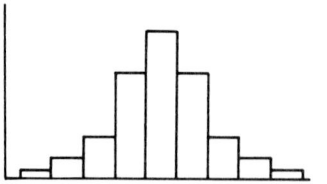 

Fig. 2.1   Symmetrical distributions.

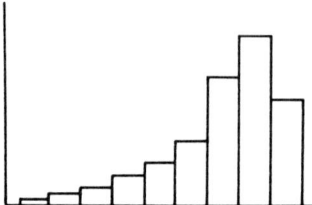 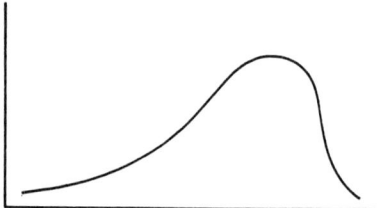

Fig. 2.2   Skewed distributions.

If the distribution is symmetrical then the mean, median and mode all coincide, but if the distribution is skewed the values differ. The mean and the centre of gravity of the distribution coincide, the median bisects the area of the distribution while the mode cuts

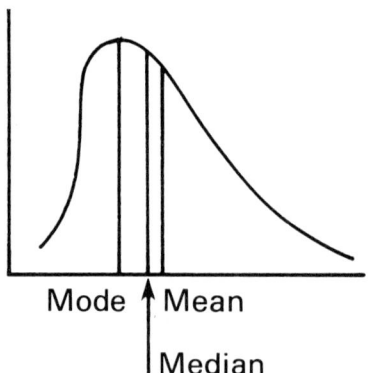

Fig. 2.3   Relationship between mean, median and mode.

the highest point on the distribution. The value obtained for the mode is not very reliable unless a continuous distribution is used, or if a very large number of discrete data values are used which approximate to a continuous distribution. For this reason an approximation is often used to calculate the mode for discrete data.

$$\text{Mean} - \text{Mode} \simeq 3\,(\text{Mean} - \text{Median})$$

Hence

$$\text{Mode} \simeq \text{Mean} - 3\,(\text{Mean} - \text{Median})$$
$$\simeq (3 \times \text{Median}) - (2 \times \text{Mean})$$

Skewness

Skewed distributions are shown in Fig. 2.2. Two features describe how skewed a distribution is:

(i) the direction of the skew;
(ii) the magnitude of the skew.

The direction of the skew may be either negative as in Fig. 2.2, or positive as in Fig. 2.3. It can be seen that the positive skew has the longer tail on the right while a negative skew has the longer tail on the left.

There are many methods of expressing the magnitude of the skew, and the most commonly used is Pearson's coefficient of skewness:

$$\text{Skewness} = \frac{\text{Mean} - \text{Mode}}{\text{Standard deviation}}$$

(An explanation of what standard deviations are, and how they are calculated is given later in this chapter.)

The drawback of this equation for skewness is that the calculated value for the mode is often unreliable. For this reason the mode is replaced using the empirical relationship

$$\text{Mean} - \text{Mode} \simeq 3\,(\text{Mean} - \text{Median})$$

14

Thus skewness is often calculated as

$$\text{Skewness} = \frac{3\,(\text{Mean}-\text{Median})}{\text{Standard deviation}}$$

Not only does the magnitude of the number indicate the degree of skew, but the sign (+ or −) of the number indicates the direction (positive or negative) of the skew.

Range, Variance and Standard Deviation of a Set of Values

While the mean and median are useful measures of the students' achievements, they give no indication as to the spread of results, and some students will have passed in 10 subjects whereas others will have passed in only one.

The simplest way of expressing the spread or precision of a set of results is to quote the range of the numbers, that is the largest value and the smallest value, or alternatively the difference between them. This quantity is not representative since it only takes account of two values from the set and may be badly distorted by a single abnormal value. A method of avoiding this problem is to use the 'inter-quartile range'. For this one arranges the values in ascending order and chooses the values one-quarter and three-quarters down the list. (For a normal distribution the inter-quartile range represents 1.35 standard deviations. The meaning of this should become apparent later.)

A better measure of the spread or precision of the set of results is given by the variance s^2, and the standard deviation s. The variance is defined as the sum of the squared differences between each of the terms and the mean value. Thus:

$$s^2 = \frac{(x_1-\mu)^2+(x_2-\mu)^2+(x_3-\mu)^2+\ \ \ +\ldots+(x_n-\mu)^2}{n}$$

$$s^2 = \frac{\displaystyle\sum_{i=1}^{i=n}(x_i-\mu)^2}{n} \qquad (2)$$

It should be noted that each of the differences is squared before it is summed. This is necessary since some of the differences are positive and some are negative, and if just the differences were added then their total would be zero as a direct consequence of the definition of the mean.

The standard deviation s is given by

$$s = \sqrt{\left[\frac{\Sigma(x_i-\mu)^2}{n}\right]} \qquad (3)$$

Clearly a large variance or a large standard deviation corresponds to a wide spread of results, and small values for s^2 and s correspond to closely grouped results. Consider a very much simplified example of five pupils who obtained passes in 6, 9, 3, 7 and 5 subjects respectively. The mean

$$\mu = \frac{6+9+3+7+5}{5} = \frac{30}{5} = 6$$

The variance is evaluated

$$s^2 = \frac{\Sigma\,(6-6)^2+(9-6)^2+(3-6)^2+(7-6)^2+\ \ \ +(5-6)^2}{5}$$

$$= \frac{0+9+9+1+1}{5} = 4$$

hence the standard deviation

$$s = \sqrt{4} = 2$$

This method of evaluating the variance is long-winded, particularly if the number of terms is large, and the calculation may be simplified. Starting with Equation 2

$$s^2 = \frac{\displaystyle\sum_{i=1}^{i=n}(x_i-\mu)^2}{n}$$

The term

$$\begin{aligned}
\Sigma(x_i-\mu)^2 &= \Sigma\,[(x_i-\mu)\cdot(x_i-\mu)] \\
&= \Sigma\,[x_i^2-2\,x_i\mu+\mu^2] \\
&= \Sigma x_i^2-2\mu\Sigma x_i+\Sigma\mu^2 \\
&= \Sigma x_i^2-2\mu\,n\mu+n\mu^2 \\
&= \Sigma x_i^2-n\mu^2
\end{aligned}$$

15

hence

$$s^2 = \frac{\Sigma x_i^2 - n\mu^2}{n}$$

or

$$s^2 = \frac{\Sigma x_i^2}{n} - \mu^2 \qquad (4)$$

$$s^2 = \frac{\Sigma x_i^2}{n} - \frac{(\Sigma x_i)^2}{n^2} \qquad (5)$$

Equations 4 and 5 are both much simpler for the calculation of the variance by hand, but Equation 4 squares any rounding error produced in calculating the mean μ, hence Equation 5 is to be preferred. This equation is always used on calculators because the individual values need not be stored as they are entered, but only the sum of the values Σx_i, the sum of the values squared Σx_i^2 and the number of terms must be collected. However, with a computer Equation 2 should be used because it is less prone to numerical rounding errors. The use of this equation requires that the numbers are stored in an array, the mean is calculated, and then the individual differences are calculated, squared and summed. Equation 2 gives the most accurate answer. Equations 4 and 5 are potentially worse since they involve the subtraction of two numbers which are approximately equal for small variances. This results in loss of accuracy. This problem of limited numerical accuracy is further discussed in the section on finding the roots of an equation (Chapter 10).

Mean, Variance and Standard Deviation Using a Sample of Readings

In most statistical work the population is very large, and it is usual to work with a sample of readings rather than the entire population. Similarly in scientific experiments one performs a limited number of readings such as titrations to find the concentration of a solution. The readings obtained are random samples from the entire population, and the mean of the sample, the variance of the sample and the standard deviation *of the sample* can be calculated as before. From these one would like to obtain the best estimate of the mean, variance and standard deviation *of the whole population*.

The mean of the sample is denoted by $\bar{x}$, and this gives the best estimate of the mean of the whole population μ

$$\bar{x} = \frac{\Sigma x_i}{n} = \text{Estimated value for } \mu$$

However, the sample variance s^2 underestimates the variance of the entire population σ^2, and for a sample of n terms the best estimate of the population variance is obtained using $(n-1)$ as the divisor rather than n as in Equation 2.

$$\text{Estimated } \sigma^2 = \frac{\Sigma (x_i - \bar{x})^2}{n-1} \qquad (6)$$

and in a similar way the standard deviation of the population is estimated by:

$$\text{Estimated } \sigma = \sqrt{\left[\frac{\Sigma (x_i - \bar{x})^2}{n-1} \right]} \qquad (7)$$

This equation is generally used with a computer, but for hand calculations it is often simplified:

$$\text{Estimated } \sigma = \sqrt{\left[\frac{\Sigma x^2}{(n-1)} - \frac{(\Sigma x)^2}{n(n-1)} \right]} \qquad (8)$$

When the sample size is large, the estimate of σ using the divisor $(n-1)$ is almost the same as that obtained using the divisor n. With a sample of 50 the difference between the true σ and the estimated σ is less than 1%, and for a sample size of 100 the difference is less than 0.5%. For large samples of perhaps 30 or more it is customary to use the divisor n.

Explanation of the Divisors n and $(n-1)$

Equation 2 for the standard deviation s of a set of numbers uses the divisor n. Equation 7 for the estimated standard deviation σ based on a random sample from the whole population uses the divisor $(n-1)$. The difference between these equations may be explained (rather than proved) in the following manner.

If the whole population is used, then the true mean μ is known, and the standard deviation can be calculated using the n divisor. If the true mean is not known (as is the case when using a sample of readings) then the estimated mean $\bar{x}$ must be used instead. However, the sum of all the differences $(x_i - \bar{x})$ is zero by the definition of $\bar{x}$. It follows that if $(n-1)$ of the differences are given, then the last $(n$th) difference can be calculated. There are thus only $(n-1)$ degress of freedom when using a sample to estimate the standard deviation of the entire parent population. Degrees of freedom are further discussed in Chapter 5.

Calculation of Confidence Limits

The probability that the mean of the whole population μ lies outside the 95% confidence limits is 5%. Similarly the probability that μ lies outside the 99% confidence limits is 1%. When there is only a small sample of data values, the confidence limits are calculated using the t-distribution as follows:

$$\text{Confidence limit} = \bar{x} \pm \frac{t \cdot \sigma}{\sqrt{n}}$$

where $\bar{x}$ is the mean of the sample, t is a constant based on the confidence level chosen and the number of points, σ is the estimated standard deviation of the sample and n is the number of data values. The value of t can be obtained from the table in Appendix 6. To use this one must select the appropriate confidence level and also the number of degrees of freedom v. In this case the number of degrees of freedom is $(n-1)$. Degrees of freedom are fully explained in Chapter 5. It should be noted that as v becomes large the t-distribution tends towards the normal distribution. For this reason it is common to use the individual t values for a small number of points but to use the infinity (normal) value for a large number of points (i.e. $n > = 30$).

Description of Standard Deviation Program (Program 2.1)

After printing a heading, the user is asked if full instructions are required. The reply must be YES or NO, and is checked by a subroutine (lines 1890–1980). No other reply is accepted. Full or abbreviated instructions are printed accordingly, but if the program is re-run then abbreviated instructions will always be given.

The user is prompted to type in the data values one at a time followed by pressing RETURN. The X array in the program can hold up to 100 values. Normally there will be fewer entries than this, and a dummy value of 999999 is typed to indicate the end of data input.

A check is then performed to ensure that at least one valid line of data has been typed (lines 230–250). Next a subroutine (lines 1140–1880) is called to print and edit the data if necessary. The user is asked if the data are correct, and if not the data are listed and instructions given to allow insertion and deletion of lines, replacement of existing values and re-listing the current data. Extensive checks are carried out to ensure that changes are valid. This subroutine is described more fully in Chapter 7.

A check is performed to ensure that at least two data values remain after editing. The average value is calculated and printed (lines 330–410). The sum of the differences (between the values and their average value) squared is accumulated, and the variance and standard deviation are calculated and printed (lines 420–570). It is worth mentioning that the divisor $(n-1)$ is used when there are less than 30 points—otherwise the divisor is n.

The user is then asked if confidence limits are required. If they are needed, they are calculated in the following manner:

(i) First the confidence limits are calculated (lines 630–650) using the inifinity values corresponding to the 95% and 99% values for the normal distribution.

(ii) Thirty t values for the 95% confidence

limit are read from a table of DATA values stored in the program (lines 660–750). If there are more than 30 readings then the infinity value is retained, otherwise a new confidence limit is calculated from the t value appropriate for the number of readings (line 700).

(iii) The 99% confidence limit is calculated in a similar way (lines 760–850).

(iv) The confidence limits are printed (lines 860–910).

The user is then asked if another run is required. If so, a choice is given between typing in a completely new set of data, or editing the old (existing) data (lines 920–1090). If another run is not required then the run is terminated and a finishing message is printed (lines 1100–1130).

Program 2.1   Trial run.

```
STANDARD DEVIATION CALCULATION
======== ========= ===========

WOULD YOU LIKE FULL INSTRUCTIONS?
  TYPE YES OR NO & PRESS RETURN.

? YES

TYPE IN DATA VALUES. PRESS RETURN AFTER EACH TERM.
YOU WILL HAVE CHANCE TO CORRECT TYPING ERRORS LATER
TERMINATE DATA WITH THE VALUE 999999
? 25.00
? 24.99
? 25.01
? 999999
ARE THE DATA VALUES ENTERED CORRECT?   TYPE YES OR NO & PRESS RETURN.

? YES

NUMBER OF READINGS = 3

AVERAGE VALUE = 25

VARIANCE = 0.000100005

STANDARD DEVIATION = 0.0100002

WOULD YOU LIKE THE CONFIDENCE LIMITS?
  TYPE YES OR NO & PRESS RETURN.

? YES

WITH 95% CONFIDENCE THE MEAN OF THE PARENT POPULATION IS IN
THE RANGE 25 ,PLUS OR MINUS 0.024844   THAT IS 24.9752 TO 25.0248

WITH 99% CONFIDENCE THE MEAN OF THE PARENT POPULATION IS IN
THE RANGE 25 ,PLUS OR MINUS 0.0573033   THAT IS 24.9427 TO 25.0573

WOULD YOU LIKE ANOTHER RUN?
  TYPE YES OR NO & PRESS RETURN.

? NO

JOB COMPLETED.
```

```
10 DIM X(100), Q$(10), I$(3)
20 PRINT "STANDARD DEVIATION CALCULATION"
30 PRINT "======== ========= ==========="
40 PRINT
50 PRINT "WOULD YOU LIKE FULL INSTRUCTIONS?"
60 GOSUB  1910
70 LET I$ = Q$
80 PRINT
90 IF I$ = "YES" THEN 120
100 PRINT "INPUT DATA"
110 GOTO  140
120 PRINT "TYPE IN DATA VALUES. PRESS RETURN AFTER EACH TERM."
130 PRINT "YOU WILL HAVE CHANCE TO CORRECT TYPING ERRORS LATER"
140 PRINT "TERMINATE DATA WITH THE VALUE 999999"
150 LET N = 0
160 FOR I = 1 TO 100
170    INPUT X(I)
180    IF X(I) = 999999 THEN 230
190    LET N = N + 1
200 NEXT I
210 PRINT
220 PRINT "PROGRAM CAN ONLY HANDLE 100 VALUES."
230 IF N > 0 THEN 270
240 PRINT "PLEASE TYPE IN SOME DATA"
250 GOTO 160
260 REM CALL SUBROUTINE TO CHECK & EDIT DATA
270 GOSUB 1150
280 REM ABANDON RUN IF LESS THAN 2 TERMS
290 PRINT
300 IF N >= 2 THEN 340
310 PRINT "WITH ONLY ONE DATA POINT THE STANDARD DEVIATION MUST BE ZERO"
320 GOTO  920
330 REM WORK OUT AVERAGE VALUE
340 LET A = 0
350 FOR I = 1 TO N
360    LET A = A + X(I)
370 NEXT I
380 LET A1 = A / N
390 PRINT "NUMBER OF READINGS ="; N
400 PRINT
410 PRINT "AVERAGE VALUE ="; A1
420 REM WORK OUT THE DIFFERENCES SQUARED BETWEEN EACH MARK AND AVERAGE,
430 REM AND COLLECT TOTAL IN D.
440 LET D = 0
450 FOR I = 1 TO N
460    LET D1 = X(I) - A1
470    LET D = D + (D1 * D1)
480 NEXT I
490 REM WORK OUT VARIANCE V & STANDARD DEVIATION S
500 LET V = D / (N - 1)
510 IF N < 30 THEN 530
520 LET V = D / N
530 PRINT
540 PRINT "VARIANCE ="; V
550 PRINT
560 LET S = SQR(V)
570 PRINT "STANDARD DEVIATION ="; S
580 REM DECIDE WHETHER TO WORK OUT CONFIDENCE LIMITS
590 PRINT
600 PRINT "WOULD YOU LIKE THE CONFIDENCE LIMITS?"
610 GOSUB  1900
```

```
620 IF Q$ = "NO" THEN 920
630 REM CALCULATE CONFIDENCE LIMITS USING INFINITY VALUES
640 LET C = 1.95996 * S / SQR(N)
650 LET C1 = 2.57582 * S / SQR(N)
660 REM RE-CALCULATE 95% CONFIDENCE LIMIT IF N<= 30
670 FOR I = 1 TO 30
680    READ T
690    IF I <> N THEN 710
700    LET C = T * S / SQR(N)
710 NEXT I
720 DATA 0, 12.706, 4.303, 3.182, 2.776, 2.571, 2.447, 2.365
730 DATA 2.306, 2.262, 2.228, 2.201, 2.197, 2.160, 2.145, 2.131
740 DATA 2.120, 2.110, 2.101, 2.093, 2.086, 2.080, 2.074, 2.069
750 DATA 2.064, 2.060, 2.056, 2.052, 2.048, 2.045
760 REM RE-CALCULATE 99% CONFIDENCE LIMIT IF N <= 30
770 FOR I = 1 TO 30
780    READ T
790    IF I <> N THEN 810
800    LET C1 = T * S / SQR(N)
810 NEXT I
820 DATA 0, 63.657, 9.925, 5.841, 4.604, 4.032, 3.707, 3.499
830 DATA 3.355, 3.250, 3.169, 3.106, 3.055, 3.012, 2.977, 2.947
840 DATA 2.921, 2.898, 2.878, 2.861, 2.845, 2.831, 2.819, 2.807
850 DATA 2.797, 2.787, 2.779, 2.771, 2.763, 2.756
860 PRINT
870 PRINT "WITH 95% CONFIDENCE THE MEAN OF THE PARENT POPULATION IS IN"
880 PRINT "THE RANGE";A1;",PLUS OR MINUS";C;"   THAT IS";A1-C;"TO";A1+C
890 PRINT
900 PRINT "WITH 99% CONFIDENCE THE MEAN OF THE PARENT POPULATION IS IN"
910 PRINT "THE RANGE";A1;",PLUS OR MINUS";C1;" THAT IS";A1-C1;"TO";A1+C1
920 PRINT
930 PRINT "WOULD YOU LIKE ANOTHER RUN?"
940 GOSUB 1900
950 IF Q$ = "NO" THEN 1110
960 RESTORE
970 LET I$ = "NO"
980 PRINT "TYPE NEW FOR A RUN WITH COMPLETELY NEW DATA"
990 PRINT "  OR OLD TO EDIT AND RERUN THE EXISTING DATA"
1000 INPUT Q$
1010 IF Q$ = "NEW" THEN 1050
1020 IF Q$ = "OLD" THEN 1080
1030 PRINT "REPLY '"; Q$; "' NOT UNDERSTOOD"
1040 GOTO 980
1050 PRINT "TYPE IN A NEW SET OF DATA"
1060 PRINT "==== == = === === == ===="
1070 GOTO  140
1080 GOSUB 1200
1090 GOTO 290
1100 REM TERMINATE JOB
1110 PRINT
1120 PRINT "JOB COMPLETED."
1130 STOP
1140 REM SUBROUTINE TO CHECK THAT DATA ARE CORRECT & ALTER IF NECESSARY
1150 PRINT "ARE THE DATA VALUES ENTERED CORRECT?";
1160 REM A4 SHOULD BE SET TO THE NUMBER OF LINES ON THE VDU
1170 LET A4 = 20
1180 GOSUB 1900
1190 IF Q$ = "YES" THEN 1880
1200 PRINT "HERE IS A LIST OF THE CURRENT DATA"
1210 PRINT "LINE NUMBER", "X"
1220 FOR I = 1 TO N
```

```
1230    PRINT I, X(I)
1240    IF INT(I / (A4 - 1)) * (A4 - 1) <> I THEN 1280
1250    PRINT "WOULD YOU LIKE TO CONTINUE LISTING";
1260    GOSUB 1900
1270    IF Q$ = "NO" THEN 1290
1280 NEXT I
1290 PRINT "TYPE R TO REPLACE";
1300 IF I$ = "NO" THEN 1320
1310 PRINT " AN EXISTING LINE OF DATA"
1320 IF N = 100 THEN 1370
1330 PRINT TAB(5); " A TO ADD";
1340 IF I$ = "NO" THEN 1360
1350 PRINT " AN EXTRA LINE"
1360 IF N = 1 THEN 1400
1370 PRINT TAB(5); " D TO DELETE";
1380 IF I$ = "NO" THEN 1400
1390 PRINT " AN EXISTING LINE"
1400 PRINT TAB(5); " L TO LIST";
1410 IF I$ = "NO" THEN 1430
1420 PRINT " THE DATA"
1430 PRINT "  OR C TO CONTINUE";
1440 IF I$ = "NO" THEN 1460
1450 PRINT " THE CALCULATION"
1460 INPUT Q$
1470 IF Q$ = "R" THEN 1570
1480 IF N = 100 THEN 1510
1490 IF Q$ = "A" THEN 1690
1500 IF N = 1 THEN 1520
1510 IF Q$ = "D" THEN 1740
1520 IF Q$ = "L" THEN 1200
1530 IF Q$ = "C" THEN 1880
1540 PRINT "REPLY '"; Q$; "' NOT UNDERSTOOD."
1550 GOTO 1290
1560 REM REPLACE LINE
1570 PRINT "TYPE THE LINENUMBER OF THE LINE TO BE REPLACED";
1580 INPUT I
1590 IF I <> INT(I) THEN 1610
1600 IF (I - 1) * (I - N) <= 0 THEN 1640
1610 PRINT "LINENUMBER MUST BE AN INTEGER IN THE RANGE 1 -"; N
1620 PRINT "RE-";
1630 GOTO 1570
1640 PRINT "TYPE THE CORRECT LINE TO REPLACE THE ONE WHICH IS WRONG:"
1650 PRINT "X"
1660 INPUT X(I)
1670 GOTO 1720
1680 REM ADD A NEW LINE
1690 LET N = N + 1
1700 PRINT "TYPE THE ADDITIONAL LINE OF DATA AS SHOWN:    X"
1710 INPUT X(N)
1720 PRINT "OK"
1730 GOTO 1290
1740 REM DELETE A LINE
1750 PRINT "TYPE THE LINENUMBER OF THE LINE TO BE DELETED"
1760 INPUT J
1770 IF (J - 1) * (J - N) > 0 THEN 1790
1780 IF J = INT(J) THEN 1810
1790 PRINT "LINENUMBER MUST BE AN INTEGER IN THE RANGE 1 -"; N
1800 GOTO 1750
1810 FOR I = J + 1 TO N
1820    LET X(I - 1) = X(I)
1830 NEXT I
```

```
1840 LET N = N - 1
1850 PRINT "OK"
1860 IF J > N THEN 1290
1870 GOTO 1200
1880 RETURN
1890 REM SUBROUTINE TO CHECK REPLIES
1900 IF I$ = "NO" THEN 1920
1910 PRINT " TYPE YES OR NO & PRESS RETURN."
1920 PRINT
1930 INPUT Q$
1940 IF Q$ = "YES" THEN 1980
1950 IF Q$ = "NO" THEN 1980
1960 PRINT "REPLY '"; Q$; "' NOT UNDERSTOOD.";
1970 GOTO 1910
1980 RETURN
1990 END
```

How to Combine Standard Deviations

Consider two independent terms x and y with standard deviation σ_x and σ_y. If x and y are used to calculate the final result z, then the standard deviation of z is σ_z.

Addition $z = x + y$

$$\text{then } \sigma_z = \sqrt{(\sigma_x^2 + \sigma_y^2)}$$

This is obtained directly from Appendix 8, Equation 4.

Subtraction $z = x - y$

$$\text{then } \sigma_z = \sqrt{(\sigma_x^2 + \sigma_y^2)}$$

This is obtained directly from Appendix 8, Equation 5.

Multiplication $z = x \cdot y$

$$\text{then } \frac{\sigma_z}{z} = \sqrt{\left(\frac{\sigma_x^2}{x^2} + \frac{\sigma_y^2}{y^2} \right)}$$

This is obtained directly from Appendix 8, Equation 6.

Division $z = x/y$

$$\text{then } \frac{\sigma_z}{z} = \sqrt{\left(\frac{\sigma_x^2}{x^2} + \frac{\sigma_y^2}{y^2} \right)}$$

This is obtained directly from Appendix 8, Equation 7.

The equations for addition and subtraction are the same, and the equations for multiplication and division are also the same.

Coefficient of Variation

The precision of a final result depends on the spread of the measurements. One common measure of precision is called the coefficient of variation, and compares the spread of the measurements with their magnitude:

Coefficient of variation =

$$\frac{\text{Standard deviation of measurements}}{\text{Mean value of measurements}} \times 100$$

This is arguably a more useful measure of precision than the standard deviation, because it takes into acount the magnitude of the numbers. As with the standard deviation, a low value for the coefficient of variation corresponds to high precision while a high value corresponds to low precision.

Mean, Variance and Standard Deviation Using Grouped Data

In many experiments which yield a large number of data values it is convenient to record the results in groups, each of which covers a range of values, rather than discrete values. For example a survey of blood alcohol readings measured in a forensic laboratory over a large period of time might be grouped into bands of 10 or 20 mg per 100 ml of sample. In other cases the large number of readings involved makes grouping almost unavoidable—for example a national survey of the annual salaries of the 50 million inhabitants of Great Britain.

It is usual practice to collect the data in groups rather than as the exact values.

Consider a simple example where the Forestry Commission measured the girths of a set of trees. Data are collected into groups using tally marks (Table 2.1). To calculate the mean girth one uses the formula:

$$\text{Mean } \bar{x} = \frac{\Sigma\,[x_i \cdot f(x_i)]}{n} \qquad (9)$$

where x_i is the mid-point of the range of the girth of the tree and $f(x_i)$ is the frequency (number of occurrences) of the girth x_i. The number of readings n is equal to the sum of the frequencies

$$n = \Sigma f(x_i)$$

Using Equation 9 the mean $\bar{x}$ is evaluated:

$$\bar{x} = \frac{[(30 \times 3) + (50 \times 13) + (70 \times 22) +}{3 + \qquad 13 + \qquad 22 +}$$

$$\frac{+\ (90 \times 5) + (110 \times 7)]}{+\qquad 5 + \qquad 7}\ \text{cm}$$

$$\bar{x} = \frac{3500}{50}\ \text{cm} = 70\ \text{cm}$$

On average in the grouping, there will be as many values rounded up to the mid-point of the range as there are values which are rounded down. The positive and negative errors thus introduced should cancel each other.

The appropriate equation for the standard deviation for a grouped sample differs from Equation 7 only in that it allows for the frequency in each band.

$$\text{Estimated } \sigma = \sqrt{\left\{\frac{\Sigma\,[(x_i - \bar{x})^2 \cdot f(x_i)]}{n-1}\right\}} \qquad (10)$$

Equation 7 may be considered as a special case for Equation 10 where all the frequencies are one. With grouped data, Equation 10 gives too high a value for the estimated standard deviation. This is because the error terms $(x_i - \bar{x})$ are squared, making all of the rounding errors, produced by grouping, into positive numbers. On average each $(x_i - \bar{x})^2$ term is too large by an amount of $c^2/12$ for each point, where c is the range of the group. In the case where all the groups have the same range (as in the example of tree girths) the equation becomes:

$$\text{Estimated } \sigma$$

$$= \sqrt{\left\{\frac{\Sigma\,[(x_i - \bar{x})^2 \cdot f(x_i)]}{n-1} - \frac{c^2}{12}\right\}} \qquad (11)$$

This is known as Sheppard's correction.

Table 2.1

Range of girths (cm)	Mid-point of range x_i (cm)	Tally	Frequency $f(x_i)$
20 to 40	30	1 1 1	3
40 to 60	50	⦀⦀ ⦀⦀ 1 1 1	13
60 to 80	70	⦀⦀ ⦀⦀ ⦀⦀ ⦀⦀ 1 1	22
80 to 100	90	⦀⦀	5
100 to 120	110	⦀⦀ 1 1	7

$\Sigma 50 = $ number of readings n

Using Equation 11 the standard deviation of tree girths is

Estimated σ

$$= \sqrt{\left[\frac{(30-70)^2 \cdot 3}{50} + \frac{(50-70)^2 \cdot 13}{50} + \right.}$$

$$+ \frac{(70-70)^2 \cdot 22}{50} + \frac{(90-70)^2 \cdot 5}{50} +$$

$$\left. + \frac{(110-70)^2 \cdot 7}{50} - \frac{20^2}{12} \right]$$

$$= \sqrt{\left(\frac{4800}{50} + \frac{5200}{50} + \frac{0}{50} + \frac{2000}{50} + \right.}$$

$$\left. + \frac{11\,200}{50} - \frac{400}{12} \right)$$

$$= \sqrt{\frac{23\,200}{50} - \frac{400}{12}} = 20.75\text{ cm}$$

It should be noted that the number of terms n has been used as the denominator rather than $n-1$. This is commonly done when the number of terms is large as discussed previously. In this book 'large' is taken to mean 30 or more. Without Sheppard's correction the estimated value for $\sigma = 21.54$ cm, hence the correction decreases the value by almost 4%. It is worth mentioning that the change in divisor only changes the estimated standard deviation by about 1%.

Description of Standard Deviation Program for Grouped Data (Program 2.2)

First a heading is printed and the user is asked if full instructions are required. The reply, which must be YES or NO is checked by a subroutine (lines 2100–2190), and either long or short instructions are printed.

A message invites the user to input data in the form: lower limit of range, higher limit of range, number of readings in the range (frequency of range)—followed by pressing RETURN. The data input loop extends from lines 190–230. A number of checks are performed in a subroutine (lines 2200–2330) to ensure that the values typed are reasonable:

(i) The frequency must be a whole number.
(ii) The frequency must be positive or zero.
(iii) The high limit must be greater than or equal to the low limit.

The end of data input is signalled by typing a dummy line of 0, 0, 0 and pressing RETURN. The arrays L, H and F are dimensioned at 100 and restrict the maximum number of lines of data to 100. A check is performed to ensure that some valid data have been entered before the terminator. When data input is complete a subroutine is called (lines 1330–2090) which asks if the data entered are correct, and if necessary it permits the addition, deletion or replacement of lines as well as the option of listing the current data. This subroutine is described more fully in Chapter 7.

If at this stage there is only one data range, the program reports that the standard deviation must be zero, and then branches to the end of the program. Usually there will be more than one data range, and the program works out the average reading (lines 360–440). A check is performed to ensure that there are at least two readings since the estimated standard deviation cannot be calculated from a single reading.

The standard deviation is then calculated in two ways (lines 610–750), that is without and with Sheppard's group correction. Both results are printed. If the number of readings is less than 30 then the divisor used is the number of readings minus one, otherwise it is the number of readings. In the unlikely case of the correction exceeding the sum of differences squared the standard deviation is set to zero and a warning message is printed.

Provided that the standard deviation is greater than zero, the user is given the option of calculating confidence limits based on the t-distribution. This is fully discussed in the description of the (non-grouped) standard deviation program.

Finally the user is asked if another run is required, and if so whether completely new data are to be input or whether the existing data are to be edited and re-run.

Program 2.2   Trial run.

```
STANDARD DEVIATION CALCULATION FOR GROUPED DATA
======== ========= =========== === ======= ====

WOULD YOU LIKE FULL INSTRUCTIONS?
 TYPE YES OR NO & PRESS RETURN.

? YES

TYPE THREE VALUES ON ONE LINE SEPARATED BY COMMAS.  THESE
ARE:  LOW LIMIT OF RANGE, HIGH LIMIT OF RANGE, FREQUENCY
THEN PRESS RETURN & TYPE THE NEXT LINE, RETURN ETC.
YOU WILL HAVE THE CHANCE TO CORRECT TYPING ERRORS LATER
TERMINATE DATA WITH THE DUMMY VALUES  0, 0, 0
LOW LIMIT, HIGH LIMIT, FREQUENCY
? 20, 40, 3
? 40, 60, 13
? 60, 80, 22
? 80, 100, 5
? 100, 120, 7
? 0, 0, 0
ARE THE DATA VALUES ENTERED CORRECT?  TYPE YES OR NO & PRESS RETURN.

? YES

NUMBER OF GROUPS = 5

NUMBER OF READINGS = 50

AVERAGE VALUE = 70

STANDARD DEVIATION = 21.5407

WITH THE GROUP CORRECTION THE BEST ESTIMATE FOR
THE STANDARD DEVIATION IS 20.7525

WOULD YOU LIKE THE CONFIDENCE LIMITS?
 TYPE YES OR NO & PRESS RETURN.

? YES

WITH 95% CONFIDENCE THE MEAN OF THE PARENT POPULATION IS IN
THE RANGE 70 PLUS OR MINUS 5.75218  THAT IS 64.2478 TO 75.7522

WITH 99% CONFIDENCE THE MEAN OF THE PARENT POPULATION IS IN
THE RANGE 70 PLUS OR MINUS 7.55964  THAT IS 62.4404 TO 77.5596

WOULD YOU LIKE ANOTHER RUN?
 TYPE YES OR NO & PRESS RETURN.

? NO

JOB COMPLETED.
```

```
10 DIM F(100), H(100), L(100), Q$(10), I$(3)
20 PRINT "STANDARD DEVIATION CALCULATION FOR GROUPED DATA"
30 PRINT "======== ========= =========== === ======= ===="
40 PRINT
50 PRINT "WOULD YOU LIKE FULL INSTRUCTIONS?"
60 GOSUB 2120
70 LET I$ = Q$
80 PRINT
90 IF I$ = "YES" THEN 120
100 PRINT "INPUT DATA"
110 GOTO 160
120 PRINT "TYPE THREE VALUES ON ONE LINE SEPARATED BY COMMAS.  THESE"
130 PRINT "ARE:  LOW LIMIT OF RANGE, HIGH LIMIT OF RANGE, FREQUENCY"
140 PRINT "THEN PRESS RETURN & TYPE THE NEXT LINE, RETURN ETC."
150 PRINT "YOU WILL HAVE THE CHANCE TO CORRECT TYPING ERRORS LATER"
160 PRINT "TERMINATE DATA WITH THE DUMMY VALUES  0, 0, 0"
170 PRINT "LOW LIMIT, HIGH LIMIT, FREQUENCY"
180 LET N = 0
190 FOR I = 1 TO 100
200    GOSUB 2220
210    IF ABS(L(I)) + ABS(H(I)) + F(I) = 0 THEN 260
220    LET N = N + 1
230 NEXT I
240 PRINT
250 PRINT "PROGRAM CAN ONLY HANDLE 100 VALUES."
260 IF N > 0 THEN 300
270 PRINT "PLEASE ENTER SOME DATA VALUES"
280 GOTO 120
290 REM CALL SUBROUTINE TO CHECK & EDIT DATA
300 GOSUB 1340
310 REM ABANDON RUN IF LESS THAN 2 TERMS
320 PRINT
330 IF N >= 2 THEN 370
340 PRINT "WITH ONLY ONE DATA RANGE THE STANDARD DEVIATION MUST BE ZERO"
350 GOTO 1110
360 REM WORK OUT AVERAGE VALUE & CORRECTION FACTOR C
370 LET A = 0
380 LET N1 = 0
390 LET C = 0
400 FOR I = 1 TO N
410    LET A = A + (L(I) + H(I)) / 2 * F(I)
420    LET C = C + (H(I) - L(I)) * (H(I) - L(I)) * F(I) / 12
430    LET N1 = N1 + F(I)
440 NEXT I
450 IF N1 >= 2 THEN 480
460 PRINT "THERE MUST BE AT LEAST TWO READINGS"
470 GOTO 1110
480 LET A1 = A / N1
490 PRINT "NUMBER OF GROUPS ="; N
500 PRINT
510 PRINT "NUMBER OF READINGS ="; N1
520 PRINT
530 PRINT "AVERAGE VALUE ="; A1
540 REM WORK OUT THE DIFFERENCES SQUARED BETWEEN EACH MARK AND AVERAGE,
550 REM AND COLLECT TOTAL IN D.
560 LET D = 0
570 FOR I = 1 TO N
580    LET D1 = (H(I) + L(I)) / 2 - A1
590    LET D = D + (D1 * D1) * F(I)
600 NEXT I
610 REM WORK OUT STANDARD DEVIATION S1
```

26

```
620 LET S1 = SQR(D / (N1 - 1))
630 LET S = (D - C) / (N1 - 1)
640 IF N1 < 30 THEN 670
650 LET S1 = SQR(D / N1)
660 LET S = (D - C) / N1
670 PRINT
680 PRINT "STANDARD DEVIATION ="; S1
690 PRINT
700 IF S >= 0 THEN 730
710 PRINT "SHEPPARDS CORRECTION IS SO LARGE THAT"
720 LET S = 0
730 LET S = SQR(S)
740 PRINT "WITH THE GROUP CORRECTION THE BEST ESTIMATE FOR"
750 PRINT "THE STANDARD DEVIATION IS"; S
760 REM DECIDE WHETHER TO WORK OUT CONFIDENCE LIMITS
770 PRINT
780 IF S = 0 THEN 1110
790 PRINT "WOULD YOU LIKE THE CONFIDENCE LIMITS?"
800 GOSUB 2110
810 IF Q$ = "NO" THEN 1110
820 REM CALCULATE CONFIDENCE LIMITS USING INFINITY VALUES
830 LET C = 1.95996 * S / SQR(N1)
840 LET C1 = 2.57582 * S / SQR(N1)
850 REM RE-CALCULATE 95% CONFIDENCE LIMIT IF N <= 30
860 FOR I = 1 TO 30
870    READ T
880    IF I <> N1 THEN 900
890    LET C = T * S / SQR(N1)
900 NEXT I
910 DATA 0, 12.706, 4.303, 3.182, 2.776, 2.571, 2.447, 2.365
920 DATA 2.306, 2.262, 2.228, 2.201, 2.197, 2.16, 2.145, 2.131
930 DATA 2.12, 2.11, 2.101, 2.093, 2.086, 2.08, 2.074, 2.069
940 DATA 2.064, 2.06, 2.056, 2.052, 2.048, 2.045
950 REM RE-CALCULATE 99% CONFIDENCE LIMIT IF N <= 30
960 FOR I = 1 TO 30
970    READ T
980    IF I <> N1 THEN 1000
990    LET C1 = T * S / SQR(N1)
1000 NEXT I
1010 DATA 0, 63.657, 9.925, 5.841, 4.604, 4.032, 3.707, 3.499
1020 DATA 3.355, 3.25, 3.169, 3.106, 3.055, 3.012, 2.977, 2.947
1030 DATA 2.921, 2.898, 2.878, 2.861, 2.845, 2.831, 2.819, 2.807
1040 DATA 2.797, 2.787, 2.779, 2.771, 2.763, 2.756
1050 PRINT
1060 PRINT "WITH 95% CONFIDENCE THE MEAN OF THE PARENT POPULATION IS IN"
1070 PRINT "THE RANGE";A1;"PLUS OR MINUS";C;" THAT IS";A1-C;"TO";A1+C
1080 PRINT
1090 PRINT "WITH 99% CONFIDENCE THE MEAN OF THE PARENT POPULATION IS IN"
1100 PRINT "THE RANGE";A1;"PLUS OR MINUS";C1;" THAT IS";A1-C1;"TO";A1+C1
1110 PRINT
1120 PRINT "WOULD YOU LIKE ANOTHER RUN?"
1130 GOSUB 2110
1140 IF Q$ = "NO" THEN 1300
1150 RESTORE
1160 LET I$ = "NO"
1170 PRINT "TYPE NEW FOR A RUN WITH COMPLETELY NEW DATA"
1180 PRINT "  OR OLD TO EDIT AND RERUN THE EXISTING DATA"
1190 INPUT Q$
1200 IF Q$ = "NEW" THEN 1240
1210 IF Q$ = "OLD" THEN 1270
1220 PRINT "REPLY '"; Q$; "' NOT UNDERSTOOD"
```

```
1230 GOTO 1170
1240 PRINT "TYPE IN A NEW SET OF DATA"
1250 PRINT "==== == = === === == ===="
1260 GOTO 160
1270 GOSUB 1390
1280 GOTO 320
1290 REM TERMINATE JOB
1300 PRINT
1310 PRINT "JOB COMPLETED."
1320 STOP
1330 REM SUBROUTINE TO CHECK THAT DATA ARE CORRECT & ALTER IF NECESSARY
1340 PRINT "ARE THE DATA VALUES ENTERED CORRECT?";
1350 REM A4 SHOULD BE SET TO THE NUMBER OF LINES ON THE VDU
1360 LET A4 = 20
1370 GOSUB 2110
1380 IF Q$ = "YES" THEN 2090
1390 PRINT "HERE IS A LIST OF THE CURRENT DATA"
1400 PRINT "LINE NUMBER", "LOW LIMIT", "HIGH LIMIT", "FREQUENCY"
1410 FOR I = 1 TO N
1420    PRINT I, L(I), H(I), F(I)
1430    IF INT(I / (A4 - 1)) * (A4 - 1) <> I THEN 1470
1440    PRINT "WOULD YOU LIKE TO CONTINUE LISTING";
1450    GOSUB 2110
1460    IF Q$ = "NO" THEN 1480
1470 NEXT I
1480 PRINT "TYPE R TO REPLACE";
1490 IF I$ = "NO" THEN 1510
1500 PRINT " AN EXISTING LINE OF DATA"
1510 IF N = 100 THEN 1560
1520 PRINT TAB(5); " A TO ADD";
1530 IF I$ = "NO" THEN 1550
1540 PRINT " AN EXTRA LINE"
1550 IF N = 1 THEN 1590
1560 PRINT TAB(5); " D TO DELETE";
1570 IF I$ = "NO" THEN 1590
1580 PRINT " AN EXISTING LINE"
1590 PRINT TAB(5); " L TO LIST";
1600 IF I$ = "NO" THEN 1620
1610 PRINT " THE DATA"
1620 PRINT "   OR C TO CONTINUE";
1630 IF I$ = "NO" THEN 1650
1640 PRINT " THE CALCULATION"
1650 INPUT Q$
1660 IF Q$ = "R" THEN 1760
1670 IF N = 100 THEN 1700
1680 IF Q$ = "A" THEN 1860
1690 IF N = 1 THEN 1710
1700 IF Q$ = "D" THEN 1930
1710 IF Q$ = "L" THEN 1390
1720 IF Q$ = "C" THEN 2090
1730 PRINT "REPLY '"; Q$; "' NOT UNDERSTOOD."
1740 GOTO 1480
1750 REM REPLACE LINE
1760 PRINT "TYPE THE LINENUMBER OF THE LINE TO BE REPLACED";
1770 INPUT I
1780 IF I <> INT(I) THEN 1800
1790 IF (I - 1) * (I - N) <=0 THEN 1830
1800 PRINT "LINENUMBER MUST BE AN INTEGER IN THE RANGE 1 -"; N
1810 PRINT "RE-";
1820 GOTO 1760
1830 PRINT "TYPE THE CORRECT LINE TO REPLACE THE ONE WHICH IS WRONG:"
```

```
1840 GOTO 1890
1850 REM ADD A NEW LINE
1860 LET N = N + 1
1870 LET I = N
1880 PRINT "TYPE THE ADDITIONAL LINE OF DATA AS SHOWN:"
1890 PRINT "LOW LIMIT, HIGH LIMIT, FREQUENCY"
1900 GOSUB 2220
1910 PRINT "OK"
1920 GOTO 1480
1930 REM DELETE A LINE
1940 PRINT "TYPE THE LINENUMBER OF THE LINE TO BE DELETED"
1950 INPUT J
1960 IF (J - 1) * (J - N) >0 THEN 1980
1970 IF J = INT(J) THEN 2000
1980 PRINT "LINENUMBER MUST BE AN INTEGER IN THE RANGE 1 -"; N
1990 GOTO 1940
2000 FOR I = J + 1 TO N
2010    LET L(I - 1) = L(I)
2020    LET H(I - 1) = H(I)
2030    LET F(I - 1) = F(I)
2040 NEXT I
2050 LET N = N - 1
2060 PRINT "OK"
2070 IF J > N THEN 1480
2080 GOTO 1390
2090 RETURN
2100 REM SUBROUTINE TO CHECK REPLIES
2110 IF I$ = "NO" THEN 2130
2120 PRINT " TYPE YES OR NO & PRESS RETURN."
2130 PRINT
2140 INPUT Q$
2150 IF Q$ = "YES" THEN 2190
2160 IF Q$ = "NO" THEN 2190
2170 PRINT "REPLY '"; Q$; "' NOT UNDERSTOOD.";
2180 GOTO 2120
2190 RETURN
2200 REM SUBROUTINE TO INPUT FREQUENCY & CHECK THAT IT IS NOT NEGATIVE
2210 REM & THAT HIGH LIMIT OF RANGE >= LOW LIMIT
2220 INPUT L(I), H(I), F(I)
2230 IF F(I) = INT(F(I)) THEN 2260
2240 PRINT "FREQUENCY MUST BE A WHOLE NUMBER"
2250 GOTO 2310
2260 IF F(I) >= 0 THEN 2290
2270 PRINT "FREQUENCY MUST BE POSITIVE OR ZERO"
2280 GOTO 2310
2290 IF H(I) >= L(I) THEN 2330
2300 PRINT "THE UPPER LIMIT MUST BE GREATER THAN THE LOWER LIMIT"
2310 PRINT "LAST LINE OF DATA REJECTED - RETYPE CORRECTLY"
2320 GOTO 2220
2330 RETURN
2340 END
```

Exercises

2.1 The following are the speeds of a sample of 24 cars in m.p.h. along a certain stretch of road at about the same time on the same day.

60, 49, 77, 66, 60, 66, 55, 65, 48, 50, 57, 63, 55, 60, 70, 51, 68, 67, 53, 60, 60, 62, 57, 61.

Calculate the mean and standard deviation of these speeds and estimate the mean and standard deviation of all the cars on this road at that time. (For simplicity Sheppard's correction should be ignored.)

2.2 The heights of 100 women are given in Table 2.2. Calculate the mean and standard deviation of these values. (Remember to use Sheppard's correction since the data are grouped.)

2.3 Two random sets of values x_1 and x_2 are drawn from a parent population of mean μ and standard deviation σ. What is the mean and standard deviation of each of the following distributions:

(a) $x_1 + x_2$ (b) $x_1 - x_2$ (c) $\frac{1}{2}(x_1 + x_2)$
(d) $\frac{1}{2}(x_1 - x_2)$

2.4 A student's class grades in English and maths are both distributed with means of 55 and standard deviations of 10. Write down the mean and standard deviation of:

(a) his total mark in English and maths;
(b) the difference between his marks in English and maths;
(c) his average mark in English and maths.

2.5 Define the mean, median and mode of a distribution. Calculate the mean and median weekly wage for a set of people using the data in Table 2.3 and use these to estimate the mode and skewness.

Table 2.2

Height (cm)	Frequency
Less than 147.5	4
147.5–152.5	9
152.5–157.5	21
157.5–162.5	32
162.5–167.5	20
167.5–172.5	11
More than 172.5	3

Table 2.3

Weekly wage (£)	Number of employees
35–45	11
45–55	35
55–65	58
65–75	64
75–85	50
85–95	33
95–105	22
105–115	12
115–125	9
125–135	6

3

Central Limit Theorem

The central limit theorem may be stated:

> If samples of size n_1 are drawn at random from a parent population of mean μ and standard deviation σ, the sample means constitute a population of mean μ and the standard deviation tends to $\sigma/\sqrt{n_1}$ as n_1 tends to infinity. Regardless of whether the parent population was normal or not, the sample means tend to a normal distribution as n_1 tends to infinity. The approximation may be quite good with n_1 as small as 5, and is generally acceptable for $n_1 \geqslant 15$.

One application of the central limit theorem is to estimate the mean and standard deviation of a parent population, given only a set of sample means. The procedure is similar to that for standard deviations described in the previous chapter. The difference in the two procedures is that the calculation of standard deviations requires *all* of the individual data values, whereas the central limit theorem uses only a set of sample means collected from the original data. (A sample mean is the mean of n_1 values drawn from the original data.) The central limit theorem should be used only if the original data are not available. If the original data are available it would be pointless to draw samples of size n_1, calculate the sample means and then use central limit theorem to estimate the mean and standard deviation of the original data, since these values can be obtained directly by the standard deviation procedure. Furthermore the standard deviation procedure is more reliable.

Example

A headmaster asked eight of his teachers to find the number of hours that their pupils watched television in a week. Each teacher questioned 12 children, and gave the headmaster the average hours of television viewing. The headmaster does not have the original data from the 96 children—he only has eight sample means. He can use the central limit theorem to estimate the mean and standard deviation of hours of television viewing by his pupils.

The eight sample means that the headmaster has are:

> 20.6, 18.8, 17.5, 19.6, 16.3, 17.1, 20.4, 17.8 hours.

The mean of these values is 18.5 hours and their standard deviation is 1.6 hours. These values can be used as *estimates* for μ and $\sigma/\sqrt{n_1}$, hence the estimated value of μ is 18.5 hours, and the estimated value of $\sigma = 1.6 \times \sqrt{12} = 5.5$ hours. It is interesting to compare these values with those obtained by the standard deviation procedure using all the viewing data collected by the teachers (see Table 3.1). (If the headmaster had all of these data he should not have used the central limit theorem.)

Using all of these figures to estimate μ and σ, the mean and standard deviation of viewing time by pupils were:

> mean viewing time $\mu = 18.5$ hours
> standard deviation of viewing time $\sigma = 4.4$ hours

Table 3.1

Teacher	Individual viewing times of pupils in hours	Sample mean
1	15, 18, 17, 17, 28, 17, 19, 19, 24, 23, 27, 23	20.6
2	19, 18, 23, 19, 13, 20, 23, 13, 25, 18, 15, 19	18.8
3	23, 18, 10, 16, 20, 18, 21, 12, 16, 22, 20, 14	17.5
4	18, 22, 20, 23, 19, 11, 21, 26, 27, 17, 14, 17	19.6
5	10, 23, 18, 15, 16, 17, 18, 20, 22, 14, 13, 10	16.3
6	11, 22, 18, 16, 23, 22, 12, 21, 13, 19, 10, 18	17.1
7	17, 16, 20, 23, 14, 25, 26, 22, 19, 25, 21, 17	20.4
8	13, 15, 18, 17, 21, 14, 27, 18, 23, 21, 16, 10	17.8

These values should be compared with the estimates obtained using the central limit theorem ($\mu = 18.5$ hours, $\sigma = 5.5$ hours). It should be noted that the means are the same, but the estimate for the standard deviation is wrong by 25%. This emphasises two points:

(i) The central limit theorem provides an *estimate* and should only be used when the full data are not available.
(ii) The sample size of 12 is rather small, and closer results would probably be obtained with a larger sample.

Outline of Central Limit Theorem

Three points emerge from the central limit theorem:

(i) The mean of the sample means tends to the mean of the parent population μ.
(ii) The standard deviation of the sample means tends to $\sigma/\sqrt{n_1}$.
(iii) The distribution of the sample means is approximately normal for large values of n_1.

These three points are discussed in turn:

(i) It is self-evident that if only a small number of samples is taken from a large parent population, it is possible that the samples are not representative of the whole population, and thus the mean of the sample means may differ appreciably from μ the true mean of the parent population. Clearly as the number of samples is increased it becomes less likely that the samples are not representative. (For example the chance of obtaining 3 'freak' samples is much larger than the chance of obtaining 30 'freak' samples.) Thus provided the number of samples is fairly large, the mean of the sample means will approximate to μ.

(ii) Consider a parent population which comprises a large number of loaves of bread produced by a bakery. A sample of two loaves is taken and each loaf is weighed giving weights x_1 and x_2. If the sampling is performed several times then different values for x_1 and x_2 will be obtained. The standard deviation of these readings will be σ_{x_1} and σ_{x_2}, and their variances will be $\sigma_{x_1}^2$ and $\sigma_{x_2}^2$ respectively. Using Appendix 8 Equation 4 the variance of the sum of the weights of the two loaves is $\sigma_{x_1}^2 + \sigma_{x_2}^2$.

If, however, each sample comprises n_1 loaves, the variance of the sum of the weights will be

$$\sigma_{x_1}^2 + \sigma_{x_2}^2 + \sigma_{x_3}^2 + \ldots + \sigma_{x_{n1}}^2$$

Since each loaf weighed is from the parent population which has a mean weight μ and standard deviation σ, the estimated standard deviation for the x_1 weights will tend to σ. Similarly the estimated standard deviation for the $x_1, x_2, x_3, \ldots, x_{n1}$ will also tend to σ. Thus the variance of the sum of the weights tends to $\sigma^2 + \sigma^2 + \sigma^2 + \ldots + \sigma^2$. Since there are n_1

terms being added, the variance of the sum of the weights is $n_1\sigma^2$.

Thus the standard deviation of the sum of the weights

$$= \sqrt{(n_1\sigma^2)}$$
$$= \sigma\sqrt{n_1}$$

Since the mean sample weight or the 'sample mean' is equal to the sum of the weights divided by the sample size n_1

Standard deviation of sample mean

$$= \text{Standard deviation of} \left(\frac{\text{sum of weights}}{n_1} \right)$$

$$= \frac{1}{n_1} \cdot \text{standard deviation of sum of weights}$$

$$= \frac{1}{n_1} \sigma\sqrt{n_1}$$

$$= \frac{\sigma}{\sqrt{n_1}}$$

(iii) In one sample of loaves it is highly likely that some loaves will weigh more than the mean weight of the parent population, and others will weigh less. Calculating a mean weight for each sample tends to cancel out these differences. However, the differences do not totally disappear, although small differences occur more frequently than large differences and the mean difference is zero. Random differences of this kind generally follow an approximately normal distribution provided that the number of terms n_1 is large. (See Chapter 1.)

Description of the Central Limit Theorem Program (Program 3.1)

The program first prints a heading, and then asks if full instructions are required. The answer is checked in a subroutine (lines 1640–1730), and must be either YES or NO. Full or abbreviated instructions are printed as requested for the first run, but shortened instructions are always given on subsequent runs.

Next the user is invited to type in up to a maximum of 100 sample means (lines 90–250). Generally there will be fewer than 100 sample means, and the user indicates the end of data input by typing the dummy value of 999999. A check is performed (lines 270–290) to ensure that at least one sample mean has been entered before the terminator. Though at least two sample means are required to perform a meaningful calculation, it is possible to add additional data in the checking/editing subroutine described in the next paragraph. The check performed here is essential to ensure the correct functioning of this subroutine.

A subroutine (lines 890–1630) is then entered which asks if the data are correct. The answer must be either YES or NO and is checked in another subroutine (lines 1640–1730). If the data are correct then the editing subroutine is exited, but otherwise the current data are listed. Instructions are then given for replacement of incorrect sample means, addition of new sample means or deletion of incorrect sample means, together with commands for re-listing the data and continuing the calculation. The operation of this subroutine is described more fully in Chapter 7.

On returning from the checking subroutine a check is performed (lines 320–350) to ensure that at least two sample means exist. Should there be only one sample mean then a warning message is printed explaining that the standard deviation must be zero. In this case no calculations are performed, and the user is asked if another run is required.

Generally there are two or more sample means, and the program next asks for the number of values which were used to calculated the sample means (i.e. the number of values in each sample). A number of checks (lines 380–480) are performed on the value typed in:

   (i) The value typed must be an integer.
  (ii) The value must be less than or equal to 1000. This is an empirical limit.
 (iii) The value must be 5 or more since

sample means with fewer than 5 values are unreliable.

(iv) If the value is less than 15, a warning message is printed as the calculated standard deviation may not be reliable.

(v) A special case is made if the value is 1. This corresponds to typing in all of the individual readings, and the results obtained will be identical to those from the standard deviation program.

Next the mean of the samples mean is calculated and printed (lines 490–560). Then the sum of the squared differences from the mean is accumulated (lines 570–610) and the variance is evaluated and printed (lines 620–660). In common with the standard deviation procedure described previously, the denominator used is $(n-1)$ if there are less than 30 sample means, or n if there are 30 or more sample means, where n is the number of

Program 3.1   Trial run.

```
            CENTRAL LIMIT THEOREM
            ======= ===== =======
WOULD YOU LIKE FULL INSTRUCTIONS
  TYPE YES OR NO & PRESS RETURN.

? YES
THIS PROGRAM ESTIMATES THE VALUES FOR THE MEAN AND STANDARD
DEVIATION OF A PARENT POPULATION, FROM WHICH A SAMPLE OF
READINGS HAVE BEEN TAKEN.   THE READINGS WERE COLLECTED INTO
GROUPS OF N VALUES.   THE ORIGINAL N VALUES ARE NO LONGER
NEEDED (OR AVAILABLE) BUT THEIR MEAN IS REQUIRED.   THIS IS
CALLED THE SAMPLE MEAN.
TYPE IN THE SAMPLE MEANS & PRESS RETURN AFTER EACH VALUE
YOU WILL BE GIVEN THE CHANCE TO EDIT INCORRECT DATA LATER
TERMINATE THE DATA WITH A DUMMY VALUE OF 999999
? 20.6
? 18.8
? 17.5
? 19.6
? 16.3
? 17.1
? 20.4
? 17.8
? 999999
ARE THE DATA VALUES ENTERED CORRECT?   TYPE YES OR NO & PRESS RETURN.

? YES
TYPE THE NUMBER OF VALUES USED TO OBTAIN EACH SAMPLE MEAN
? 12
TAKE CARE - THE STANDARD DEVIATION MAY BE UNRELIABLE
SINCE THE SAMPLE SIZE IS LESS THAN 15

THE AVERAGE OF THE SAMPLE MEANS TYPED IN IS 18.5125
AND THIS IS THE BEST ESTIMATE FOR MEAN OF PARENT POPULATION

VARIANCE OF SAMPLE MEANS = 2.51553
ESTIMATED STANDARD DEVIATION OF SAMPLE MEANS = 1.58604

BEST ESTIMATE FOR STANDARD DEVIATION OF PARENT POPULATION   IS 5.49421

WOULD YOU LIKE ANOTHER RUN
  TYPE YES OR NO & PRESS RETURN.

? NO
END OF JOB
```

```
10 DIM M(100), Q$(10), I$(3)
20 PRINT TAB(10); "CENTRAL LIMIT THEOREM"
30 PRINT TAB(10); "======= ===== ======="
40 PRINT
50 PRINT "WOULD YOU LIKE FULL INSTRUCTIONS"
60 GOSUB 1660
70 LET I$ = Q$
80 IF I$ = "NO" THEN 180
90 PRINT "THIS PROGRAM ESTIMATES THE VALUES FOR THE MEAN AND STANDARD"
100 PRINT "DEVIATION OF A PARENT POPULATION, FROM WHICH A SAMPLE OF"
110 PRINT "READINGS HAVE BEEN TAKEN.  THE READINGS WERE COLLECTED INTO"
120 PRINT "GROUPS OF N VALUES.  THE ORIGINAL N VALUES ARE NO LONGER"
130 PRINT "NEEDED (OR AVAILABLE) BUT THEIR MEAN IS REQUIRED.  THIS IS"
140 PRINT "CALLED THE SAMPLE MEAN."
150 PRINT "TYPE IN THE SAMPLE MEANS & PRESS RETURN AFTER EACH VALUE"
160 PRINT "YOU WILL BE GIVEN THE CHANCE TO EDIT INCORRECT DATA LATER"
170 GOTO 190
180 PRINT "TYPE THE SAMPLE MEANS"
190 PRINT "TERMINATE THE DATA WITH A DUMMY VALUE OF 999999"
200 LET N = 0
210 FOR I = 1 TO 100
220    INPUT M(I)
230    IF M(I) = 999999 THEN 270
240    LET N = N + 1
250 NEXT I
260 PRINT "PROGRAM CAN ONLY HANDLE 100 SAMPLE MEANS"
270 IF N > 0 THEN 310
280 PRINT "PLEASE ENTER SOME SAMPLE MEANS"
290 GOTO 210
300 REM CHECK THAT DATA ARE CORRECT
310 GOSUB 900
320 IF N > 1 THEN 360
330 PRINT "SINCE THERE IS ONLY ONE SAMPLE MEAN THE STANDARD DEVIATION"
340 PRINT "MUST BE ZERO"
350 GOTO 720
360 PRINT "TYPE THE NUMBER OF VALUES USED TO OBTAIN EACH SAMPLE MEAN"
370 INPUT N1
380 IF N1 <> INT(N1) THEN 410
390 IF N1 = 1 THEN 430
400 IF (N1 - 5) * (N1 - 1000) <= 0 THEN 460
410 PRINT "RETYPE AN INTEGER NUMBER IN THE RANGE 5 - 1000"
420 GOTO 370
430 PRINT "WITH A SAMPLE OF SIZE 1 THE RESULTS ARE THE SAME AS"
440 PRINT "FROM THE STANDARD DEVIATION PROGRAM."
450 GOTO 490
460 IF N1 >= 15 THEN 490
470 PRINT "TAKE CARE - THE STANDARD DEVIATION MAY BE UNRELIABLE"
480 PRINT "SINCE THE SAMPLE SIZE IS LESS THAN 15"
490 LET S = 0
500 FOR I = 1 TO N
510    LET S = S + M(I)
520 NEXT I
530 PRINT
540 LET M1 = S / N
550 PRINT "THE AVERAGE OF THE SAMPLE MEANS TYPED IN IS"; M1
560 PRINT "AND THIS IS THE BEST ESTIMATE FOR MEAN OF PARENT POPULATION"
570 LET S = 0
580 FOR I = 1 TO N
590    LET S1 = M(I) - M1
600    LET S = S + S1 * S1
```

```
610 NEXT I
620 LET V = S / (N - 1)
630 IF N < 30 THEN 650
640 LET V = S / N
650 PRINT
660 PRINT "VARIANCE OF SAMPLE MEANS ="; V
670 LET S = SQR(V)
680 PRINT "ESTIMATED STANDARD DEVIATION OF SAMPLE MEANS ="; S
690 PRINT
700 PRINT "BEST ESTIMATE FOR STANDARD DEVIATION OF PARENT POPULATION";
710 PRINT " IS"; S * SQR(N1)
720 PRINT
730 PRINT "WOULD YOU LIKE ANOTHER RUN"
740 GOSUB 1650
750 LET I$ = "NO"
760 IF Q$ = "NO" THEN 870
770 PRINT "WOULD YOU LIKE TO USE COMPLETELY NEW DATA"
780 PRINT "OR EDIT AND RE USE THE OLD EXISTING DATA"
790 PRINT "TYPE NEW OR OLD & PRESS RETURN"
800 INPUT Q$
810 IF Q$ = "NEW" THEN 180
820 IF Q$ = "OLD" THEN 850
830 PRINT "REPLY '"; Q$; "' NOT UNDERSTOOD.   RE-";
840 GOTO 790
850 GOSUB 950
860 GOTO 320
870 PRINT "END OF JOB"
880 STOP
890 REM SUBROUTINE TO CHECK THAT DATA ARE CORRECT AND ALTER IF NECESSARY
900 PRINT "ARE THE DATA VALUES ENTERED CORRECT?";
910 REM A4 SHOULD BE SET TO THE NUMBER OF LINES ON THE VDU
920 LET A4 = 20
930 GOSUB 1650
940 IF Q$ = "YES" THEN 1630
950 PRINT "HERE IS A LIST OF THE CURRENT DATA"
960 PRINT "LINE NUMBER", "SAMPLE MEAN"
970 FOR I = 1 TO N
980    PRINT I, M(I)
990    IF INT(I / (A4 - 1)) * (A4 - 1) <> I THEN 1030
1000    PRINT "WOULD YOU LIKE TO CONTINUE LISTING";
1010    GOSUB 1650
1020    IF Q$ = "NO" THEN 1040
1030 NEXT I
1040 PRINT "TYPE R TO REPLACE";
1050 IF I$ = "NO" THEN 1070
1060 PRINT " AN EXISTING SAMPLE MEAN"
1070 IF N = 100 THEN 1120
1080 PRINT TAB(5); " A TO ADD";
1090 IF I$ = "NO" THEN 1110
1100 PRINT " AN EXTRA SAMPLE MEAN"
1110 IF N = 1 THEN 1150
1120 PRINT TAB(5); " D TO DELETE";
1130 IF I$ = "NO" THEN 1150
1140 PRINT " AN EXISTING SAMPLE MEAN"
1150 PRINT TAB(5); " L TO LIST";
1160 IF I$ = "NO" THEN 1180
1170 PRINT " THE DATA"
1180 PRINT "   OR C TO CONTINUE";
1190 IF I$ = "NO" THEN 1210
1200 PRINT " THE CALCULATION"
1210 INPUT Q$
```

```
1220 IF Q$ = "R" THEN 1320
1230 IF N = 100 THEN 1260
1240 IF Q$ = "A" THEN 1440
1250 IF N = 1 THEN 1270
1260 IF Q$ = "D" THEN 1490
1270 IF Q$ = "L" THEN 950
1280 IF Q$ = "C" THEN 1630
1290 PRINT "REPLY '"; Q$; "' NOT UNDERSTOOD."
1300 GOTO 1040
1310 REM REPLACE LINE
1320 PRINT "TYPE THE LINENUMBER OF THE LINE TO BE REPLACED";
1330 INPUT I
1340 IF I <> INT(I) THEN 1360
1350 IF (I - 1) * (I - N) <= 0 THEN 1390
1360 PRINT "LINENUMBER MUST BE AN INTEGER IN THE RANGE 1 -"; N
1370 PRINT "RE-";
1380 GOTO 1320
1390 PRINT "TYPE THE CORRECT VALUE TO REPLACE THE ONE WHICH IS WRONG:"
1400 PRINT "SAMPLE MEAN"
1410 INPUT M(I)
1420 GOTO 1470
1430 REM ADD A NEW LINE
1440 LET N = N + 1
1450 PRINT "TYPE THE ADDITIONAL SAMPLE MEAN"
1460 INPUT M(N)
1470 PRINT "OK"
1480 GOTO 1040
1490 REM DELETE A LINE
1500 PRINT "TYPE THE LINENUMBER OF THE LINE TO BE DELETED"
1510 INPUT J
1520 IF (J - 1) * (J - N) > 0 THEN 1540
1530 IF J = INT(J) THEN 1560
1540 PRINT "LINENUMBER MUST BE AN INTEGER IN THE RANGE 1 -"; N
1550 GOTO 1500
1560 FOR I = J + 1 TO N
1570    LET M(I - 1) = M(I)
1580 NEXT I
1590 LET N = N - 1
1600 PRINT "OK"
1610 IF J > N THEN 1040
1620 GOTO 950
1630 RETURN
1640 REM SUBROUTINE TO CHECK REPLIES
1650 IF I$ = "NO" THEN 1670
1660 PRINT " TYPE YES OR NO & PRESS RETURN."
1670 PRINT
1680 INPUT Q$
1690 IF Q$ = "YES" THEN 1730
1700 IF Q$ = "NO" THEN 1730
1710 PRINT "REPLY '"; Q$; "' NOT UNDERSTOOD.";
1720 GOTO 1660
1730 RETURN
1740 END
```

sample means. The estimated standard deviation of the sample means is calculated as the square root of the variance, and is printed (lines 670–680). The best estimate for the standard deviation of the parent population, i.e. the estimate for σ is calculated and printed (lines 700–710).

The user is then asked if another run is required. If the answer is NO, then the run is finished, but if the answer is YES the user is invited to choose between typing in completely new data, or editing and re-running using the old (existing) data.

Exercises

3.1 On five consecutive days the weight of fish landed by a trawler was 500, 700, 600, 800, 650 lbs. Each day's catch was packaged into 25 boxes. Use the central limit theorem to estimate the mean and standard deviation of the weight of fish in a box.

3.2 A lift is designed to carry a maximum load of 1 tonne (1000 kg). The manufacturers claim that it will carry up to 13 people. If people have a mean weight of 70 kg with a standard deviation of 10 kg is the claim fair, and what is the chance of overloading the lift with 13 people?

3.3 The weights of men travelling by air from London to Edinburgh were found to have a mean value of 75 kg and a standard deviation of 8 kg. What is the probability that 64 men travelling on this aircraft have a combined weight greater than 4925 kg?

3.4 A factory produces washers which should be of uniform thickness. Quality control consists of taking 100 washers at random from each day's production, measuring their total thickness, and calculating the average thickness of these 100. Estimate the mean and standard deviation of the thickness of a washer from the 20 days' records given in Table 3.2.

Table 3.2

Thickness of 100 washers (mm)				
253.6	246.8	249.3	251.7	252.4
251.4	250.8	249.5	248.3	245.4
254.5	251.1	248.9	248.1	246.5
247.2	250.4	250.1	251.8	248.5

4

Data and Distributions

Discrete and Continuous Data

Some experiments and all opinion polls yield discrete data. For example the result of tossing a coin is either 'heads' or 'tails', while a poll on political affiliations would yield data on the numbers of Conservative, Labour, Liberal and other supporters. The essential feature of such data is that there is only a limited number of possible outcomes or results.

In contrast other experiments yield data on a continuous scale. Examples of such data include the speed of motor cars, the heights of men or the weights of laboratory animals. The essential feature of this type of data is that there is a continuum of possibilities for each of the examples.

These two different types of data must be handled differently. This is because when using discrete data it is possible to give the probability of an event occurring— for example the chance that a tossed coin will land 'heads' uppermost. In contrast, the probability that a laboratory animal weighed *exactly* 3 kg is infinitessimally small. Instead of quoting the probability for an exact value, when using continuous data probabilities are associated with intervals or ranges. One might reasonably ask for the probability of a laboratory animal weighing between 2.5 kg and 3.5 kg, or a car travelling at a speed of between 35 m.p.h. and 40 m.p.h. The difference between these two types of data is shown in Figs. 4.1 and 4.2. Figure 4.1 shows the results obtained by tossing a coin 10 times, recording the number of 'heads', and repeating the proce-

dure many times. Graphs such as this are called bar charts. Figure 4.2 shows the distribution of the weights of a large number of dogs. Curves such as this are called probability density curves and represent continuous distributions.

The shaded area on the bar chart (Fig. 4.1) represents the number of occurrences of 'heads' appearing exactly 3 times in 10 tosses, while the shaded area in the graph (Fig. 4.2) gives the probability of a dog weighing between 2.5 and 3.5 kg. For a continuous distribution, the probability of obtaining a value between x_1 and x_2 is the area under the probability density curve between the limits x_1

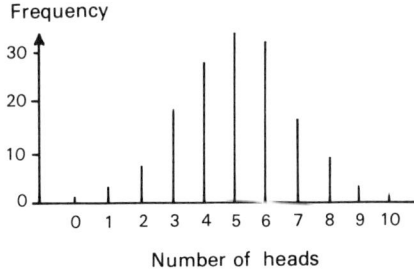

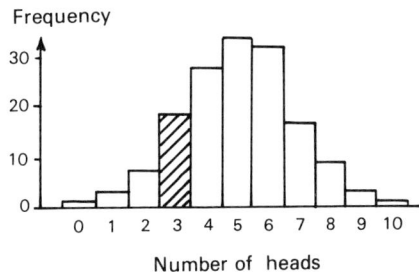

Fig. 4.1   Bar charts showing the number of 'heads'.

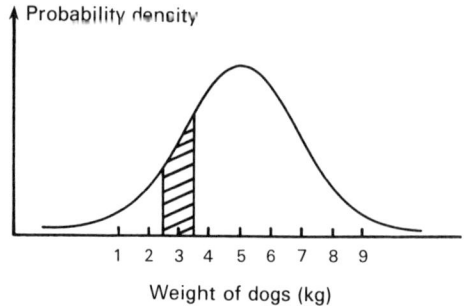

Weight of dogs (kg)

Fig. 4.2 Graph showing the distribution of the weights of dogs.

and x_2. The total area under the probability density curve from minus infinity to plus infinity is one since this represents every possible outcome.

The area under the bar chart in Fig. 4.1 increases with the number of times that the procedure (in this case tossing a coin 10 times), is repeated. This introduces difficulties which are avoided by plotting the relative frequency rather than frequency and obtaining a histogram.

Relative frequency of result

$$= \frac{\text{Frequency of result}}{\text{Number of times procedure is repeated}}$$

A histogram of the results is shown in Fig. 4.3, and the important difference from the bar chart in Fig. 4.1 is that the area under the histogram is always one.

The shaded area on the histogram (Fig. 4.3) represents the relative frequency of 'heads' appearing 3 times in 10 tosses. Figures 4.2 and 4.3 are similar in that areas represent probabilities, but they differ in two ways. Firstly, Fig. 4.2 uses probability density whereas Fig. 4.3 uses relative frequency. Secondly, Fig. 4.2 is a smooth (continuous) curve, while Fig. 4.3 is a stepped (discrete) curve.

The distinction between discrete and continuous data becomes less important if the number of discrete outcomes and the number of times the procedure was repeated are both large. This case is illustrated by tossing 250 coins at a time, counting the number of 'heads', and repeating the procedure 2000 times. The results are shown in Fig. 4.4, and it can be seen that the discrete data of the histogram approximate quite closely to a continuous curve.

The sharp distinction between discrete and continuous data is often blurred for another reason. The speeds of motor cars travelling along a road clearly form a continuous distribution. However, if the instrument measuring the speeds is only accurate to the nearest 1 m.p.h., then the continuous speeds are actually recorded as discrete data. Plotting such data would produce a histogram

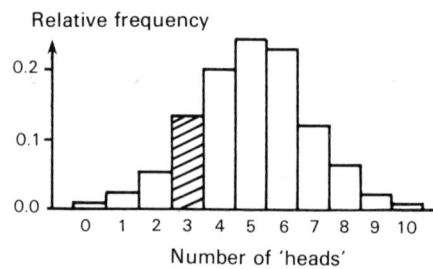

Number of 'heads'

Fig. 4.3 Histogram showing relative frequency of number of 'heads'.

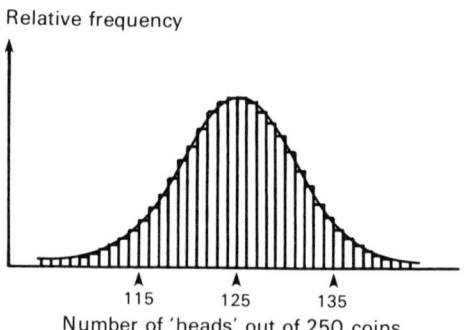

Number of 'heads' out of 250 coins

Fig. 4.4 Histogram approximating to a continuous distribution.

approximating to a continuous curve as in Fig. 4.4.

In this chapter, four different distributions are discussed: normal distribution, t-distribution, Poisson distribution and binomial distribution, and the first two of these are used extensively elsewhere in the book.

Elementary Probability

The concept of probability, that is the chance that an event will occur, is used in many places in this book. Some of the simple ideas and laws are outlined.

The probability that an event will occur is a number in the range 0 to 1. A probability of 0 means that the event will never occur, whereas a probability of 1 means that it is certain to occur. A probability of $\frac{1}{2}$ means that there is an equal chance of the event occurring or not occurring, for example the chance of getting 'heads' when tossing an unbiased coin or of getting an even number when rolling a fair die. The probability of rolling any one particular number in the range 1 to 6 (for example a 4) is $\frac{1}{6}$. These probabilities are written symbolically as:

$$P(\text{heads}) = \frac{1}{2}$$

$$P(\text{even}) = \frac{1}{2}$$

$$P(4) = \frac{1}{6}$$

If all the possible outcomes of an event are listed, then one of these outcomes must happen, so the sum of the individual probabilities must be one (otherwise there would be a chance of some other outcome). In coin tossing experiments there are two possible outcomes: heads and tails, hence

$$P(\text{heads}) + P(\text{tails}) = 1$$

Similarly in rolling a die there are six possible outcomes:

$$1, 2, 3, 4, 5 \text{ or } 6$$

hence

$$P(1) + P(2) + P(3) + P(4) + P(5) + P(6) = 1$$

If the die is fair then each of these individual probabilities is equal to $\frac{1}{6}$, but the sum of the individual probabilities is always 1 regardless of whether the die is fair or not.

Consider the probability of obtaining a score of 5 *or* 6 when rolling a die. Clearly

$$P(5 \text{ or } 6) = P(5) + P(6) \qquad (1)$$

Let A represent getting a score of 5 or 6

then $P(A) = P(5) + P(6)$

Let B represent getting an even score

then $P(B) = P(2) + P(4) + P(6)$

From Equation 1 it would appear that the probability of A or B is equal to the probability of A plus the probability of B. Thus

$P(A \text{ or } B)$ would appear to be
$P(5) + P(6) + P(2) + P(4) + P(6)$.

Intuitively this is wrong since the left-hand side is the probability of being even, or 5 or 6 that is the probability of shaking a 2, 4, 6, 5 or 6 and the number 6 appears twice in the list. $P(A \text{ or } B) = P(A) + P(B)$ *only* when the outcomes A and B are mutually exclusive (complementary). When A and B are not mutually exclusive, any outcomes which occurs in both A and B is counted twice. In the above example 6 is counted twice, and

$$P(A \text{ or } B) = P(A) + P(B) - P(6)$$

Generally $P(A \text{ or } B) = P(A) + P(B) - P(A \text{ and } B)$. This is illustrated in the Venn diagram (Fig. 4.5). Consider the probability of tossing a 'head' *and* rolling a 6 in an experiment where one fair coin is tossed and one fair die is rolled. Intuitively the probability is one-twelfth. Thus it would appear that

$$P(A \text{ and } B) = P(A) \times P(B) \qquad (2)$$

This result is true provided that the events A and B are independent, that is the probability of one is unaffected by the occurrence or non-occurrence of the other. An example of this result failing is the probability of a coin being simultaneously heads and tails. Plainly the probability is zero, yet $P(\text{heads}) = \frac{1}{2}$ and $P(\text{tails}) = \frac{1}{2}$ so $P(\text{heads and tails}) = \frac{1}{2} \times \frac{1}{2} = \frac{1}{4}$ from Equation 2. Equation 2 is only valid if A and B are independent.

Normal Distribution

The normal distribution is one of the most widely used continuous distributions in statistics (see Fig. 4.6). It is sometimes called the 'Gaussian distribution', or 'the normal curve of errors', because the frequencies of observed random errors in the repeated measurement

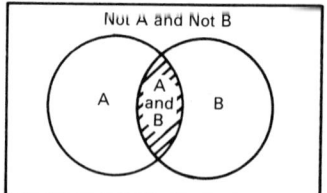
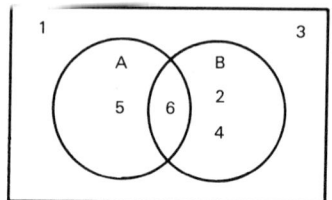

Fig. 4.5   Venn diagram.

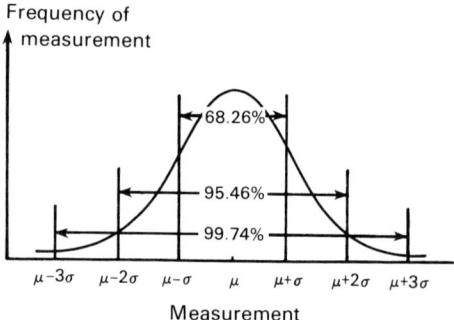

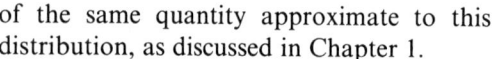

Fig. 4.6   Graph of a normal distribution.

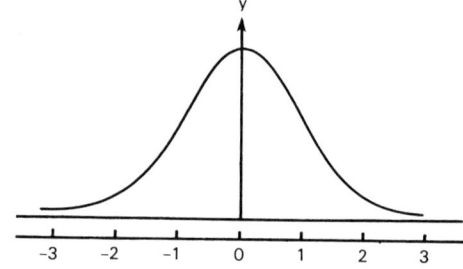

Fig. 4.7   Graph of standard normal curve.

of the same quantity approximate to this distribution, as discussed in Chapter 1.

One important feature of the normal distribution is that it is symmetrical about μ. The curve is bell-shaped, and extends to infinity in both directions, coming closer and closer to the horizontal axis without ever touching it. The horizontal axis is calibrated in terms of σ; the standard deviation of the measurement. It is not necessary to extend the tails of the curve very far, and because the area under the curve beyond ± 4 standard deviations is only 0.000 06 this is ignored for most practical purposes.

Normal distributions can have different shapes by stretching the x axis (and squashing the y axis to keep the area equal to one), or vice versa. The whole curve may be translated (moved) to the left or right, but there is only one normal curve with a given mean μ and standard deviation σ. The most commonly used normal curve has $\mu = 0$ and $\sigma = 1$. This is called the standard normal curve (Fig. 4.7).

The equation of the standard normal curve is

$$y = \frac{1}{\sqrt{2\pi}} e^{-\frac{1}{2}x^2} \qquad (3)$$

where x is the number of standard deviations. The integral of Equation 3 is used to calculate the area under the standard normal curve, and is tabulated in Appendix 4. The area tabulated is the area from minus infinity up to the number of standard deviations specified x, as shown in Fig. 4.8.

If the area from the given number of standard deviations to plus infinity is required, this is calculated as one minus the table value, since the total area under the curve is by definition one.

The table does not give the areas for negative standard deviations (Fig. 4.9a).

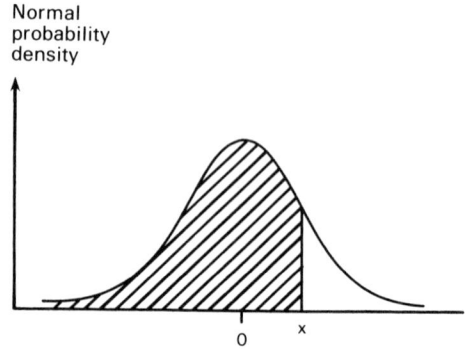

Fig. 4.8   Area under standard normal curve tabulated in Appendix 4.

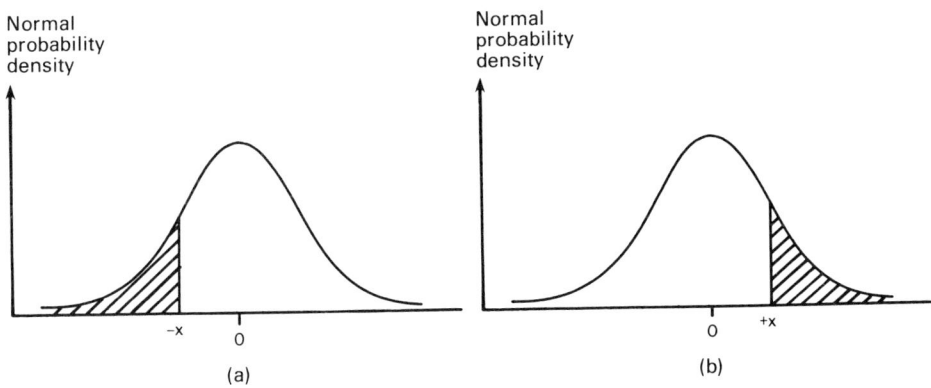

Fig. 4.9   Areas for negative standard deviations.

Clearly the shaded area in Fig. 4.9a is equal to the shaded area in Fig. 4.9b, which is equal to one minus the shaded area in Figure 4.8.

Area below $(-x)$ standard deviations
$= 1 -$ area below $(+x)$ standard deviations

The normal distribution is widely used for comparing two large samples, and for calculating confidence limits.

t-Distribution

For comparing small samples (number of readings less than 30), or for calculating confidence limits for small sets of data, the normal distribution is not adequate, and the t-distribution should be used. Its properties are similar to the normal distribution (symmetrical, total area equals one, and mean equals zero), but its shape varies depending on the number of degrees of freedom. In many

situations the number of degrees of freedom is the number of readings minus one, but this may vary in individual cases, and is defined with each example. A table of t values for varying numbers of degrees of freedom is given in Appendix 6. It should be noted that the t-distribution tends to the normal distribution as the number of degrees of freedom becomes large. Care should be exercised to avoid confusion between one- and two-tailed possibilities.

Figure 4.10a shows the one-tailed probability of 10%, while Fig. 4.10b shows the two-tailed probability of 20%. Two-tailed tests are used to establish if the samples are significantly different, regardless of which is the larger, while one-tailed tests are used to establish either if sample 1 is significantly greater than sample 2, or if sample 1 is significantly smaller than sample 2, but *NOT* both.

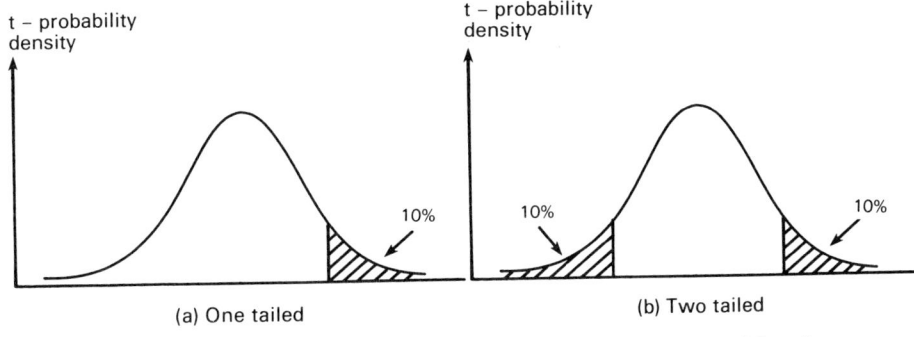

Fig. 4.10   One- and two-tailed probabilities for 25 degrees of freedom.

Poisson Distribution

The Poisson distribution is used to calculate the number of occurrences of a particular event for discrete data, for example the number of defective transistors in a packet. The Poisson distribution assumes that the events occur randomly and independently. It can be derived from the binomial distribution, and may be stated:

Probability of n occurrences of event in a given sample

$$= \frac{e^{-\mu} . \mu^n}{n!}$$

where μ is the mean number of occurrences of the event per sample, and $n!$ is factorial $n = 1 \cdot 2 \cdot 3 \ldots n$. Three points should be borne in mind:

(i) The derivation of the Poisson distribution assumes that the probability of the event occurring is small, hence large samples are required.

(ii) The variance of the Poisson distribution is equal to the mean μ.

(iii) The Poisson distribution tends to the normal distribution with mean μ and variance μ for large values of n.

A Poisson distribution is calculated in Chapter 5, Example 6.

Binomial Distribution

The binomial distribution relates to discrete data. In a single trial, an event either occurs with a probability p, or does not occur with a probability q. Clearly

$$p + q = 1$$

The probability of i occurrences of the event in n independent trials is given by the coefficient of t^i in $(q + pt)^n$.

Exercises

4.1 The weights of individual apples from a particular tree are found to be normally distributed. In one year, the crop constituted 150 apples, of which 15 were below 71 g, in mass and 30 were above 103 g. Estimate the mean and standard deviation of the crop, and calculate how many apples are likely to weigh above 96 g.

4.2 What is meant by the inter-quartile range of a distribution? Verify for a 'normal' distribution with mean $= 0$ and standard deviation $= 1$ that the quartiles are ± 0.675. (See Chapter 2.)

4.3 An intelligence quotient (IQ) test is standardised to give a 'normal' distribution with mean 100 and standard deviation 16. Calculate the probability of an individual having an IQ in the following ranges:

(a) less than 70
(b) 70–80
(c) 80–90
(d) 90–100
(e) 100–110
(f) 110–120
(g) 120–130
(h) greater than 130

4.4 In a particular town the number of houses struck by lightning over a period of 100 years had the following distribution:

Number of houses struck	0	1	2	3 or more
Number of years	36	37	17	10

Calculate the mean and variance for this distribution, and calculate the Poisson distribution with the same mean. Without performing calculations, do the data appear to fit a Poisson distribution, and could this have been guessed from the mean and variance?

5

Chi-Squared Test

In many experiments the results obtained are compared with those predicted by a theory which is under test. For example if a die is tossed 600 times, then in theory one would expect 100 occurrences of each of the numbers 1 to 6. If this experiment is carried out (or simulated on a computer) it is extremely unlikely that the exact theoretical result will be obtained. One must therefore ask how far the observed frequencies must differ from the theoretical frequencies before one can reasonably claim that the die is biased or the method of throwing is unfair.

A measure of how far the observed and expected frequencies differ is given by the chi-squared χ^2 statistic

$$\chi^2 = \Sigma \left[\frac{(O-E)^2}{E} \right]$$

where O are the observed frequencies and E the expected frequencies.

Example 1—Die Throwing Experiment and Chi-Squared

The way in which χ^2 is calculated is illustrated with the results from the die throwing experiment (Table 5.1). Thus the value of χ^2 is calculated as 1.96. Given the number of degrees of freedom v, this value of χ^2 can be looked up in χ^2 tables for various probability levels. In this example there are six pairs of O and E values (1, 2, 3, 4, 5 and 6) that is there are six classes. There is one restriction in calculating the expected frequencies in that the expected frequencies have the same total

as the observed frequencies. The number of degrees of freedom v is calculated:

$$v = \text{Number of classes} - \text{Number of restrictions}$$

$$= 6 - 1 = 5$$

Mathematicians have calculated for a random sample with five degrees of freedom the probabilities of obtaining values of χ^2 greater than or equal to certain values:

Probability $P = 99\%$ 95% 90% 80%

Chi-squared $\chi^2 > 0.55$ 1.15 1.61 2.34

It can be seen that the χ^2 value of 1.96 corresponds to a probability of between 80% and 90%. This means that there is between an 80% and 90% chance that results as bad (different from the predicted) or worse could have arisen by chance. Since one would only expect a better result (agreeing more closely with the theoretical) between 10% and 20% of the time there are no statistical grounds for suspecting the fairness of the die.

If the value of χ^2 evaluated as a large number (for example 12), then the probability of a deviation greater than or equal to χ^2 is less than 5%. Since there is less than a 1 in 20 chance of obtaining this χ^2 result by chance one would suspect that the die was unfairly balanced. Moreover if the value of χ^2 exceeded 15, there is less than a 1% chance of a fair die giving this result hence the die used is highly suspect.

Conversely if the value of χ^2 evaluates as a very small number (for example 1) then the

Table 5.1

Score	Observed frequency O	Expected frequency E	$O-E$	$(O-E)^2$	$(O-E)^2/E$
1	105	100	5	25	0.25
2	92	100	-8	64	0.64
3	103	100	3	9	0.09
4	95	100	-5	25	0.25
5	97	100	-3	9	0.09
6	108	100	8	64	0.64
	Σ 600	Σ 600			$\Sigma\ 1.96 = \chi^2$

probability of a deviation greater than or equal to χ^2 is greater than 95%. Since there is less than a 1 in 20 chance of obtaining a result this good one starts to suspect that the data are not random in that 'only good results' have been selected by the experimenter and 'bad' results discarded. If χ^2 is smaller than 0.5 which corresponds to a probability of 99% then the data are almost too good to be true and serious doubts exist as to whether the data are truly random or may even be fictitious.

A complete table of χ^2 values for certain probabilities and varying numbers of degrees of freedom is given in Appendix 5. This should be used to verify the examples given in this chapter.

Example 2—Chi-Squared Applied to Blood Groups

There are four main blood groups in man—groups A, B, AB and O. The genes responsible for types A and B are dominant while the gene for type O is recessive. It follows that a person belonging to group A (phenotype A) may be either homozygous with two A genes, or heterozygous with an A gene and an O gene. In an identical way a person who is phenotype B may have either the genotype BB or BO. People who are phenotype AB must be genotype AB, and similarly phenotype O must be

genotype OO (see Table 5.2). Simple genetic theory predicts that the blood groups of children of two AB parents should be in ratio 1 AA:2 AB:1 BB.

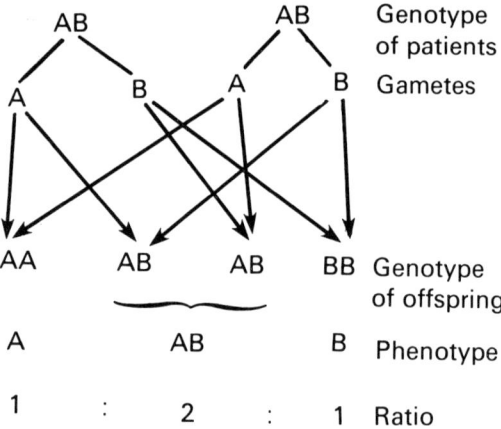

In a survey of 100 children born to such parents the following results were obtained A = 18, AB = 53 and B = 29. Do these results constitute evidence that the theory is false?

Table 5.2

Phenotype	Possible genotypes	
A	AA	AO
B	BB	BO
AB	AB	
O	OO	

Table 5.3

Phenotype (observed blood group)	Observed frequency O	Expected frequency E	$O-E$	$(O-E)^2$	$(O-E)^2/E$
A	18	25	-7	49	1.96
AB	53	50	3	9	0.18
B	29	25	4	16	0.64
	Σ 100	Σ 100			Σ 2.78 $= \chi^2$

Chi-squared is evaluated as shown in Table 5.3. There are three classes A, AB, B, and one restriction (the totals of O and E have been made to agree). The number of degrees of freedom v is given by

$$v = \text{Number of classes}$$
$$\quad - \text{Number of restrictions}$$
$$= 3-1 = 2$$

Reference to χ^2 significance tables (Appendix 5) shows that

Probability P = 50%   30%   20%   10%
Chi-squared $\chi^2 > 1.39$ 2.41   3.22   4.61

The calculated value of χ^2 of 2.78 lies between the 20% and 30% probability levels, and it follows that assuming the genetic theory is correct there is between a 20% and 30% chance that results as bad or worse than this would be obtained because of random errors. Though the observed frequencies differ appreciably from the predicted ones, one would expect results as bad about every fourth survey hence there is no statistical evidence to suspect the genetic theory.

Example 3—Chi-Squared and Contingency Tables

A doctor has 200 patients who suffer from the same disease. The patients may be treated with an old drug, a new drug, or no drug at all. The disease may result in considerable pain, slight pain, or no pain, and the number of patients in each category is shown in the contingency table (Table 5.4). The doctor would like to know if the treatment has any statistical effect on the degree of pain experienced. First, one makes the assumption that the treatment has no effect on the level of pain. Using this assumption one calculates how many people would be expected in each of the categories, that is one produces a contingency table of expected frequencies. This is done as follows.

The proportion of people experiencing considerable pain is $70/200 = 35\%$. The proportion of people having no drug is $85/200 = 42.5\%$. The expected proportion of people having both considerable pain and no drug is $35\% \times 42.5\% = 14.875\%$ which corresponds to 29.75 people out of the 200 sampled. It is quite valid in this context to have a fraction of a person since expected frequencies

Table 5.4

Observed frequencies	No drug	New drug	Old drug	Row totals
Considerable pain	40	16	14	70
Slight pain	30	17	18	65
No pain	15	32	18	65
Column totals	85	65	50	200

do not have to be integers. The other entries in the expected contingency table are generated in a similar manner. The results are shown in Table 5.5. Chi-squared is then calculated in the usual way taking each of the nine pairs of observed and expected frequencies (see Table 5.6). To calculate the number of degrees of freedom one requires the number of classes and the number of restrictions. Since there are nine pairs of O and E frequencies the number of classes is nine. The number of restrictions is slightly more difficult. The total of each horizontal row in the expected table equals that in the observed table. Thus each row constitutes one restriction (in this case there are three restrictions). In addition the total of

cach vertical row is the same in both expected and observed tables. Though this would seem to suggest a further three restrictions in the example given, it in fact only adds a further two restrictions. This is because by adding the row totals (70, 65 and 65) one obtains the total number of patients (200). Since the sum of the column totals (85, 65 and 50) must also equal the number of patients, one can easily calculate one column total from three row totals and two column totals, hence in this case there are $3+2=5$ restrictions. In general for an $m \times n$ contingency table there are $m+n-1$ restrictions and $m \cdot n$ classes. The number of degrees of freedom v is given by

$$\text{or} \quad \left. \begin{array}{ll} v = (m \cdot n)-(m+n-1) = 9-5 \\ v = (m-1) \cdot (n-1) \qquad = 2 \times 2 \end{array} \right\} = 4$$

Reference to the χ^2 distribution table (Appendix 5) shows that for four degrees of freedom a χ^2 value of 18.99 is greater than the value (18.46) for a probability $P=0.1\%$. This means that there is less than 0.1% chance (that is less than 1 chance in 1000) that results which differ from the theory as badly as these could have arisen by chance. This provides extremely strong evidence that the hypothesis assumed is incorrect. The doctor should therefore reject the hypothesis that the treatment has no effect on the level of pain. Conversely this indicates that it is 99.9% certain that one or both of the drugs are beneficial. This does not resolve whether the new, the old or both drugs are beneficial, and this is left as a challenge to the reader. (Hint—calculate χ^2 from a 3×2 contingency table comprising no drug, old drug, and three pain levels and look up significance. Then repeat for no drug and new drug.) Should a problem require a 2×2 contingency table, then it is necessary to use Yates's correction.

Table 5.5

Expected frequencies	No drug	New drug	Old drug	Row totals
Considerable pain	29.75	22.75	17.5	70
Slight pain	27.625	21.125	16.25	65
No pain	27.625	21.125	16.25	65
Column totals	85	65	50	200

Table 5.6

Observed frequency O	Expected frequency E	$(O-E)^2/E$
40	29·75	3·53
16	22.75	2.00
14	17.5	0.70
30	27.625	0.20
17	21.125	0.81
18	16.25	0.19
15	27.625	5.77
32	21.125	5.60
18	16.25	0.19
		$\Sigma \; 18.99 = \chi^2$

Example 4—Use of Yates's Correction when $v=1$

In all cases when the number of degrees of freedom $v=1$ it is necessary to apply Yates's correction for continuity. This states that when $v=1$ the absolute values of the $(O-E)$ differences must each be reduced by 0.5. This will always be necessary with a 2×2 contingency table and also in other cases. Though the reason for this correction is beyond the scope of this book, it is sufficient to observe that χ^2 is a continuous distribution and it is being used with discrete results. The correction is unnecessary when there are several observed and expected frequencies (i.e. $v>1$).

For example if a penny is tossed 100 times, one would predict that it would land showing 'heads' on 50/100 occasions and 'tails' on 50/100 occasions provided that the coin was not biased or the method of tossing unfair. In practice the result may differ slightly from the theoretical value, and the chi-squared test is used to find if the differences between experimental and theoretical frequencies are significant or not. Suppose the result of the experiment was 'heads' 55 times and 'tails' 45 times—can one conclude that the coin is biased, or is the result reasonable for an unbiased coin? (See Table 5.7.) Reference to the χ^2 distribution table (Appendix 5) for $\chi^2=0.81$ and $v=1$ gives a probability of a large deviation P between 30% and 50% which implies a good chance of such a result occurring by chance with a fair coin.

How to Handle Continuous Data

In each of the four examples considered so far there have been only a limited number of possible outcomes. For example when tossed a coin must land with either a 'head' or a 'tail'

uppermost, and a die can show only one of the digits 1–6. Such data are usually termed discrete by mathematicians or discontinuous by biologists.

Many experiments yield different types of data with continuous variation. Some examples of these sorts of experimental data are:

  (i) the heights of a group of men;
 (ii) the weights of individual hen's eggs;
(iii) the girths of tree trunks;
 (iv) a set of titration results;
  (v) a set of amplification factors from apparently identical transistors;
 (vi) the speeds of cars travelling along a particular road.

With such continuous data it is necessary to group the data into a number of discrete classes when performing statistical tests. Grouping of data is commonly performed, for example, when plotting a bar chart. When data are grouped in preparation for the chi-squared test the following points should be observed:

  (i) A large number of measurements should be made. A minimum of at least 30 measurements is essential.
 (ii) To obtain reasonable discrimination (resolution) there should be at least 6–8 classes (i.e. groups of data).
(iii) No class or group should be so small that it contains less than five expected values, that is the expected frequency must be five or more in each class. This limitation is a direct result of the derivation of the chi-squared distribution.

Table 5.7

	Observed frequencies O	Expected frequencies E	$(O-E)$	$Y=$ $\|O-E\|-0.5$	Y^2/E
Heads	55	50	5	4.5	0.405
Tails	45	50	-5	4.5	0.405
					$\overline{\quad\quad}$
					$\Sigma\, 0.81 = \chi^2$

(iv) Though it is common to group data into bands which cover an equal range, this is not essential. If one considers the traffic speed data in Example 5, it is seen that most of the classes cover a speed range of 10 m.p.h., but one class covers a range of 5 m.p.h. and another class covers an infinite range. Should a class contain less than five expected values (restriction iii) then two classes are merged into one with a greater range than before.

It should be noted that unless the number of measurements is large, the value of χ^2 will vary appreciably depending on how the measurements are arranged into different groups. It is partly for this reason that a very high value of χ^2 corresponding to a low probability P is required before a hypothesis is rejected. In general if $P < 5\%$ the hypothesis is suspect, if $P < 1\%$ the hypothesis is highly suspect, and if $P < 0.1\%$ the hypothesis is almost certainly false. These rejection limits are severe compared with the limit of one standard deviation from the mean which is used in other branches of statistics (31.7% of a normal population lie beyond a limit of one standard deviation).

Example 5—Comparison of Observed Frequencies with a Normal Distribution

A civil engineer has monitored the speeds of cars travelling along a main road to decide whether road improvements are necessary. The results are shown in Table 5.8, and by plotting a bar chart of the frequency of various speeds the results appear to be approximately normally distributed (see Fig. 5.1). To enable reasonable predictions the engineer requires a model of traffic speeds, and the problem is to establish whether the normal distribution model is realistic. The observed results are shown in Table 5.8. The mean speed of the cars is 40 m.p.h. and the standard deviation of the speeds is 14.49 m.p.h. These figures can be obtained from the standard deviation program described in

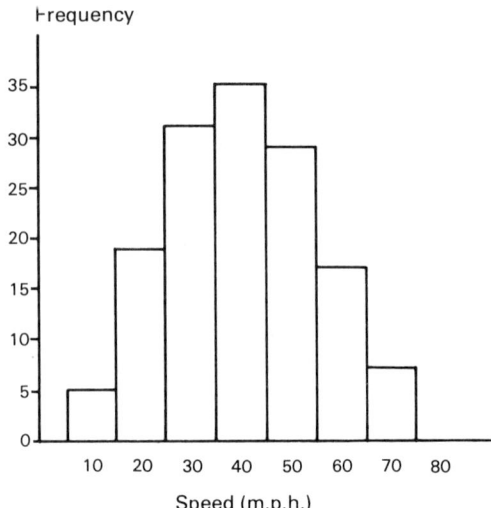

Fig. 5.1

Table 5.8

Traffic speed (m.p.h.)	Observed frequencies O
0–5	0
5–15	5
15–25	19
25–35	31
35–45	35
45–55	29
55–65	17
65–75	7
over 75	0

Σ 143 = number of cars recorded

Chapter 2. It should be noted that this value for the standard deviation involves Sheppard's correction because the speeds have been grouped into intervals of 10 m.p.h. resulting in a slightly smaller standard deviation than the value of 14.77 m.p.h. which would be obtained if grouping was ignored.

A normal population is generated which has the same mean speed, standard deviation of speed and also the same number of cars.

Once this has been done the observed and expected frequencies may be compared to give chi-squared.

Method of Generating Normal Population

(i) A table is prepared showing the various speed ranges.

(ii) The speeds are then expressed as the number of standard deviations from the mean speed. Speeds below the mean give rise to negative values while speeds above the mean give positive values.

(iii) Each of these values (standard deviations from mean) is looked up in a table showing the area under a normal probability curve starting at the left-hand side up to the number of standard deviations specified. (For example looking up the value of one standard deviation in the normal table given in Appendix 4 gives a value of 0.841. This means that 84.1% of any normal population are less than one standard deviation above the mean.) Tables do not usually give negative values for the standard deviation. This is discussed in Chapter 4 and may be handled as follows: firstly, the normal curve is symmetrical. In consequence the area below a given negative value is identical to the area above the same positive value. Secondly, the total area under the normal curve represents all possible outcomes and must by definition be equal to one. The area above a certain value (which corresponds to the area below the required negative value) can be evaluated as $1 -$ the area below the positive value which can be obtained directly from the tables. Thus:

Area below $(-x)$ standard deviations $= 1 -$ Area below $(+x)$ standard deviations (see Fig. 5.2).

(iv) To obtain the area under the normal curve in each speed range one subtracts

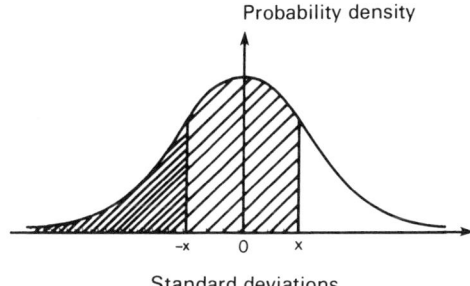

Probability density

Standard deviations

Fig. 5.2

the area below the low speed from the area below the high speed (see Fig. 5.3).

(v) The expected frequencies are derived by multiplying the area (probability) in each speed range by the total number of cars (143 in this example).

This is illustrated in Table 5.9. It must be noted that the sum of the expected frequencies is not exactly 143 cars as would be expected. There are two reasons for this:

(a) Small arithmetic rounding errors have accumulated.

(b) More important the sum of all the areas is 0.997 rather than 1.000. This is caused by the lower speed limit of 0 m.p.h. While this is a perfectly reasonable physical restriction, mathematically with a normal distribution there is a small probability (0.003) that cars travel at less than 0 m.p.h. since the normal probability curve extends to minus infinity. This problem can be hidden and overcome by re-labelling the first speed range as less than 5

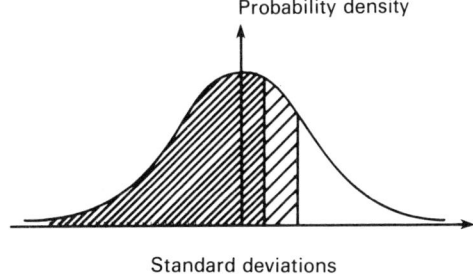

Probability density

Standard deviations

Fig. 5.3

51

Table 5.9

Speed m.p.h.	Speeds as standard deviations from mean	Area of normal curve below this standard deviation	Area within this speed range	Expected frequencies E
0–5	−2.76 to −2.42	0.003 to 0.008	0.005	0.72
5–15	−2.42 to −1.73	0.008 to 0.042	0.034	4.86
15–25	−1.73 to −1.04	0.042 to 0.149	0.107	15.30
25–35	−1.04 to −0.35	0.149 to 0.363	0.214	30.60
35–45	−0.35 to +0.35	0.363 to 0.637	0.274	39.18
45–55	+0.35 to +1.04	0.637 to 0.851	0.214	30.60
55–65	+1.04 to +1.73	0.851 to 0.958	0.107	15.30
65–75	+1.73 to +2.42	0.958 to 0.992	0.034	4.86
over 75	over +2.42	0.992 to 1.000	0.008	1.14
			Σ 0.997	Σ 142.56

m.p.h. rather than 0–5 m.p.h., and this results in an extra 0.003×143 cars in this speed range thus changing the expected frequency for this range from 0.72 to 1.15.

It is now possible to perform the chi-squared test in the usual way (see Table 5.10). The value of χ^2 is thus 1.96. The number of degrees of freedom v is calculated

v = Number of classes

    − Number of restrictions

The number of classes was originally nine, but merging of classes has reduced this to seven. The number of restrictions is three (same total of 143, same mean speed of 40 m.p.h. and same standard deviation of 14.49 m.p.h). Thus

$v = 7 - 3 = 4$

Reference to the χ^2 distribution table in Appendix 5 for $\chi^2 = 1.96$ and $v = 4$ gives a probability P between 0.70 and 0.80. This means that there is between a 70% and 80% chance of obtaining worse results than this by chance if the traffic is normally distributed. χ^2 can never prove a hypothesis but in this case considerable support has been given to the hypothesis that the traffic flow is normally distributed.

Table 5.10

Observed frequencies O	Expected frequencies E	$(O-E)^2/E$
0 ⎫ 5 ⎱ 5	1.15 ⎫ 4.86 ⎱ 6.01	0.17
19	15.30	0.89
31	30.60	0.01
35	39.18	0.45
29	30.60	0.08
17	15.30	0.19
7 ⎫ 0 ⎱ 7	4.86 ⎫ 1.14 ⎱ 6.00	0.17
		Σ 1.96 $= \chi^2$

Example 6—Comparison of Observed Frequencies and Poisson Distribution

A Poisson distribution is useful for analysis of discontinuous (discrete) data (see Chapter 4) and is applicable when the chance of a particular result is small, and the chance is independent of the previous results. Because the chance of the result occurring is small, a large number of tests must be performed.

If one considers the number of defective transistors found in each packet of 100, then the chance that any one transistor is working or defective is totally independent of whether the one previously examined was working or defective, or of how many have already been found to be defective. The Poisson distribution is only applicable if the chance of any transistor being faulty is small and the number of transistors tested is large. The Poisson distribution is very easy to calculate, and this is a great advantage over the normal distribution. It should be noted that for *all* Poisson distributions the mean value is always equal to the variance. The Poisson distribution is calculated using the equation:

$$\text{Probability of } n \text{ occurrences} = \frac{e^{-\mu} \cdot \mu^n}{n!}$$

where μ is the mean and $n!$ is factorial n (i.e. $1 \cdot 2 \cdot 3 \ldots n$). To convert the probabilities obtained in this way into expected frequencies E (for comparison with the observed frequencies O in the chi-squared test), one multiplies the calculated probability by the number of readings, i.e. the number of packets opened.

A quality control department examined the data for the number of defective transistors in a bag. They wished to establish whether faulty components were produced at random, or if the production process tended to have 'bad runs'. If the process produces bad components at random the distribution of defective transistors should approximate to Poisson whereas with 'bad runs' the results will not fit the Poisson distribution.

Eighty bags each containing 100 transistors were examined. The number of transistors in each bag is irrelevant to calculation provided all bags contain the same number, and provided the proportion of faulty transistors is small. The results are as shown in Table 5.11. The mean number of defective transistors per bag is two (160 defective transistors in 80 bags). The Poisson frequencies are calculated as shown in Table 5.12.

The following points should be noted:

(i) By definition factorial O ($O!$) equals one so the Poisson probability for no defective transistors ($n=0$) reduces to $e^{-\mu}$.

Table 5.11

Defective transistors n	Frequency (number of bags) O
0	8
1	18
2	25
3	24
4	5
over 4	0
	Σ 80 = number of bags opened

Table 5.12

Defective transistors n	Poisson probability $e^{-\mu} \cdot \mu^n/n!$		Expected frequencies E
0	e^{-2}	= 0.135	10.8
1	$e^{-2} \cdot 2/1$	= 0.271	21.7
2	$e^{-2} \cdot 2^2/(2 \cdot 1)$	= 0.271	21.7
3	$e^{-2} \cdot 2^3/(3 \cdot 2 \cdot 1)$	= 0.180	14.4
4	$e^{-2} \cdot 2^4/(4 \cdot 3 \cdot 2 \cdot 1)$	= 0.090	7.2
Over 4		0.053	4.2
	Total	1.000	Total 80.0

(ii) The next and subsequent lines in the table can be generated by multiplying the probability on the previous line by μ (2 in this case) and dividing by n. With the exception of the last line, the entire table can be speadily generated in this way.

(iii) The probability for the last line ($n > 4$ in this case) is obtained indirectly by subtracting all the previously calculated probabilities from 1, since the sum of all probabilities must be 1 by definition.

The chi-squared statistic is calculated in a similar manner to the previous examples. It should be noted that expected frequency for more than four defective transistors per bag is less than five. The mathematical derivation of χ^2 requires that all the expected frequencies should be large. In practice large means at least five. To overcome this the last two classes (that is the lines where $n = 4$ and $n > 4$) have been combined to make a single class (see Table 5.13). The value of χ^2 is thus 11.85. The number of degrees of freedom v is calculated:

$$v = \text{Number of classes}$$

$$- \text{Number of restrictions}$$

The number of classes is five. Though there were originally six classes corresponding to $n = 0$, 1, 2, 3, 4 and $n > 4$ defective transistors, $n = 4$ and $n > 4$ have been combined into a single class. The number of restrictions is two

Table 5.13

n	Observed frequency O	Expected frequency E		$(O-E)^2/E$
0	8	10.8		0.73
1	18	21.7		0.63
2	25	21.7		0.50
3	24	14.4		6.40
4	5 } 5	7.2 } 11.4		3.59
>4	0	4.2		
	Σ 80	Σ 80.0		Σ 11.85 $= \chi^2$

(the totals of both O and E are 80 bags, and the mean number defective per bag is two for both O and E). Thus

$$v = 5 - 2 = 3$$

Reference to the chi-squared distribution table in Appendix 5 for $\chi^2 = 11.85$ and three degrees of freedom gives a probability P between 0.01 and 0.001 that is between 1% and 0.1%. If the observed distribution is indeed Poisson then there is less than a 1% chance that results which disagree as badly or worse than this could have arisen by chance. It is therefore reasonable to conclude that the observed results have not come from a Poisson distribution, and that the production of defective transistors is not random.

Finally it is worth checking that the mean and variance (standard deviation squared) of the observed data are nearly equal, since the expected (Poisson) frequencies will by definition have these two terms identical. It is plainly unreasonable to expect two sets of values to agree if their variances are very different. In this example the variance for the observed frequencies is 1.18 compared with the value of 2 for the expected frequencies. It is therefore not surprising that the Poisson distribution is not found to fit!

Interpretation of the Probability Results

The χ^2 calculation together with the number of degrees of freedom eventually yield a probability P. This probability corresponds to the chance that results as different from the expected values (or even more different) could have arisen by chance assuming that the hypothesis is correct. The P value gives an indication of how likely it is that the hypothesis is false. It should be noted that χ^2 may be used as evidence to disprove a hypothesis if the observed and expected values differ significantly. Conversely agreement shows that the observed results could have arisen from the hypothesis, but this does not prove that the hypothesis is true (see Tables 5.14–5.16). Table 5.15 shows the usual range where the

Table 5.14   When to Reject the Hypothesis

Value of χ^2	Difference between observed and expected values	The hypothesis
Between $P=5\%$ and $P=1\%$ values	Significant	Probably untrue
Between $P=1\%$ and $P=0.1\%$ values	Highly significant	Most probably untrue
Greater than $P=0.1\%$ value	Exceedingly significant	Almost certainly untrue

Table 5.15   When the Hypothesis May be True

Value of χ^2	Difference between observed and expected values	Evidence to reject the hypothesis
Between $P=10\%$ and $P=5\%$ values	Barely significant	Very slight
Between $P=95\%$ and $P=10\%$ values	Not significant	None

Table 5.16   When to Suspect the Data

Value of χ^2	*Agreement* between observed and expected values	Data
Between $P=99\%$ and 95% values	Unbelievably good	Suspect
Less than $P=99\%$ values	Too good to be true	Highly suspect

hypothesis is accepted, but one must remember that this does not prove that the hypothesis is true.

If χ^2 is in the range shown in Table 5.16 the agreement is so good that it is improbable that such results could have arisen by chance. In these circumstances one should suspect:

(i) that the data are totally fictitious or have been 'improved' by the experimenter removing 'bad' results;

(ii) that the sample is not random, and the sampling technique should be examined;

(iii) that the hypothesis has been designed to fit the data too perfectly.

Null Hypothesis

Some books refer to the 'null hypothesis'. The null hypothesis states that there is no significant difference between the observed and expected values. Chi-squared provides a method of rejecting or not rejecting the null hypothesis. Since confusion may arise between the scientific hypothesis under test and the null hypothesis, the foregoing examples and discussion refer only to the scientific hypothesis under test.

Details of the Computer Program (Program 5.1 and Trial Runs 5.1–5.5)

First the program prints the title (line 20), then asks if the user requires full instructions. A subroutine (lines 2560–2650) checks that an answer YES or NO has been given, and continues to prompt the user if any other reply is given. Depending on the reply, long or shortened instructions are printed during the first run with the program, but a second or subsequent run always gets shortened messages.

The user is instructed to input the data values, and up to 100 pairs of observed and expected frequencies may be typed in (lines 190–290). Each pair of values is checked to ensure that the numbers typed are valid using a subroutine (lines 1600–1790). The observed frequency must be an integer and positive or

Trial run 5.1

```
      CHI-SQUARED TEST
      === ======= ====
WOULD YOU LIKE FULL INSTRUCTIONS?   TYPE YES OR NO & PRESS RETURN.

? YES
THE PURPOSE OF THE CHI-SQUARED TEST IS TO COMPARE A SET OF
OBSERVED FREQUENCY READINGS WITH THOSE PREDICTED BY THE
HYPOTHESIS UNDER TEST.  A HIGH VALUE SUGGESTS THAT THE
HYPOTHESIS IS INCORRECT, WHILST A LOW VALUE INDICATES GOOD
AGREEMENT WITH THE HYPOTHESIS.
TYPE IN A PAIR OF OBSERVED AND EXPECTED DATA FREQUENCIES
SEPARATED BY A COMMA.
PRESS RETURN AFTER EACH PAIR OF VALUES
YOU WILL BE GIVEN THE CHANCE TO CORRECT TYPING ERRORS LATER

INPUT DATA
TERMINATE THE DATA WITH 999999, 999999
OBS FREQ, THEOR FREQ
? 105, 100
? 92, 100
? 103, 100
? 95, 100
? 97, 100
? 108, 100
? 999999, 999999
ARE THE DATA VALUES ENTERED CORRECT?   TYPE YES OR NO & PRESS RETURN.

? YES
VALUE OF CHI-SQUARED = 1.96
YOU HAVE PROVIDED 6 CLASSES (DATA PAIRS)
TYPE NUMBER OF DEGREES OF FREEDOM, OR 0 FOR AN EXPLANATION
? 5

PROBABILITY THAT EXPERIMENTAL DATA WHICH AGREES AS BADLY
OR WORSE THAN THIS COULD HAVE ARISEN BY CHANCE IS 85  %

THERE IS NO EVIDENCE TO REJECT THE HYPOTHESIS

WOULD YOU LIKE ANOTHER RUN?   TYPE YES OR NO & PRESS RETURN.

? NO
END OF JOB
```

Trial run 5.2

```
        CHI-SQUARED TEST
        === ======= ====
WOULD YOU LIKE FULL INSTRUCTIONS?    TYPE YES OR NO & PRESS RETURN.

? NO

INPUT DATA
TERMINATE THE DATA WITH 999999, 999999
OBS FREQ, THEOR FREQ
? 18, 2500
? 18, 25
? 53, 50
? 29, 25
? 999999, 999999
ARE THE DATA VALUES ENTERED CORRECT?
? NO
HERE IS A LIST OF THE CURRENT DATA
LINE NUMBER    OBS FREQ         THEOR FREQ
1                18             2500
2                18             25
3                53             50
4                29             25
TYPE R TO REPLACE  A TO ADD  D TO DELETE  L TO LIST   OR C TO CONTINUE ? D
TYPE THE LINENUMBER OF THE LINE TO BE DELETED
? 1
OK
HERE IS A LIST OF THE CURRENT DATA
LINE NUMBER    OBS FREQ         THEOR FREQ
1                18             25
2                53             50
3                29             25
TYPE R TO REPLACE  A TO ADD  D TO DELETE  L TO LIST   OR C TO CONTINUE ? C
VALUE OF CHI-SQUARED = 2.78
YOU HAVE PROVIDED 3 CLASSES (DATA PAIRS)
TYPE NUMBER OF DEGREES OF FREEDOM, OR 0 FOR AN EXPLANATION
? 2

PROBABILITY THAT EXPERIMENTAL DATA WHICH AGREES AS BADLY
OR WORSE THAN THIS COULD HAVE ARISEN BY CHANCE IS 25  %

THERE IS NO EVIDENCE TO REJECT THE HYPOTHESIS

WOULD YOU LIKE ANOTHER RUN?
? NO
END OF JOB
```

zero. The theoretical frequency is checked to ensure that it is positive, and also that it is sufficiently large (greater than or equal to five). If any of these checks fail, the data pair is rejected and the user is told to re-type the correct values. In all of these cases except where the theoretical frequency is less than five the line of data is incorrect, but in the case of a theoretical frequency below five the user

must decide whether to combine the data with that from another group, or omit it altogether. The number of valid data pairs is counted, and the end of data input is signalled by the user typing the terminator 999999, 999999.

Next a subroutine is entered to check the data which have been typed in, and to alter them if necessary (lines 1800–2550). The user is asked if the data entered are correct, and the

Trial run 5.3

```
      CHI-SQUARED TEST
      === ======= ====
WOULD YOU LIKE FULL INSTRUCTIONS?   TYPE YES OR NO & PRESS RETURN.

? NO

INPUT DATA
TERMINATE THE DATA WITH 999999, 999999
OBS FREQ, THEOR FREQ
? 40, 29.75
? 16, 22.75
? 14, 17.5
? 30, 27.625
? 17, 21.125
? 18, 16.25
? 15, 27.625
? 32, 21.125
? 18, 16.25
? 999999, 999999
ARE THE DATA VALUES ENTERED CORRECT?
? YES
VALUE OF CHI-SQUARED = 18.989
YOU HAVE PROVIDED 9 CLASSES (DATA PAIRS)
TYPE NUMBER OF DEGREES OF FREEDOM, OR 0 FOR AN EXPLANATION
? 4

PROBABILITY THAT EXPERIMENTAL DATA WHICH AGREES AS BADLY
OR WORSE THAN THIS COULD HAVE ARISEN BY CHANCE IS 0.1  %

THE HYPOTHESIS IS ALMOST CERTAINLY UNTRUE

WOULD YOU LIKE ANOTHER RUN?
? NO
END OF JOB
```

YES/NO subroutine (lines 2560–2650) is used to obtain an answer of YES or NO. If the data are correct the program returns from the check subroutine, but otherwise the following procedure is adopted. The data are listed in three columns—line number, observed frequency and calculated frequency. It should be noted that if there are a lot of data, the program stops the listing when the screen contains 20 lines. This is to allow the user to examine the data before they scroll off the top of the screen on a visual display unit. The user is asked if he would like to continue listing, and if so the next 20 lines are displayed. The value of 20 is chosen by setting the variable $A4$ equal to 20 in line 1830, and this value was chosen since many visual display units show 20 lines of 80 characters. For VDUs which display 16 lines of 64 characters the value of $A4$ should be changed to 16, and for continuous listing of all the data on a printing terminal $A4$ should be set to 999.

After listing the data, instructions are printed to explain how the user may modify an existing line of data, add an extra line, delete an existing line, list the data or continue the calculation. New data are checked to ensure that they are reasonable by calling the check subroutine (lines 1600–1790). In general any number of alterations may be made to the data except that one is not allowed to add data if the arrays already hold 100 data pairs, and one is not allowed to delete all the data. If a line other than the last line is deleted, the current data are automatically listed since the deletion changes the line numbers. Extensive

Trial run 5.4

```
      CHI-SQUARED TEST
      === ======= ====
WOULD YOU LIKE FULL INSTRUCTIONS?   TYPE YES OR NO & PRESS RETURN.

? NO

INPUT DATA
TERMINATE THE DATA WITH 999999, 999999
OBS FREQ, THEOR FREQ
? 55, 50
? 45, 50
? 999999, 999999
ARE THE DATA VALUES ENTERED CORRECT?
? NO
HERE IS A LIST OF THE CURRENT DATA
LINE NUMBER    OBS FREQ       THEOR FREQ
1                55              50
2                45              50
TYPE R TO REPLACE  A TO ADD  D TO DELETE  L TO LIST   OR C TO CONTINUE ? C
VALUE OF CHI-SQUARED = 1
YOU HAVE PROVIDED 2 CLASSES (DATA PAIRS)
TYPE NUMBER OF DEGREES OF FREEDOM, OR 0 FOR AN EXPLANATION
? 1

SINCE THERE IS ONLY ONE DEGREE OF FREEDOM
CHI-SQUARED WILL BE RECALCULATED USING YATES CORRECTION
RECALCULATED VALUE FOR CHI-SQUARED = 0.81

PROBABILITY THAT EXPERIMENTAL DATA WHICH AGREES AS BADLY
OR WORSE THAN THIS COULD HAVE ARISEN BY CHANCE IS 37   %

THERE IS NO EVIDENCE TO REJECT THE HYPOTHESIS

WOULD YOU LIKE ANOTHER RUN?
? NO
END OF JOB
```

checks prevent the user altering lines which do not exist. Eventually the user will continue with the calculation.

A check is performed to ensure that there are at least two data pairs (lines 360–380), and the value of chi-squared is calculated (lines 390–420) and printed (line 430).

The user is then asked to type the number of degrees of freedom. The value typed is checked to ensure that it is an integer, less than or equal to the number of data pairs, and greater than zero. If any of these tests fail, full instructions explaining how to calculate the number of degrees of freedom are printed out, and the user is requested to retype the correct value. Instructions may be obtained by typing 0 for the number of degrees of freedom.

If the number of degrees of freedom is 1 then the value of the chi-squared is recalculated using Yates's correction (lines 700–830).

In the unlikely event that the observed and theoretical frequencies agree exactly the run is abandoned. Otherwise an empirical polynomial equation is used to calculate the probability P that results with as bad or worse agreement as the experimental frequencies could have arisen by chance (lines 890–1150). This is equivalent to manually looking up a table of probabilities for the appropriate value of chi-squared and the particular number of degrees of freedom. With tables one might say, for example, that the value was within the 95% limit. The program evaluates the exact probability and rounds the answer to give

Trial run 5.5

```
    CHI-SQUARED TEST
    === ======= ====
WOULD YOU LIKE FULL INSTRUCTIONS?   TYPE YES OR NO & PRESS RETURN.

? NO

INPUT DATA
TERMINATE THE DATA WITH 999999, 999999
OBS FREQ, THEOR FREQ
? 5, 6.01
? 19, 15.3
? 31, 30.6
? 35, 39.18
? 29, 30.6
? 17, 15.3
? 7, 6.00
? 999999, 999999
ARE THE DATA VALUES ENTERED CORRECT?
? YES
VALUE OF CHI-SQUARED = 1.9549
YOU HAVE PROVIDED 7 CLASSES (DATA PAIRS)
TYPE NUMBER OF DEGREES OF FREEDOM, OR 0 FOR AN EXPLANATION
? 4

PROBABILITY THAT EXPERIMENTAL DATA WHICH AGREES AS BADLY
OR WORSE THAN THIS COULD HAVE ARISEN BY CHANCE IS 74  %

THERE IS NO EVIDENCE TO REJECT THE HYPOTHESIS

WOULD YOU LIKE ANOTHER RUN?
? NO
END OF JOB
```

either an integer or one decimal figure in the printed probability. The program then prints a comment on the significance of the value and the validity of the hypothesis.

Finally the user is asked if he would like another run (lines 1410–1570), and the YES/NO subroutine is used to check the reply. If another run is required, the user is offered the choice of typing in completely new data, or editing the data already typed in prior to another run.

Exercises

5.1 (a) Use the chi-squared test to establish if the results from a die throwing experiment suggest that the die is fair.

Score	1	2	3	4	5	6
Frequency	47	44	69	48	45	47

(b) Test whether the die gives an abnormal proportion of 3s.

Score	3	others
Frequency	69	231

Explain the results.

5.2 The values below are extracted from 100 one digit numbers taken from a table claiming to be random numbers:

98133	55804	84863	08022	96684
22037	11087	40257	33483	10143
94299	66246	29286	92984	67425
22266	86541	77191	64578	17755

Test whether the frequencies of the digits differ significantly from random.

5.3 A laboratory assistant is responsible for growing batches of 100 pea seeds, and has to record the number of dwarf plants from each batch. From theoretical considerations it is expected that on average 25 out of each 100 grown will be dwarf. The number of dwarfs claimed for 8 batches of 100 plants were

17, 31, 21, 29, 30, 16, 20, 36

Does this support the suspicion that the laboratory assistant is careless or is manufacturing results?

5.4 A seaside resort has three beaches. A survey of the three beaches was made at the same time on the same day, with the following results:

Beach	A	B	C
Number of males	71	82	87
Number of females	79	68	113

Test whether the proportion of females differs significantly between the beaches.

5.5 A roulette wheel is suspected of being unfair. There are 37 possible scores which are labelled 0 to 36 respectively, and the gaming house wins on the score of zero. Of 999 trial spins, the house won (that is zero came up) on 44 occasions. Does this constitute evidence that the roulette wheel is biased? Would it be fair to suspect the wheel if zero had been the outcome on 35 occasions? (Remember to use Yates's correction since $v = 1$.)

5.6 Explain why the χ^2 statistic calculated from a 2×2 contingency table requires Yates's correction. 100 guinea pigs were fed with diet 1, and another 100 similar guinea pigs were fed with diet 2. Vitamin deficiency was observed in 33 animals fed with diet 1 and 45 animals fed with diet 2. Does the proportion of animals suffering vitamin deficiency differ significantly?

Program 5.1   Trial run.

```
    CHI-SQUARED TEST
    === ======= ====
WOULD YOU LIKE FULL INSTRUCTIONS?   TYPE YES OR NO & PRESS RETURN.

? NO

INPUT DATA
TERMINATE THE DATA WITH 999999, 999999
OBS FREQ, THEOR FREQ
? 8, 10.8
? 18, 21./
? 25, 21.7
? 24, 14.4
? 5, 11.4
? 999999, 999999
ARE THE DATA VALUES ENTERED CORRECT?
? YES
VALUE OF CHI-SQUARED = 11.8516
YOU HAVE PROVIDED 5 CLASSES (DATA PAIRS)
TYPE NUMBER OF DEGREES OF FREEDOM, OR 0 FOR AN EXPLANATION
? 3

PROBABILITY THAT EXPERIMENTAL DATA WHICH AGREES AS BADLY
OR WORSE THAN THIS COULD HAVE ARISEN BY CHANCE IS 0.8  %

THE HYPOTHESIS IS MOST PROBABLY UNTRUE

WOULD YOU LIKE ANOTHER RUN?
? NO
END OF JOB
```

```
10  DIM Q$(10), I$(3), F(100), T(100)
20  PRINT TAB(8); "CHI-SQUARED TEST"
30  PRINT TAB(8); "=== ======= ===="
40  REM F ARRAY CONTAINS OBSERVED & T CONTAINS THEORETICAL FREQUENCIES
50  PRINT "WOULD YOU LIKE FULL INSTRUCTIONS?";
60  GOSUB 2580
70  LET I$ = Q$
80  IF I$ = "NO" THEN 180
90  PRINT "THE PURPOSE OF THE CHI-SQUARED TEST IS TO COMPARE A SET OF"
100 PRINT "OBSERVED FREQUENCY READINGS WITH THOSE PREDICTED BY THE"
110 PRINT "HYPOTHESIS UNDER TEST.  A HIGH VALUE SUGGESTS THAT THE"
120 PRINT "HYPOTHESIS IS INCORRECT, WHILST A LOW VALUE INDICATES GOOD"
130 PRINT "AGREEMENT WITH THE HYPOTHESIS."
140 PRINT "TYPE IN A PAIR OF OBSERVED AND EXPECTED DATA FREQUENCIES"
150 PRINT "SEPARATED BY A COMMA."
160 PRINT "PRESS RETURN AFTER EACH PAIR OF VALUES"
170 PRINT "YOU WILL BE GIVEN THE CHANCE TO CORRECT TYPING ERRORS LATER"
180 PRINT
190 REM INPUT & CHECK VALIDITY OF INPUT FREQUENCIES
200 PRINT "INPUT DATA"
210 PRINT "TERMINATE THE DATA WITH 999999, 999999"
220 PRINT "OBS FREQ, THEOR FREQ"
230 LET N = 0
240 FOR I = 1 TO 100
250    REM ENTER SUBROUTINE TO INPUT DATA PAIR & CHECK THAT IT IS VALID
260    GOSUB 1620
270    IF ABS(F(I) - 999999) + ABS(T(I) - 999999) = 0 THEN 310
280    LET N = N + 1
290 NEXT I
300 PRINT "THIS PROGRAM CAN ONLY HANDLE 100 VALUES"
310 IF N > 0 THEN 350
320 PRINT "YOU MUST ENTER SOME VALID DATA"
330 GOTO 240
340 REM ENTER SUBROUTINE TO CHECK & EDIT DATA IF NECESSARY
350 GOSUB 1810
360 IF N > 1 THEN 390
370 PRINT "THERE MUST BE AT LEAST 2 DATA VALUES"
380 GOTO 870
390 LET S = 0
400 FOR I = 1 TO N
410    LET S = S + (F(I) - T(I)) * (F(I) - T(I)) / T(I)
420 NEXT I
430 PRINT "VALUE OF CHI-SQUARED ="; S
440 PRINT "YOU HAVE PROVIDED"; N; "CLASSES (DATA PAIRS)"
450 PRINT "TYPE NUMBER OF DEGREES OF FREEDOM, OR 0 FOR AN EXPLANATION"
460 INPUT D
470 IF D < N THEN 500
480 PRINT "THE NUMBER OF DEGREES OF FREEDOM MUST BE LESS THAN"; N
490 GOTO 530
500 IF D <= 0 THEN 530
510 IF D = INT(D) THEN 710
520 PRINT "THE NUMBER OF DEGREES OF FREEDOM MUST BE A WHOLE NUMBER"
530 PRINT "THE NUMBER OF DEGREES OF FREEDOM IS THE NUMBER OF CLASSES IN"
540 PRINT "THE DATA PROVIDED MINUS THE NUMBER OF RESTRICTIONS IMPOSED"
550 PRINT "IN THE CALCULATION OF THE THEORETICAL FREQUENCY.  EG. IF A"
560 PRINT "NORMAL DISTRIBUTION IS BEING TESTED FOR THEN THE THEORETICAL"
570 PRINT "FREQUENCIES WILL HAVE (1) THE SAME TOTAL, (2) SAME MEAN &"
580 PRINT "(3) THE SAME STANDARD DEVIATION AS THE OBSERVED FREQUENCIES."
590 PRINT "THUS THERE ARE THREE RESTRICTIONS. SIMILARLY IF THE POISSON"
600 PRINT "OR BINOMIAL DISTRIBUTIONS ARE BEING TESTED THERE WILL BE"
610 PRINT "ONE OR TWO RESTRICTIONS DEPENDING ON WHETHER JUST THE TOTALS"
```

```
620 PRINT "OR BOTH THE TOTALS & THE MEANS HAVE BEEN FORCED TO AGREE."
630 PRINT
640 PRINT "IF YOU ARE USING A CONTINGENCY TABLE OF H ROWS AND K COLUMNS"
650 PRINT "NUMBER OF DEGREES OF FREEDOM IS CALCULATED AS (H-1)*(K-1)"
660 PRINT "WHICH MAKES ALLOWANCE FOR AGREEMENT OF ROW AND COLUMN TOTALS"
670 PRINT "BETWEEN OBSERVED AND CALCULATED TABLES."
680 PRINT
690 GOTO 440
700 REM APPLY YATES CORRECTION TO CHI-SQUARED IF DEGREES FREEDOM = 1
710 IF D > 1 THEN 840
720 PRINT
730 PRINT "SINCE THERE IS ONLY ONE DEGREE OF FREEDOM"
740 PRINT "CHI-SQUARED WILL BE RECALCULATED USING YATES CORRECTION"
750 IF I$ = "NO" THEN 780
760 PRINT "ABSOLUTE DIFFERENCE OF EACH OBSERVED FREQ - EXPECTED FREQ"
770 PRINT "TERM HAS BEEN REDUCED BY 0.5"
780 LET S = 0
790 FOR I = 1 TO N
800    IF ABS(F(I) - T(I)) < 0.5 THEN 820
810    LET S = S + (ABS(F(I)-T(I))-0.5) * (ABS(F(I)-T(I))-0.5) / T(I)
820 NEXT I
830 PRINT "RECALCULATED VALUE FOR CHI-SQUARED ="; S
840 IF S <> 0 THEN 890
850 PRINT "THE OBSERVED FREQUENCY VALUES ALL AGREE"
860 PRINT "EXACTLY WITH THE THEORETICAL FREQUENCY"
870 PRINT "RUN ABANDONED ON THIS DATA."
880 GOTO 1410
890 LET E2 = EXP(-10)
900 LET G2 = S / 2
910 LET S1 = 0
920 LET W = 1
930 LET J = 2
940 LET M1 = D + 1
950 LET E1 = 0
960 IF D = 2 * INT(D / 2) THEN 1070
970 LET E1 = 1
980 LET J = 3
990 GOTO 1070
1000 LET S1 = S1 + W
1010 LET W = W * S / J
1020 LET J = J + 2
1030 IF W < 100000 THEN 1070
1040 LET S1 = S1 * E2
1050 LET W = W * E2
1060 LET G2 = G2 - 10
1070 IF J < M1 THEN 1000
1080 LET P2 = EXP(-G2) * S1
1090 LET P = P2
1100 IF E1 = 0 THEN 1160
1110 LET Z = SQR(S)
1120 REM EMPIRICAL POLYNOMIAL TO EVALUATE PROBABILITY
1130 LET P1 = (0.005711 * Z - 0.006523) * Z + 0.038704
1140 LET P1 = ((P1 * Z + 0.094513) * Z + 0.200039) * Z + 1
1150 LET P = 1 / (P1 * P1 * P1 * P1) + SQR(2 * S / 3.14159) * P2
1160 PRINT
1170 LET P = P * 100
1180 PRINT "PROBABILITY THAT EXPERIMENTAL DATA WHICH AGREES AS BADLY"
1190 PRINT "OR WORSE THAN THIS COULD HAVE ARISEN BY CHANCE IS";
1200 LET K = 1
1210 IF (P - 10) * (P - 95) < 0 THEN 1230
1220 LET K = 10
```

```
1230 PRINT INT(K * P + 0.5) / K; " %"
1240 PRINT
1250 REM PRINT COMMENTS ON THE VALIDITY OF THE HYPOTHESIS
1260 IF P > 0.1 THEN 1280
1270 PRINT "THE HYPOTHESIS IS ALMOST CERTAINLY UNTRUE"
1280 IF (P - 0.1) * (P - 1) > 0 THEN 1300
1290 PRINT "THE HYPOTHESIS IS MOST PROBABLY UNTRUE"
1300 IF (P - 1) * (P - 5) > 0 THEN 1320
1310 PRINT "THE HYPOTHESIS IS PROBABLY UNTRUE"
1320 IF (P - 5) * (P - 10) > 0 THEN 1340
1330 PRINT "EVIDENCE TO REJECT THE HYPOTHESIS IS VERY SLIGHT"
1340 IF (P - 10) * (P - 95) > 0 THEN 1360
1350 PRINT "THERE IS NO EVIDENCE TO REJECT THE HYPOTHESIS"
1360 IF (P - 95) * (P - 99) > 0 THEN 1380
1370 PRINT "THE AGREEMENT IS UNBELIEVABLY GOOD & THE DATA ARE SUSPECT"
1380 IF P < 99 THEN 1410
1390 PRINT "THE AGREEMENT IS TOO GOOD TO BE TRUE & THE DATA"
1400 PRINT "ARE HIGHLY SUSPECT"
1410 PRINT
1420 PRINT "WOULD YOU LIKE ANOTHER RUN?";
1430 GOSUB 2570
1440 IF Q$ = "NO" THEN 1580
1450 LET I$ = "NO"
1460 PRINT "TYPE NEW FOR A RUN WITH COMPLETELY NEW DATA"
1470 PRINT "  OR OLD TO EDIT & RERUN THE EXISTING DATA"
1480 INPUT Q$
1490 IF Q$ = "NEW" THEN 1550
1500 IF Q$ = "OLD" THEN 1530
1510 PRINT "REPLY '"; Q$; "' NOT UNDERSTOOD"
1520 GOTO 1460
1530 GOSUB 1860
1540 GOTO 360
1550 PRINT
1560 PRINT "NEW SET OF DATA"
1570 GOTO 180
1580 PRINT "END OF JOB"
1590 STOP
1600 REM SUBROUTINE TO INPUT & CHECK VALIDITY OF INPUT FREQUENCIES
1610 PRINT "OBS FREQ, THEOR FREQ"
1620 INPUT F(I), T(I)
1630 IF F(I) = INT(F(I)) THEN 1660
1640 PRINT "OBSERVED FREQUENCY MUST BE A WHOLE NUMBER"
1650 GOTO 1770
1660 IF F(I) >= 0 THEN 1690
1670 PRINT "OBSERVED FREQUENCY MUST BE POSITIVE"
1680 GOTO 1770
1690 IF T(I) >= 0 THEN 1720
1700 PRINT "A NEGATIVE THEORETICAL FREQUENCY IS IMPOSSIBLE"
1710 GOTO 1770
1720 IF T(I) >= 5 THEN 1790
1730 PRINT "THE CHI-SQUARED DERIVATION REQUIRES THAT ALL EXPECTED"
1740 PRINT "FREQUENCIES ARE SUFFICIENTLY LARGE.  THIS IS USUALLY TAKEN"
1750 PRINT "TO MEAN A MINIMUM OF FIVE."
1760 PRINT "EITHER OMIT THE DATA PAIR, OR MERGE IT WITH ANOTHER GROUP."
1770 PRINT "DATA PAIR REJECTED - RETYPE CORRECTLY"
1780 GOTO 1620
1790 RETURN
1800 REM SUBROUTINE TO CHECK THAT DATA ARE CORRECT & ALTER IF NECESSARY
1810 PRINT "ARE THE DATA VALUES ENTERED CORRECT?";
1820 REM A4 SHOULD BE SET TO THE NUMBER OF LINES ON THE VDU
1830 LET A4 = 20
```

```
1840  GOSUB 2570
1850  IF Q$ = "YES" THEN 2550
1860  PRINT "HERE IS A LIST OF THE CURRENT DATA"
1870  PRINT "LINE NUMBER","OBS FREQ","THEOR FREQ"
1880  FOR I = 1 TO N
1890     PRINT I, F(I), T(I)
1900     IF INT(I / (A4 - 1)) * (A4 - 1) <> I THEN 1940
1910     PRINT "WOULD YOU LIKE TO CONTINUE LISTING";
1920     GOSUB 2570
1930     IF Q$ = "NO" THEN 1950
1940  NEXT I
1950  PRINT "TYPE R TO REPLACE";
1960  IF I$ = "NO" THEN 1980
1970  PRINT " AN EXISTING LINE OF DATA"
1980  IF N = 100 THEN 2030
1990  PRINT TAB(5); " A TO ADD";
2000  IF I$ = "NO" THEN 2020
2010  PRINT " AN EXTRA LINE"
2020  IF N = 1 THEN 2060
2030  PRINT TAB(5); " D TO DELETE";
2040  IF I$ = "NO" THEN 2060
2050  PRINT " AN EXISTING LINE"
2060  PRINT TAB(5); " L TO LIST";
2070  IF I$ = "NO" THEN 2090
2080  PRINT " THE DATA"
2090  PRINT "   OR C TO CONTINUE";
2100  IF I$ = "NO" THEN 2120
2110  PRINT " THE CALCULATION"
2120  INPUT Q$
2130  IF Q$ = "R" THEN 2230
2140  IF N = 100 THEN 2170
2150  IF Q$ = "A" THEN 2330
2160  IF N = 1 THEN 2180
2170  IF Q$ = "D" THEN 2400
2180  IF Q$ = "L" THEN 1860
2190  IF Q$ = "C" THEN 2550
2200  PRINT "REPLY '"; Q$; "' NOT UNDERSTOOD."
2210  GOTO 1950
2220  REM REPLACE LINE
2230  PRINT "TYPE THE LINENUMBER OF THE LINE TO BE REPLACED";
2240  INPUT I
2250  IF I <> INT(I) THEN 2270
2260  IF (I - 1) * (I - N) <= 0 THEN 2300
2270  PRINT "LINENUMBER MUST BE AN INTEGER IN THE RANGE 1 -"; N
2280  PRINT "RE-";
2290  GOTO 2230
2300  PRINT "TYPE THE CORRECT LINE TO REPLACE THE ONE WHICH IS WRONG:"
2310  GOTO 2370
2320  REM ADD A NEW LINE
2330  LET N = N + 1
2340  LET I = N
2350  PRINT "TYPE THE ADDITIONAL LINE OF DATA AS SHOWN:"
2360  REM ENTER SUBROUTINE TO INPUT DATA PAIR & CHECK THAT IT IS VALID
2370  GOSUB 1610
2380  PRINT "OK"
2390  GOTO 1950
2400  REM DELETE A LINE
2410  PRINT "TYPE THE LINENUMBER OF THE LINE TO BE DELETED"
2420  INPUT J
2430  IF (J - 1) * (J - N) > 0 THEN 2450
2440  IF J = INT(J) THEN 2470
```

```
2450 PRINT "LINENUMBER MUST BE AN INTEGER IN THE RANGE 1 -"; N
2460 GOTO 2410
2470 FOR I = J + 1 TO N
2480    LET F(I - 1) = F(I)
2490    LET T(I - 1) = T(I)
2500 NEXT I
2510 LET N = N - 1
2520 PRINT "OK"
2530 IF J > N THEN 1950
2540 GOTO 1860
2550 RETURN
2560 REM SUBROUTINE TO CHECK REPLIES
2570 IF I$ = "NO" THEN 2590
2580 PRINT " TYPE YES OR NO & PRESS RETURN."
2590 PRINT
2600 INPUT Q$
2610 IF Q$ = "YES" THEN 2650
2620 IF Q$ = "NO" THEN 2650
2630 PRINT "REPLY '"; Q$; "' NOT UNDERSTOOD.";
2640 GOTO 2580
2650 RETURN
2660 END
```

5.7 The number of deaths recorded in the obituary column of a newspaper were recorded over a period of 700 publications, and yielded the following results:

Number of deaths recorded on a particular day

0	1	2	3	4	5 or more

Number of days

205	240	165	70	15	5

Test whether the number of deaths differs significantly from a Poisson distribution with the same mean.

5.8 When studying plant genetics, Mendel found 315 round and yellow peas, 108 round and green, 101 wrinkled and yellow, and 32 wrinkled and green. His theory of dominant and recessive characters in heredity predicts that these numbers should be in the ratio $9:3:3:1$. Do the observed results agree with the theory, and are the results so good that one must suspect their authenticity?

6

Comparison of Two Samples

Two sets of data have been collected. The first set comprises n_1 readings and has a mean m_1. The second set has n_2 readings and a mean of m_2. The estimated standard deviations s_1 and s_2 of the parent populations from which the two samples were drawn are calculated:

$$s_1 = \sqrt{\Sigma(x_1 - m_1)^2/(n_1 - 1)}$$

and

$$s_2 = \sqrt{[\Sigma(x_2 - m_2)^2/(n_2 - 1)]}$$

The problem is to establish if the two sets of data differ significantly, that is whether the difference in means $|m_1 - m_2|$ is significantly large compared with the standard deviations s_1 and s_2.

With large sets of data the method of doing the comparison may be summarised:

(i) The mean m_1 for the first set of data is known. However, if another sample of n_1 readings was drawn from the same parent population, it is probable that a slightly different mean m_1 would be obtained. The first step is to estimate by how much m_1 varies, that is to estimate the standard error of m_1.

(ii) In a similar way an estimate is made of the standard error of m_2 for the second set of data.

(iii) The estimated values for the standard errors for m_1 and m_2 are then used to estimate the standard error of the difference in means $|m_1 - m_2|$.

(iv) The value of $|m_1 - m_2|$ is divided by the standard errors of the difference in means calculated in (iii) to give the number of standard errors variation.

(v) This value is looked up in a *normal distribution table* (Appendix 4) to find the probability of obtaining a difference in means $|m_1 - m_2|$ as large or larger than this.

Derivation of the Test for Comparing Large Samples

'If samples of size n are drawn at random from a parent population of mean μ and standard deviation σ, the sample means constitute a population of mean μ and whose standard deviation tends to $\sigma/\sqrt{n}$.' (See Chapter 3.)

(i) For the first set of data, the standard deviation s_1 is the best estimate for σ the standard deviation of the parent population. The mean value m_1 is a sample mean of n_1 values from the parent population. If further sets of data are taken from the parent population, further values of m_1 will be obtained. From the central limit theorem, the standard error of the m_1 values tends to $\sigma/\sqrt{n_1}$ which equals $s_1/\sqrt{n_1}$.

The best estimate of the standard error of m_1 is $s_1/\sqrt{n_1}$.

(ii) The best estimate of the standard error of m_2 is $s_2/\sqrt{n_2}$.

(iii) It is shown in Appendix 8 that:

The variance of the *sum* of two terms = The *sum* of the variances of the two terms.

The variance of the *difference* of two terms = The *sum* of the variances of the two terms.

Thus the variance of $m_1 - m_2$ is the variance of m_1 plus the variance of m_2. Since variance is standard error squared, the variance of $m_1 - m_2$ is:

$$s_1^2/n_1 + s_2^2/n_2$$

and hence the standard error of $m_1 - m_2$ is:

$$\sqrt{\left(\frac{s_1^2}{n_1} + \frac{s_2^2}{n_2}\right)} \qquad (1)$$

(iv) The number of standard errors variation of this particular mean difference $|m_1 - m_2|$ is calculated:

$$= \frac{\text{Particular } |m_1 - m_2|}{\text{Standard error for } m_1 - m_2} \qquad (2)$$

$$= \frac{|m_1 - m_2|}{\sqrt{\left(\frac{s_1^2}{n_1} + \frac{s_2^2}{n_2}\right)}} \qquad (3)$$

(v) The number of standard errors calculated from Equation 3 is looked up in a two-tailed normal distribution table (Appendix 4) to obtain a probability. This probability is the chance that a mean difference smaller than $|m_1 - m_2|$ would occur if the two parent populations have in fact the same mean value.

For example if the value calculated from Equation 3 exceeds 1.96, then there is less than a 5% chance that so large a difference between m_1 and m_2 could have arisen if the means of the two parent populations are the same. (This is because 1.96 standard deviations correspond to a 5% two-tailed normal probability.) Since there is less than a 1 in 20 chance of this occurring, one would suspect that the means of the two parent populations are different.

Example 1

Fifty pupils entered school 1 and sixty pupils

of the same age entered school 2. On leaving school both groups were given a common mathematics examination, which yielded the statistical results shown in Table 6.1. It is required to know if the two groups of pupils

Table 6.1

	School 1	School 2
Number of pupils	50	60
Mean mark obtained	62	58
Estimated standard deviation	12	8

differ significantly in attainment, or whether they are essentially as good and the observed variations attributed to random chance.

Using Equation 3 the difference $(62 - 58 = 4)$ in the mean marks is converted into a number of standard errors:

Number of standard errors

$$= \frac{|62 - 58|}{\sqrt{\left(\frac{12^2}{50} + \frac{8^2}{60}\right)}} = 2.01$$

Reference to the table of areas under a normal curve given in Appendix 4 shows that this corresponds to a one-tailed probability of 97.8%. This indicates that if the pupils from both schools were really equal in attainment then a result such as the one obtained in favour of school 1 would only occur 2.2% of the time. (There is also a 2.2% chance that school 2 would be superior by the same margin.) Since this results will only occur once in about 45 surveys, it lends moderately strong support to the statement that 'pupils at school 1 are better than those at school 2 *in that particular type of mathematics examination*'.

Description of Program to Compare Large Samples (See Program 6.1)

First a heading is printed (lines 20–30). Next a

loop from lines 50–200 is executed twice to input values of mean, standard deviation and number of readings for the two sets. (These values can be obtained using the standard deviation program in Chapter 3.) A number of checks are performed on the input data:

(i) There must be a whole number of readings.
(ii) The number of readings must be large, that is at least 30. (For small samples the *t*-test should be used—see later in this chapter.)
(iii) The standard deviation must not be negative since this is physically impossible!

Unacceptable data values are rejected, with warning messages, and the user is asked to re-type the correct value.

A check is performed (line 220) and a warning message printed (lines 230–290) if both the standard deviations are zero. Generally this is not the case, and a further check is performed at line 300 to see if both means are different. If the means are the same, a warning message is printed (line 310). Line 320 calculates the number of standard errors variation using Equation 3.

A subroutine (lines 610–770) is called to calculate the area under the normal curve up to the appropriate number of standard errors. This saves the user the effort of looking the number of standard errors up in a 'normal' table. The subroutine uses an order 11 empirical polynomial, and is based on the constants and method used by the Numerical Algorithms Group. The subroutine differs only slightly from that used in Appendix 4.

The probability is printed (lines 360–410) rounded to a whole number if it is in the range 5%–95%, or rounded to give one decimal figure if it is outside this range. A message which interprets the probability is then printed (lines 420–500). These explain that there is no evidence, some evidence or strong evidence to support the theory that the two parent populations have different means.

Finally, the user is offered another run (lines 520–530). The answer must be YES or NO and is checked in lines 550–580.

Program 6.1 Trial run.

```
SIGNIFICANCE OF THE DIFFERENCE IN MEAN BETWEEN TWO LARGE SETS
============ == === ========== == ==== ======= === ===== ====

TYPE IN THE NUMBER OF READINGS IN SET 1
? 50
TYPE THE MEAN VALUE FOR SET 1
? 62
TYPE IN THE STANDARD DEVIATION OF SET 1
? 12

TYPE IN THE NUMBER OF READINGS IN SET 2
? 60
TYPE THE MEAN VALUE FOR SET 2
? 58
TYPE IN THE STANDARD DEVIATION OF SET 2
? 8

THE PROBABILITY THAT THE TWO MEANS COULD BE SO DIFFERENT
IF THEIR PARENT POPULATIONS HAVE THE SAME MEAN IS 2.2 %

THERE IS SOME  EVIDENCE TO SUPPORT THE THEORY
THAT THE TWO PARENT POPULATIONS HAVE DIFFERENT MEANS

WOULD YOU LIKE ANOTHER RUN  TYPE YES OR NO & PRESS RETURN
? NO
END OF JOB
```

```
 10  DIM Q$(10), N(2), M(2), S(2)
 20  PRINT "SIGNIFICANCE OF THE DIFFERENCE IN MEAN BETWEEN TWO LARGE SETS"
 30  PRINT "============ == === ========== == ==== ======= === ===== ===="
 40  PRINT
 50  FOR I = 1 TO 2
 60     PRINT "TYPE IN THE NUMBER OF READINGS IN SET"; I
 70     INPUT N(I)
 80     IF N(I) <> INT(N(I)) THEN 100
 90     IF N(I) >= 30 THEN 120
100     PRINT "THE NUMBER OF READINGS MUST BE A WHOLE NUMBER AT LEAST 30"
110     GOTO 60
120     PRINT "TYPE THE MEAN VALUE FOR SET"; I
130     INPUT M(I)
140     PRINT "TYPE IN THE STANDARD DEVIATION OF SET"; I
150     INPUT S(I)
160     IF S(I) >= 0 THEN 190
170     PRINT "A STANDARD DEVIATION MUST BE POSITIVE - RETYPE CORRECTLY"
180     GOTO 150
190     PRINT
200  NEXT I
210  REM CHECK THAT BOTH STANDARD DEVIATIONS ARE NOT ZERO
220  IF S(1) + S(2) > 0 THEN 300
230  PRINT "SINCE BOTH STANDARD DEVIATIONS ARE ZERO, THE CHANCE OF"
240  PRINT "RESULTS SUCH AS THESE OCCURRING BY CHANCE IS";
250  IF M(1) = M(2) THEN 280
260  PRINT "0%"
270  GOTO 510
280  PRINT "100%"
290  GOTO 510
300  IF M(1) <> M(2) THEN 320
310  PRINT "BOTH MEANS ARE THE SAME HENCE"
320  LET S = ABS(M(1)-M(2)) / SQR(S(1)*S(1) / N(1) + S(2)*S(2) / N(2))
330  REM ***CALCULATE AREA UNDER NORMAL CURVE UP TO S STANDARD
340  REM ***ERRORS ABOVE THE MEAN
350  GOSUB 630
360  PRINT "THE PROBABILITY THAT THE TWO MEANS COULD BE SO DIFFERENT"
370  PRINT "IF THEIR PARENT POPULATIONS HAVE THE SAME MEAN IS";
380  LET K = 1
390  IF (P - 0.05) * (P - 0.95) < 0 THEN 410
400  LET K = 10
410  PRINT INT(P * 100 * K + 0.5) / K; "%"
420  PRINT
430  IF P < 0.05 THEN 450
440  PRINT "THERE IS NO";
450  IF (P - 0.05) * (P - 0.01) >= 0 THEN 470
460  PRINT "THERE IS SOME";
470  IF P > 0.01 THEN 490
480  PRINT "THERE IS STRONG";
490  PRINT " EVIDENCE TO SUPPORT THE THEORY"
500  PRINT "THAT THE TWO PARENT POPULATIONS HAVE DIFFERENT MEANS"
510  PRINT
520  PRINT "WOULD YOU LIKE ANOTHER RUN ";
530  PRINT "TYPE YES OR NO & PRESS RETURN"
540  INPUT Q$
550  IF Q$ = "YES" THEN 40
560  IF Q$ = "NO" THEN 590
570  PRINT "REPLY '"; Q$; "' NOT UNDERSTOOD.   RE-";
580  GOTO 530
590  PRINT "END OF JOB"
600  STOP
610  REM CALC CUMULATIVE AREA UNDER NORMAL CURVE
```

```
620 REM CONSTANTS SET FOR 8 FIGURE ACCURACY
630 LET X = S * 0.707107
640 LET P = 0
650 IF X >= 9.5 THEN 770
660 LET T = 1 - 7.5 / (ABS(X) + 3.75)
670 LET Y = 0
680 FOR I = 1 TO 12
690    READ C
700    LET Y = Y * T + C
710 NEXT I
720 RESTORE
730 DATA 3.14753E-05, -0.000138746, -6.41279E-06, 0.00178663
740 DATA -0.00823169, 0.0241519, -0.0547992, 0.102602
750 DATA -0.163572, 0.226008, -0.273422, 0.14559
760 LET P = 0.5 * EXP(-X * X) * Y
770 RETURN
780 END
```

t-Test

The t-test should be used for comparing the mean values of two small samples, and the procedure is as follows. *The assumption is made that both samples have been drawn from populations with the same standard deviation* (and hence the same variance), even if the means of the two parent populations differ.

(a) An estimate of the standard deviations of the two parent populations is calculated using n_1, n_2, s_1 and s_2.

(b) The value of s thus obtained is used to estimate the standard error of the difference between the means, that is the standard error of $|m_1 - m_2|$.

(c) The value of $|m_1 - m_2|$ is divided by the standard error of the means calculated in (b) to give the number of standard errors variation.

(d) This value is looked up in a *t-table* (Appendix 6) to find the probability of obtaining a difference in means $|m_1 - m_2|$ as large or larger than this. The t-distribution must be used because there are only a small number of readings, and a normal approximation is no longer applicable. It should be noted that the t-distribution tends to the normal distribution as the number of readings becomes large.

Derivation of the t-test for comparing the means of small samples

(a) The equation to calculate s the estimated standard deviation of the two parent populations is:

$$s = \sqrt{\left[\frac{\Sigma(x_1-m_1)^2+\Sigma(x_2-m_2)^2}{(n_1-1)+(n_2-1)}\right]}$$
$$= \sqrt{\left[\frac{(n_1-1)s_1^2+(n_2-1)s_2^2}{(n_1-1)+(n_2-1)}\right]} \quad (4)$$

The numerator represents the sum of the squared differences of each of the x_1 values from the mean m_1 plus the sum of the squared differences of each of the x_2 values from the mean m_2. This is similar to the term $\Sigma(x_1-\bar{x})^2$ used in the usual calculation of standard deviations (Chapter 2, Equation 7). The denominator comprises the number of terms in the first group minus one, and the number of terms in the second group minus one. The minus one corresponds to the loss of one degree of freedom from each group. This is because if one is given n_1-1 of the differences (x_1-m_1), the last difference can be calculated since the sum of all the differences is zero (because of the definition of the mean.) The same applies to the second set of data. Further discussion of this point is given in Chapter 2 (explanation of the divisors n and $n-1$).

(b) Since a single standard deviation s (for

71

both parent populations) is to be used instead of s_1 and s_2 (for the individual sets of data), Equation 1 may be re-written

Standard error of $m_1 - m_2$

$$= \sqrt{\left(\frac{s^2}{n_1} + \frac{s^2}{n_2}\right)} = s\sqrt{\left(\frac{1}{n_1} + \frac{1}{n_2}\right)} \qquad (5)$$

(c) Substituting Equation 5 into Equation 2

Number of standard errors variation of $m_1 - m_2$

$$= \frac{|m_1 - m_2|}{s\sqrt{\left(\frac{1}{n_1} + \frac{1}{n_2}\right)}} \qquad (6)$$

(d) The number of standard errors calculated in Equation 6 is looked up in a t-table (Appendix 6) for the appropriate number of degrees of freedom v. The value of v may be calculated

$$v = (n_1 - 1) + (n_2 - 1)$$
$$= n_1 + n_2 - 2$$

If for example v is 10 and the number of standard errors is 2.76, the table yields a two-tailed probability of 2%. This means that there is only a 1 in 50 chance that the means of the two parent populations are the same, thus providing strong evidence that the means are different.

It should be noted that in the derivation of the t-test it was assumed that the two parent populations both had the same standard deviation. If there is a large difference in the two standard deviations for the samples (s_1 and s_2), then the assumption of a single standard deviation for the two parent populations is unjustified, and application of the t-test is inappropriate.

Example 2

A dealer has tested motor car tyres from two different manufacturers fitted to the same model of car, to find if one make gives a significantly better mileage than the other.

The mileage covered by each tyre before it reached the legal limit is shown to the nearest 100 miles in Table 6.2. Using sample 1 the estimated standard deviation s_1 for tyres from manufacturer 1 is calculated as

$$s_1 = \sqrt{\left[\frac{\Sigma(x_1 - m_1)^2}{(n_1 - 1)}\right]} = 800 \text{ miles}$$

Similarly $s_2 = 600$ miles.

A superficial examination of these values might suggest that since tyres from manufacturer 2 give on average 1000 miles more wear, they must be better.

The statistical examination of these results requires first the calculation of the estimated standard deviation of both parent populations from Equation 4. This gives a value of $s = 727$. Equation 6 is then used to calculate the number of standard errors variation of $m_1 - m_2$, giving a value of 3.17. Reference to the t-table given in Appendix 6 shows that for $(13 - 1) + (9 - 1) = 20$ degrees of freedom, the value of 3.17 lies in between the values for 1% and 0.1% probability. This means that there is less than a 1% (two-tailed) chance of such a large discrepancy occurring between the two makes of tyres if the two parent populations have the same mean mileage. This provides strong evidence that the two parent populations do not have the same mean, and that tyres from manufacturer 2 last longer.

Table 6.2

Manufacturer 1		Manufacturer 2	
25 800	27 600	28 400	27 500
27 200	25 600	26 900	27 200
26 400	27 000	28 400	
25 800	28 000	27 500	
28 000	26 400	28 400	
27 200	26 800	27 500	
26 600		28 400	
Number of terms		Number of terms	
$n_1 = 13$		$n_2 = 9$	
Mean mileage		Mean mileage	
$m_1 = 26\ 800$		$m_2 = 27\ 800$	

F-Test (Variance Ratio)

The F-test is used to compare the variances (or standard deviations) of two set of data, to determine whether they differ significantly. This test may be applied to any size of set, and is particularly useful to establish whether the assumption made in the t-test can be justified for a particular set of data. (The assumption made in the t-test is that both samples have been drawn from populations with the same variance and hence the same standard deviation.)

The procedure for applying the F-test is as follows:

(i) Adopt the hypothesis that the variances of the two parent populations, from which the two sets of data were drawn, are the same. This is often referred to as the null hypothesis.

(ii) The F-statistic is calculated

$$F = s_1^2/s_2^2 \qquad (7)$$

where s_1 and s_2 are the estimated standard deviations of the two parent populations.

For convenience the values are arranged so that s_1 is greater than s_2 which results in a value of $F > 1$. As a consequence only half as many values need tabulating in significance tables.

(iii) The estimated standard deviations for the two parent populations can be calculated

$$s_1 = \sqrt{[\Sigma(x_1 - m_1)^2/(n_1 - 1)]}$$

and

$$s_2 = \sqrt{[\Sigma(x_2 - m_2)^2/(n_2 - 1)]}$$

(iv) The calculated F value is looked up in the tables given in Appendix 7. First the table showing the appropriate significance level is selected. (Tables are provided for 10%, 5%, 1% and 0.1% significance levels.) The number of degrees of freedom in the two sets v_1 and v_2 are calculated from the number of readings n_1 and n_2

$$v_1 = n_1 - 1 \qquad (8)$$

and

$$v_2 = n_2 - 1 \qquad (9)$$

The calculated F value is then compared with the value from the table for the appropriate values of v_1 and v_2. For example if $n_1 = 21$, $n_2 = 6$, $s_1 = 2$ and $s_2 = 5$. Then s_1 is smaller then s_2, hence the sets 1 and 2 are interchanged giving

$$n_1 = 6, n_2 = 21, s_1 = 5 \text{ and } s_2 = 2$$

$$F = 5^2/2^2 = 6.25$$

$$v_1 = 6 - 1 = 5$$

$$v_2 = 21 - 1 = 20$$

Using the 1% significance table with $v_1 = 5$ and $v_2 = 20$ yields an F value of 4.1. Since the calculated F value of 6.25 is greater than 4.1, there is less than a 1% chance that results as divergent as this could have arisen by chance if the variances of the two parent populations are the same. This provides strong evidence that the two parent populations have different variances. (The null hypothesis is therefore rejected.)

Comparison with the 0.1% significance table yields an F value of 6.46. There is therefore more than 0.1% chance of obtaining the observed result by chance if the parent population variances are the same.

It is interesting to note that the F values with $v_1 = 1$ correspond to the t value (with $v = v_2$) squared.

For example:

the 5% F value for $v_1 = 1$ and $v_2 = 20$ is 4.35

the 5% t value for $v = 20$ is 2.086

and $2.086^2 = 4.351$.

Example 3

The analysis in Example 2 was based on the assumption that the variance and standard deviation of both parent populations were the same. Superficially there appears to be a large difference in the standard deviations s_1 and s_2 which were estimated to be 800 and 600 miles respectively for manufacturers 1 and 2. (The variances show an even bigger difference: 640 000 and 360 000.) The F-test provides a statistical means of determining whether the difference in standard deviations s_1 and s_2 is so large that the assumption must be rejected, and the t-test results invalidated.

Using Equation 7

$$F = 800^2/600^2 = 1.78$$

Using equations 8 and 9

$$v_1 = 13-1 = 12$$

$$v_2 = 9-1 = 8$$

Referring to Appendix 7.1 (10% F-test probability) yields a critical value of 2.50. Since the calculated F of 1.78 is less than 2.50, then there is more than a 10% chance of such results occurring if the two parent populations have the same standard deviation. There is therefore no evidence to reject the hypothesis that the standard deviations of both parent populations are the same. It follows that the assumption made in the t-test was valid.

Had the calculated F value been 5.7, then this is larger than the critical value from the 1% table (Appendix 7.3), then there is less than a 1% chance that such a result could have occurred if the hypothesis (that the standard deviations of both parent populations are the same) is true. This would provide strong evidence that the standard deviations are in fact different, and the t-test result would be invalidated.

Description of Program for Comparing Two Samples by the F- and t-Tests

The program (Program 6.2) first prints a heading (lines 20–30), and then executes a loop twice from lines 60–260. Inside this loop the data values for each of the two groups are input, the total number of points in each group is counted, the sum of errors squared is calculated, and the mean is evaluated. The data values are not stored in arrays, and hence there is, in principle, no limit on the number of data points. However, in this program the F-test calculation cannot be performed if either group has more than 60 values, for reasons which are discussed later. This restriction does not apply to the t-test, but if the samples are large it is recommended that the program for comparison of large samples be used instead.

Using a loop from line 280–380, the mean, sum of errors squared, estimated standard deviation of parent population, number of data points and the number of degrees of freedom are printed for the two groups in turn.

Next three checks are performed (lines 390–500) to ensure that the data provided are suitable for the F- and t-tests.

(i) There must be some data values in both groups.
(ii) There must be a minimum of three data values in the two groups combined in order to calculate the standard deviation s of the two parent populations. (A value of 2 would cause failure through attempting to divide by zero in Equation 4.)
(iii) All of the values entered must not be identical.

If the data fail any of these checks, a warning message is printed, calculation of both the F- and t-tests is skipped, and a message (lines 1570–1580) asks if another run is required. Provided that the data are acceptable, a message (lines 570–580) asks whether an F-test is to be performed. The reply must be either YES or NO, and is checked in a subroutine (lines 1710–1770). If an F-test is requested, three additional checks are carried out on the data:

(i) Each group must contain at least 2 numbers so that the group has a standard deviation.
(ii) A maximum of 60 values in each group is imposed by the program. This is to prevent underflow and overflow errors, which occurred at 10^{-18} and 10^{18} respectively on one of the test computers. Many computers handle a

74

Program 6.2 Trial run.

```
     F  AND  T  TESTS
     =  ===  =  =====

INPUT  NUMBERS  IN  GROUP  1
PRESS  RETURN  AFTER  EACH  NUMBER   &  TERMINATE  DATA  WITH  999999
?  25800
?  27200
?  26400
?  25800
?  28000
?  27200
?  26600
?  27600
?  25600
?  27000
?  28000
?  26400
?  26800
?  999999
INPUT  NUMBERS  IN  GROUP  2
PRESS  RETURN  AFTER  EACH  NUMBER   &  TERMINATE  DATA  WITH  999999
?  28400
?  26900
?  28400
?  27500
?  28400
?  27500
?  28400
?  27500
?  27200
?  999999

GROUP  1
 MEAN  =  26800
 SUM  OF  ERRORS  SQUARED  =  7.68E+06
 STANDARD  DEVIATION  =  800
 NUMBER  OF  DATA  POINTS  =  13
 NUMBER  OF  DEGREES  OF  FREEDOM  =  12

GROUP  2
 MEAN  =  27800
 SUM  OF  ERRORS  SQUARED  =  2.88E+06
 STANDARD  DEVIATION  =  600
 NUMBER  OF  DATA  POINTS  =  9
 NUMBER  OF  DEGREES  OF  FREEDOM  =  8

WOULD  YOU  LIKE  TO  PERFORM  AN  F  TEST?  (YES/NO)
?  YES
CALCULATED  VALUE  OF  F  =  1.77778
PROBABILITY  THAT  SUCH  A  DIFFERENCE  IN  VARIANCES  COULD  OCCUR
BY  CHANCE  IF  THE  PARENT  POPULATIONS  HAVE  THE  SAME  VARIANCE
IS  21.1  %

WOULD  YOU  LIKE  TO  PERFORM  A  T  TEST?
TYPE  YES  OR  NO  AND  PRESS  RETURN
?  YES
THIS  TEST  IS  ONLY  MEANINGFUL  WHEN  THE  STANDARD  DEVIATIONS
OF  THE  TWO  GROUPS  DO  NOT  DIFFER  SIGNIFICANTLY
```

CALCULATED VALUE OF T = 3.17369
PROBABILITY THAT SUCH A DIFFERENCE IN MEANS COULD OCCUR BY
CHANCE IF THE PARENT POPULATIONS HAVE THE SAME MEAN AND
VARIANCE IS 0.478 %

WOULD YOU LIKE ANOTHER RUN? (YES/NO)
? NO
END OF JOB


```
10 DIM K(2), A(2), Y(2), B(4), Q$(10)
20 PRINT TAB(6); "F AND T TESTS"
30 PRINT TAB(6); "= === = ====="
40 PRINT
50 REM START LOOP TO INPUT DATA
60 FOR J = 1 TO 2
70     LET A(J) = 0
80     LET Y(J) = 0
90     LET I = 1
100    LET Z = 0
110    PRINT "INPUT NUMBERS IN GROUP"; J
120    PRINT "PRESS RETURN AFTER EACH NUMBER ";
130    PRINT "& TERMINATE DATA WITH 999999"
140    INPUT X
150    IF X = 999999 THEN 250
160    LET Z = Z + X
170    LET X1 = X - Y(J)
180    REM CALCULATE SUM OF ERRORS SQUARED
190    LET A(J) = A(J) + X1 * X1 * (I - 1) / I
200    REM CALCULATE MEAN
210    LET Y(J) = Z / I
220    LET I = I + 1
230    GOTO 140
240    REM K(J) = NUMBER OF POINTS IN CURRENT GROUP
250    LET K(J) = I - 1
260 NEXT J
270 REM LOOP TO PRINT STATISTICS FOR EACH GROUP
280 FOR J = 1 TO 2
290    PRINT
300    PRINT "GROUP"; J
310    IF K(J) = 0 THEN 360
320    PRINT TAB(2); "MEAN ="; Y(J)
330    PRINT TAB(2); "SUM OF ERRORS SQUARED ="; A(J)
340    IF K(J) = 1 THEN 360
350    PRINT TAB(2); "STANDARD DEVIATION ="; SQR(A(J) / (K(J) - 1))
360    PRINT TAB(2); "NUMBER OF DATA POINTS ="; K(J)
370    PRINT TAB(2); "NUMBER OF DEGREES OF FREEDOM ="; K(J) - 1
380 NEXT J
390 LET V1 = K(1) - 1
400 IF V1 > -1 THEN 430
410 PRINT "NO NUMBERS IN FIRST GROUP"
420 GOTO 1560
430 LET V2 = K(2) - 1
440 IF V2 > -1 THEN 470
450 PRINT "NO NUMBERS IN SECOND GROUP"
460 GOTO 1560
470 LET V = V1 + V2
480 IF V > 0 THEN 510
490 PRINT "THERE MUST BE AT LEAST 3 NUMBERS IN BOTH GROUPS COMBINED"
500 GOTO 1560
```

```
510 IF A(1) + A(2) > 0 THEN 560
520 IF Y(1) <> Y(2) THEN 560
530 PRINT "F AND T TEST RESULTS INDETERMINATE"
540 PRINT "BECAUSE ALL THE DATA VALUES ARE EQUAL."
550 GOTO  1560
560 PRINT
570 PRINT "WOULD YOU LIKE TO PERFORM AN F TEST? (YES/NO)"
580 GOSUB  1720
590 IF Q$ = "NO" THEN 1340
600 IF V1 > 0 THEN 630
610 PRINT "THERE MUST BE AT LEAST 2 NUMBERS IN FIRST GROUP FOR F TEST"
620 GOTO  1340
630 IF V2 > 0 THEN 660
640 PRINT "THERE MUST BE AT LEAST 2 NUMBERS IN SECOND GROUP FOR F TEST"
650 GOTO  1340
660 IF V1 < 61 THEN 690
670 PRINT "TOO MANY NUMBERS IN FIRST GROUP FOR F TEST"
680 GOTO  1340
690 IF V2 < 61 THEN 720
700 PRINT "TOO MANY NUMBERS IN SECOND GROUP FOR F TEST"
710 GOTO  1340
720 IF A(1) * A(2) > 0 THEN 750
730 PRINT "F TEST CANNOT BE PERFORMED WITH A STANDARD DEVIATION OF ZERO"
740 GOTO  1340
750 LET F = (A(1) / V1) / (A(2) / V2)
760 PRINT "CALCULATED VALUE OF F ="; F
770 LET E = 0
780 IF V1 = 2 * INT(V1 / 2) THEN 820
790 IF V2 = 2 * INT(V2 / 2) THEN 870
800 GOTO  1050
810 REM CALCULATE PROBABILITY IF V1 EVEN
820 LET U = 1 / (1 + V2 / (F * V1))
830 LET P1 = V1 + 1
840 LET Q = V2 - 2
850 GOTO  910
860 REM CALCULATE PROBABILITY IF V2 EVEN
870 LET E = 1
880 LET U = 1 / (1 + F * V1 / V2)
890 LET P1 = V2 + 1
900 LET Q = V1 - 2
910 LET S = 0
920 LET W = 1
930 LET J = 2
940 LET S = S + W
950 LET W = W * U * (J + Q) / J
960 LET J = J + 2
970 IF J < P1 THEN 940
980 LET Z = SQR(1 - U)
990 IF E = 0 THEN 1020
1000 LET P = 100 * S * (Z ^ V1)
1010 GOTO  1280
1020 LET P = 100 * S * (Z ^ V2)
1030 GOTO  1280
1040 REM CALCULATE PROBABILITY IF V1 & V2 BOTH ODD
1050 LET U = 1 / (1 + F * V1 / V2)
1060 LET X = 1 - U
1070 LET S = 0
1080 LET W = 1
1090 LET J = 2
1100 LET P1 = V2
1110 GOTO  1150
```

```
1120 LET S = S + W
1130 LET W = W * U * J / (J + 1)
1140 LET J = J + 2
1150 IF J < P1 THEN 1120
1160 LET W = W * V2
1170 LET J = 3
1180 LET P1 = V1 + 1
1190 LET Q = V2 - 2
1200 GOTO  1240
1210 LET S = S - W
1220 LET W = W * X * (J + Q) / J
1230 LET J = J + 2
1240 IF J < P1 THEN 1210
1250 LET T1 = ATN(SQR(F * V1 / V2))
1260 LET S1 = S * SQR(X * U)
1270 LET P = 100 * (1 - 2 * (T1 + S1) / 3.14159)
1280 IF P <= 50 THEN 1300
1290 LET P = 100 - P
1300 GOSUB  1640
1310 PRINT "PROBABILITY THAT SUCH A DIFFERENCE IN VARIANCES COULD OCCUR"
1320 PRINT "BY CHANCE IF THE PARENT POPULATIONS HAVE THE SAME VARIANCE"
1330 PRINT "IS"; P; "%"
1340 PRINT
1350 PRINT "WOULD YOU LIKE TO PERFORM A T TEST?"
1360 PRINT "TYPE YES OR NO AND PRESS RETURN"
1370 GOSUB  1720
1380 IF Q$ = "NO" THEN 1560
1390 PRINT "THIS TEST IS ONLY MEANINGFUL WHEN THE STANDARD DEVIATIONS"
1400 PRINT "OF THE TWO GROUPS DO NOT DIFFER SIGNIFICANTLY"
1410 PRINT
1420 IF A(1) + A(2) > 0 THEN 1450
1430 LET P = 0
1440 GOTO  1530
1450 LET S = SQR((A(1) + A(2)) / (V1 + V2))
1460 LET T = ABS(Y(1) - Y(2)) / (S * SQR(1 / K(1) + 1 / K(2)))
1470 PRINT "CALCULATED VALUE OF T ="; T
1480 LET N2 = K(1) - 1 + K(2) - 1
1490 REM CALCULATE T PROBALITY
1500 GOSUB  1790
1510 REM ROUND ANSWER
1520 GOSUB  1640
1530 PRINT "PROBABILITY THAT SUCH A DIFFERENCE IN MEANS COULD OCCUR BY"
1540 PRINT "CHANCE IF THE PARENT POPULATIONS HAVE THE SAME MEAN AND"
1550 PRINT "VARIANCE IS"; P; "%"
1560 PRINT
1570 PRINT "WOULD YOU LIKE ANOTHER RUN? (YES/NO)"
1580 GOSUB  1720
1590 RESTORE
1600 IF Q$ = "YES" THEN 60
1610 PRINT "END OF JOE"
1620 STOP
1630 REM SUBROUTINE TO ROUND OFF ANSWERS.
1640 IF P < 5 THEN 1660
1650 LET P = INT(P * 10 + .5) * .1
1660 IF (P - 5) * (P - .5) > 0 THEN 1680
1670 LET P = INT(P * 100 + .5) * .01
1680 IF P > .5 THEN 1700
1690 LET P = INT(P * 1000 + .5) * .001
1700 RETURN
1710 REM SUBROUTINE TO CHECK REPLIES
1720 INPUT Q$
```

```
1730 IF Q$ = "YES" THEN 1770
1740 IF Q$ = "NO" THEN 1770
1750 PRINT "REPLY '"; Q$; "' NOT UNDERSTOOD. RETYPE"
1760 GOTO  1720
1770 RETURN
1780 REM *** SUBROUTINE TO CALCUATE T PROBABILITY
1790 READ B(1), B(2), B(3), E(4), P
1800 DATA 1E6, 10000, 1000, 100, 0
1810 IF N2 > 4 THEN 1840
1820 IF T > B(N2) THEN 2050
1830 GOTO  1850
1840 IF T > 50 THEN 2050
1850 LET A = T / SQR(N2)
1860 LET B = N2 / (N2 + T * T)
1870 LET J = N2 - 2
1880 LET K = N2 - INT(N2 / 2) * 2 + 2
1890 LET S = 1
1900 IF J < 2 THEN 1980
1910 LET C = 1
1920 LET F2 = K
1930 FOR I = K TO J STEP 2
1940    LET C = C * B * (F2 - 1) / F2
1950    LET S = S + C
1960    LET F2 = F2 + 2
1970 NEXT I
1980 IF K > 2 THEN 2010
1990 LET P = .5 - .5 * A * SQR(B) * S
2000 GOTO 2050
2010 IF N2 > 1 THEN 2030
2020 LET S = 0
2030 LET P = .5 - (A * B * S + ATN(A)) / 3.14159
2040 REM *** CONVERT TO TWO TAILED PERCENTAGE
2050 LET P = 100 * 2 * P
2060 RETURN
2070 END
```

wider range of numbers than this, and the limit of 60 values may be increased with care.

(iii) Neither group may have a standard deviation of zero because attempted division by zero would cause failure with Equation 7.

If any of these tests fail, the F-test is abandoned, and the user is asked if the t-test is required.

Provided that the data pass the extra checks, the variance ratio F is calculated and printed (lines 750–760). This value could be looked up in the F-tables (Appendix 7), but for convenience the program calculates the probability (lines 770–1300). Three different methods are employed depending on whether the number of degrees of freedom v_1 is even, or v_2 is even or both v_1 and v_2 are odd. The

derivation of the equations used is not given here, but may be found in a paper by Lee, J.D. and Hayes, D.G. (*Computers and Education*, 1978, **2,** 165–176). It should be noted that the program does not exchange the two sets of data to guarantee that $s_1 > s_2$ as recommended in the discussion and in Equation 7. This guarantee ensures that the F probability is in the range 0–50%. The program calculates the probability in the range 0%–100%, and values above 50% are appropriately converted. (A probability of 90% is equivalent to a probability of 10%, since a variance ratio of 0.4 is equally significant to a variance ratio of 2.5, since 2.5 = 1/0.4.) From this it is apparent that the maximum F-test probability will be 50% corresponding to the standard deviations of the two groups being identical.

The calculated F-probability is rounded to give 1, 2 or 3 decimal figures as appropriate in a subroutine (lines 1630–1700), and is printed (lines 1310–1330).

Next a message (lines 1350–1360) asks whether a t-test is required. The answer which must be YES or NO is checked in a subroutine (lines 1710–1770).

If the t-test is requested then the estimated standard deviation s of the two parent populations is calculated (line 1450) using Equation 4. The number of standard errors variation t of $|m_1 - m_2|$ is calculated in line 1460 using Equation 6, and is printed in line 1470. Next a subroutine is entered (lines 1780–2060) to calculate the probability of such a t-value occurring by chance if the parent populations have the same mean. (This subroutine is the same as that used in the Pearson's correlation coefficient program.) The probability is rounded in a subroutine (lines 1630–1700) to give 1, 2 or 3 decimal figures as appropriate. The probability is then printed out (lines 1530–1550).

Finally a message (line 1570) asks whether the user would like another run. The answer must be YES or NO and is checked by a subroutine (lines 1710–1770).

It should be noted that it is always valid to perform an F-test, but that the result from a t-test is meaningful only if the standard deviations of the two groups do not differ significantly.

Exercises

6.1 Firm A manufactures electric light bulbs and claims that its product has a longer life than that of firm B. One hundred bulbs from firm A had an average life of 1234 hours, with a standard deviation of 84 hours, whereas 75 bulbs from firm B had an average life of 1210 hours with a standard deviation of 72 hours. Use the large sample test to see if bulbs from A are significantly better than bulbs from B.

6.2 Compare the electric bulbs made by firm A in Question 6.1 with those of firm C. In a test of 150 bulbs from C, the mean life was 1210 hours and the standard deviation was 110 hours.

6.3 A survey was conducted to establish whether the average height of eleven-year-old boys has increased from 1950 to 1980. The following data were collected

1950: 600 boys, mean height 149 cm with standard deviation 6.1 cm.

1980: 500 boys, mean height 150 cm with standard deviation 5.9 cm.

6.4 The Army has tested two types of anti-tank missiles. Type A missed the target by an average of 5.3 metres with a standard deviation of 1.2 metres in a test of 11 missiles. Eight type B missiles were tested and missed by an average of 4.2 metres with a standard deviation of 1.4 metres. Use the t-test to determine if missile B is significantly better than missile A.

6.5 The speeds of nine cars travelling along road A were found to be 29.6, 31.1, 30.4, 29.0, 29.9, 30.3, 29.4, 30.1 and 30.2 m.p.h. Estimate the mean speed and the standard deviation. At the same time the speeds of seven cars travelling along road B were measured, and were found to be 31.8, 30.0, 31.9, 29.7, 32.1, 30.3 and 31.2 m.p.h. Estimate the mean and standard deviation. Use a t-test to find if the means of A and B differ significantly. Perform an F-test to find if the standard deviations of A and B differ significantly. Are the results from the t-test still valid?

7

Correlation Coefficients

Pearson's Correlation Coefficient r

Data from many surveys or experiments are collected in the form of pairs of readings (called x and y). The purpose of this correlation coefficient is to establish if the x and y values are related in a linear manner. A simple way of doing this is to plot a scatter diagram. Fig. 7.1 shows that there is an approximately linear relationship between x and y (i.e. the

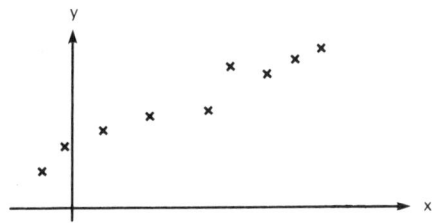

Fig. 7.1   Scatter diagram

points lie close to a straight line). In many cases the fit is less good than in the above example, and a non-subjective value is required to indicate how closely related or correlated are the x and y values. Pearson's correlation coefficient r provides such a non-subjective indicator, and is defined:

Pearson's correlation coefficient

$$r = \frac{s_{xy}}{s_x \cdot s_y} \quad (1)$$

where s_{xy} is the covariance of x and y

$$s_{xy} = \frac{\Sigma(x_i - \bar{x})(y_i - \bar{y})}{n} \quad (2)$$

(In the above expression $\bar{x}$ and $\bar{y}$ are the mean

(average) values of x and y, and n is the number of (x, y) points. The terms x_i and y_i are the values of point i and Σ indicates the summation of $(x_i - \bar{x})(y_i - \bar{y})$ over all of the (x, y) points —that is from $i = 1, 2, 3, \ldots, n$.)

s_x is the standard deviation of the x_i values (see Chapter 2 on standard deviations).

$$s_x = \sqrt{\left[\frac{\Sigma(x_i - \bar{x})^2}{n}\right]} \quad (3)$$

and s_y is the standard deviation of the y_i values

$$s_y = \sqrt{\left[\frac{\Sigma(y_i - \bar{y})^2}{n}\right]} \quad (4)$$

Substituting Equations 2, 3 and 4 into 1 gives:

$$r = \frac{\Sigma(x_i - \bar{x})(y_i - \bar{y})/n}{\sqrt{\left[\frac{\Sigma(x_i - \bar{x})^2}{n}\right]} \cdot \sqrt{\left[\frac{\Sigma(y_i - \bar{y})^2}{n}\right]}}$$

hence

$$r = \frac{\Sigma(x_i - \bar{x})(y_i - \bar{y})}{\sqrt{[\Sigma(x_i - \bar{x})^2 \Sigma(y_i - \bar{y})^2]}} \quad (5)$$

Equation 5 is used in the computer program.

It should be noted that if the n pairs of (x, y) values constitute a sample from a larger population, then to estimate the standard deviations of the x and y values of the population the divisor in Equations 3 and 4 should be $(n-1)$ rather than n. In the same way Equation 2 would require the divisor $(n-1)$ to give the estimated covariance from a sample of readings. It can be seen that the denominator, whether it is $(n-1)$ or n, cancels out in Equation 5.

An alternative to Equation 5 for evaluating Pearson's r is:

$$r = \frac{n\, \Sigma x_i y_i - \Sigma x_i \Sigma y_i}{\sqrt{[(n\Sigma x_i^2 - (\Sigma x_i)^2)\,(n\Sigma y_i^2 - (\Sigma y_i)^2)]}}$$

This equation is mathematically equivalent to Equation 5, and is commonly used on electronic calculators because it is not necessary to store the (x_i, y_i) values. However, Equation 5 gives a more accurate result if only a limited number of significant figures are carried.

The numerical value of r is zero if there is absolutely no linear correlation between the x and y values. This does not preclude the existence of a non-linear relationship. If there is some linear correlation, then a positive value for r indicates direct correlation (y increases as x increases) while a negative value for r indicates inverse correlation (y decreases as x increases). Should all of the points lie exactly on a straight line then this will result in a value for r of either $+1$ or -1. It can be seen that the numerical value of Pearson's correlation coefficient must lie in the range $+1$ to -1. Generally the calculated value of r is not exactly ± 1 or 0.

It cannot be emphasised too strongly that correlation does NOT imply causality. For example the number of colour television sets has increased over the last 10 years, and the number of whales has decreased. Though there is a negative correlation, no reasonable person would suggest that one of these factors had caused the other!

It is worth noting that Pearson's r does not depend on the scale of the x or y values. Because of this, calculations may sometimes be simplified by adding a suitable constant to the x or y values (or both), or by multiplying the x and y values by *positive* constants.

Significance of r

Table 7.1 gives the 5% significance values for varying numbers of points. Its use is best illustrated by considering an example using 10 (x, y) points. If 10 random points are taken then there is a 95% chance that the calculated

Table 7.1

Number of (x, y) points from which r is calculated n	5% significance value for Pearson's r (two tailed)
3	0.997
4	0.950
5	0.878
6	0.811
7	0.754
8	0.707
9	0.666
→10	0.632←
11	0.602
12	0.576

value of r lies in the range -0.632 to $+0.632$. If the value of r calculated from 10 experimental points lies outside this range (that is larger than 0.632 or smaller than -0.632) then there is less than a 5% chance that this degree of correlation could have occurred from random points. Hence one concludes that it is likely that x and y are linearly related (correlated). A fuller table of 5% significance values is given in Appendix 1. Similar significance tables exist for the 1% value, and if the calculated value for r lies outside the 1% limits then there is less than a 1% chance that such a degree of correlation could have occurred from random points, hence it is highly likely that x and y are linearly related.

Finally, it should be noted that Pearson's r only indicates a linear (straight line) relationship.

Care should be exercised when using significance tables, since some tables are 'one-tailed' and others are 'two-tailed'. In the example above there is a 95% chance that the value of r lies between -0.632 and $+0.632$ (Fig. 7.2). There is therefore a 5% chance that the value of r lies outside this range, that is a $2\frac{1}{2}$% chance that the value of r lies between -1 and -0.632, and a $2\frac{1}{2}$% chance that r lies between 0.632 and 1. The value of 0.632 is thus the 5%

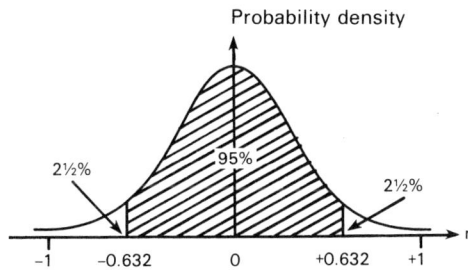

Probability density

2½%

95%

2½%

-1   -0.632   0   +0.632   +1   r

Fig. 7.2

two-tailed significance value *and* the $2\frac{1}{2}\%$ one-tailed significance value.

In some cases it is appropriate to use a two-tailed test, while in other cases a one-tailed test is appropriate. A one-tailed test should be used when only a direct relationship *or* only an inverse relationship between the x and y values is of importance, while a two-tailed test should be used whenever *both* direct *and* inverse relationships between the x and y values are equally important.

Example 1

An experiment was performed to investigate whether the rate of growth of a mould *(mucor)* is linearly related to the concentration of glucose present in the nutrient medium. Five cultures were grown for three days on nutrient solutions containing 10, 20, 30, 40 and 50 mg per litre of glucose, and the diameter of the colonies was measured.

x: Concentration of glucose mg l^{-1}

    10 20 30 40 50

y: Diameter of colony mm

    12 23 22 25 30

Mean value of x

$$= (10+20+30+40+50)/5 = 30$$

Mean value of y

$$= (12+23+22+25+30)/5 = 22.4$$

$$\Sigma(x_i-\bar{x})^2 = (-20)^2+(-10)^2+(0)^2+ \\ +(10)^2+(20)^2 = 1000$$

$$\Sigma(y_i-\bar{y})^2 = (-10.4)^2+(0.6)^2+ \\ +(-0.4)^2+(2.6)^2+(7.6)^2 \\ = 173.2$$

$$\Sigma(x_i-\bar{x})(y_i-\bar{y}) = (-20\times-10.4)+ \\ +(-10\times0.6)+ \\ +(0\times-0.4)+ \\ +(10\times2.6)+ \\ +(20\times7.6) = 380$$

using Equation 5

$$r = \frac{380}{\sqrt{(1000\times173.2)}} = 0.913$$

If this r value is looked up in a significance table (Appendix 1) for three degrees of freedom (the number of degrees of freedom is the number of x, y pairs minus two), it is found to lie between the two-tailed 5% value of 0.8783 and the 2% value of 0.93433. This means that there is between a 2% and 5% probability of obtaining a value of r greater than 0.913 or less than -0.913 from random values. It is thus somewhat unlikely that these results have occurred by chance, and consequently some support is given to a linear relationship between rate of growth and glucose concentration. In statistical terms the hypothesis that there is no linear relationship is rejected at the 5% level, but cannot be rejected at the 2% level.

Description of Program to Calculate Pearson's Correlation Coefficient, r (see Program 7.1)

After printing a heading the program asks if full instructions are required. The answer which must be YES or NO is checked in a subroutine (lines 1830–1920). Any other reply is rejected by the program which prints a message requesting an answer of YES or NO. Depending on the reply, either long or short instructions are printed out during the first run, but on a second or subsequent run only short instructions are provided.

Next (lines 100–200) the user is asked to type in the number of data values, that is the number of (x, y) pairs. The value typed is checked first to ensure that it is an integer, and secondly to ensure that it is in the range 2–100 inclusive. The upper limit of 100 is imposed by the program for two reasons:

(i) The X and Y arrays are dimensioned at 100 in line 10.
(ii) The accuracy of the method used to calculate the significance is only guaranteed up to this limit.

If a number outside the range 2–100 is typed, the number is rejected, and a message invites the user to re-type an acceptable value.

The user is then invited to type in the data values, one (x, y) pair at a time, with a comma between the terms (lines 210–320). Next a sub-routine is entered (lines 1070–1820) to permit the verification, correction or alteration of the data which have just been input.

Subroutine to Check Data

This subroutine is common to many of the programs in this book. A full explanation of its operation is given here, but an abbreviated description is given in several other sections.

A message asks if the data values entered are correct. The reply which must be YES or NO is checked by a subroutine (lines 1830–1920). If the answer is YES then the rest of the subroutine is skipped. Otherwise a list of the current data is printed in the form:

line number x y

The line numbers run sequentially 1, 2, 3 . . . and are used by the program to identify a particular line (X and Y in this case). Listing is formatted to fit on a 20 line VDU screen. When 19 lines of data have been displayed, the last line of the screen is used to ask whether to continue listing. A reply of YES or NO is checked in a subroutine. Stopping the listing is essential to allow time for the data to be read and checked before the next 19 lines are displayed. Some VDUs display a different number of lines. To make the program run satisfactorily on different sizes (number of lines) of VDU the variable A4 (line 1100) should be set to the number of lines which can be displayed, for example with a 16 line screen

LET A4 = 16

If a printing terminal is used, then it is not necessary to stop the listing of data, and A4 should be set to 999. Either when listing is complete, or when the user replies that he does not wish to continue listing then a list of options for altering the data is displayed.

The list of options is as follows:

Type R to replace an existing line of data
     A to add an extra line
     D to delete an existing line
     L to list the current data
or C to continue the calculation.

Any reply other than R, A, D, L or C is rejected and the user is instructed to re-type a valid command letter.

Replace:
    The user is asked to type the line number of the line to be replaced. This is checked (lines 1490–1560) to ensure that it is an integer in the range 1 to the number of points. Provided the line number is valid, the user is prompted to type in two numbers (lines 1570–1600) separated by a comma, to replace the old (incorrect) X, Y values.

Add:
    This option is only available if the arrays hold less than 100 values. Provided that there is space in the arrays for an additional value, the user is invited to type in a pair of values for X and Y separated by a comma (lines 1610–1660). This line of data is added at the end of the existing data.

Delete:
    This option is only available if more than one line of data exists, that is one is not allowed to delete all the data. Deletion of a line is accomplished by specifying the line number of the line of data to be removed. The line number is checked (lines 1670–1730) to ensure that it is an integer, and that it actually exists. If the line to be deleted is the last in the data list, it is just removed. Otherwise following the deletion of a line, all subsequent lines

of data are moved one place (lines 1740–1790) to fill the gap in the table. Since this changes the line numbers of lines which have been moved, the data are automatically re-listed showing the new line numbers.

List:

After performing any editing function, the current data may be re-listed to permit inspection for other errors.

Continue:

This is typed when the user is satisfied that the data are correct. It finishes the editing, and allows calculations in the main program to continue.

Calculation of r

Before attempting to calculate r, the program verifies that at least two data points remain (lines 350–380). If only one point remains the run is terminated, and the user is asked if another run is required. A warning message is printed (lines 390–400) if there are only two data points since the correlation coefficient must be either $+1$ or -1. Next the mean of the X and the mean of the Y values are calculated (lines 440–500). A loop (lines 550–590) calculates the three terms $\Sigma(x_i-\bar{x})\cdot(y_i-\bar{y})$, $\Sigma(x_i-\bar{x})^2$ and $\Sigma(y_i-\bar{y})^2$ used to calculate r from Equation 5. Checks are performed (lines 600–650) to ensure that all the x values are not equal (corresponding to a vertical straight line) and also that all the y values are not equal (which corresponds to a horizontal straight line). These checks are essential to avoid division by zero when evaluating Equation 5. The correlation coefficient is then calculated and printed (lines 660–670).

Significance of the r *Value Obtained*

A subroutine (lines 1930–2260) is used to calculate the significance of the r value just evaluated. This converts the Pearson's r value to a Student's t value using:

$$t = \frac{r\cdot\sqrt{\text{Number of degrees of freedom}}}{\sqrt{(1-r^2)}}$$

where the number of degrees of freedom is the number of x, y pairs minus two. If one was performing the calculation manually, this t value would be looked up in significance tables with the appropriate number of degrees of freedom to determine if it was significant at the 5% or 1% levels. The computer does not look up a table of values, but evaluates the probability from the t value. The method used was derived from that used by the Numerical Algorithms Group (NAG) Library.

The one-tailed probability is printed (lines 720–770), rounded to the nearest 1% if the probability is not significant, and rounded to the nearest $\frac{1}{2}$% if the probability is significant. One of the five messages shown in Table 7.2 is printed:

Finally the user is asked (lines 900–910) if another run is required, and if so whether (lines 960–1060) to use completely new data, or to edit and re-run the data already typed in.

Table 7.2

Probability range	Message
0%–1%	There is strong evidence for a direct relation between x and y
1%–5%	There is some evidence for a direct relation between x and y
5%–95%	There is no evidence for a relation between x and y
95%–99%	There is some evidence for an inverse relation between x and y
99%–100%	There is strong evidence for an inverse relation between x and y

Correlation by Ranks

Two different methods of rank correlation are developed. Both use the relative positions (i.e. orders or ranks) of the x and y values, rather than the actual x and y values. This idea was originally introduced by C. Spearman in 1906, and later developed by M. G. Kendall in 1948. Spearman's method is simply Pearson's correlation applied to ranks.

Numeric data which could be tested with Pearson's correlation coefficient could be arranged in rank order and either Spearman's or Kendall's test applied. The last two tests have the advantage that they may be used in situations where numerical data are not available, for example

  (i) judging the contestants in a beauty competition;

 (ii) judging the whiteness of laundry using different detergents;

(iii) judging the entries in a painting competition;

(iv) judging the fragrance of roses;

 (v) judging the flavour of different brews of beer.

It is because the judging of these attributes is subjective rather than quantitative that numeric data are not available. Nevertheless each judge can arrange the contestants, laundry, paintings, roses or beers in order of preference, though a different judge may well choose a different order of preference. The reason for performing correlation by ranks is to establish how closely the ranked order from one judge resembles that from a second judge.

Consider an example where a brewer has

Program 7.1   Trial run.

```
PEARSON'S CORRELATION COEFFICIENT R
======= = =========== =========== =

WOULD YOU LIKE FULL INSTRUCTIONS?
  TYPE YES OR NO & PRESS RETURN.

? YES
TEST TO MEASURE HOW CLOSELY TWO SETS OF DATA ARE RELATED

TYPE IN THE NUMBER OF DATA VALUES ? 5

TYPE IN A PAIR OF X & Y VALUES SEPARATED BY A COMMA
THEN PRESS RETURN, TYPE THE NEXT PAIR OF VALUES, RETURN ETC
YOU WILL HAVE THE CHANCE TO CORRECT TYPING ERRORS LATER
? 10, 12
? 20, 23
? 30, 22
? 40, 25
? 50, 30
END OF DATA INPUT
ARE THE DATA VALUES ENTERED CORRECT?   TYPE YES OR NO & PRESS RETURN.

? YES
CORRELATION COEFFICIENT = 0.913032

THE ONE-TAILED PROBABILITY OF OBTAINING A CORRELATION AS
GOOD OR BETTER THAN THIS BY CHANCE FROM RANDOM RANKS IS 1.5 %
THERE IS SOME  EVIDENCE FOR A DIRECT  RELATION BETWEEN X & Y

WOULD YOU LIKE ANOTHER RUN?
  TYPE YES OR NO & PRESS RETURN.

? NO
JOB FINISHED
```

```
10 DIM X(100), Y(100), Q$(10), I$(3), B(4)
20 PRINT "PEARSON'S CORRELATION COEFFICIENT R"
30 PRINT "======= = =========== =========== ="
40 PRINT
50 PRINT "WOULD YOU LIKE FULL INSTRUCTIONS?"
60 GOSUB 1850
70 LET I$ = Q$
80 IF I$ = "NO" THEN 110
90 PRINT "TEST TO MEASURE HOW CLOSELY TWO SETS OF DATA ARE RELATED"
100 PRINT
110 PRINT "TYPE IN THE NUMBER OF DATA VALUES";
120 INPUT N
130 IF N = INT(N) THEN 180
140 PRINT "VALUE MUST BE A WHOLE NUMBER"
150 PRINT "RE-";
160 GOTO 110
170 REM CHECK THAT THE NUMBER OF POINTS IS BETWEEN 2 & 100
180 IF (N - 2) * (N - 100) <= 0 THEN 220
190 PRINT "NUMBER OF DATA PAIRS MUST BE IN THE RANGE 2 - 100"
200 GOTO 100
210 REM INPUT THE DATA
220 PRINT
230 IF I$ = "YES" THEN 260
240 PRINT "TYPE IN THE DATA"
250 GOTO 290
260 PRINT "TYPE IN A PAIR OF X & Y VALUES SEPARATED BY A COMMA"
270 PRINT "THEN PRESS RETURN, TYPE THE NEXT PAIR OF VALUES, RETURN ETC"
280 PRINT "YOU WILL HAVE THE CHANCE TO CORRECT TYPING ERRORS LATER"
290 FOR I = 1 TO N
300    INPUT X(I), Y(I)
310 NEXT I
320 PRINT "END OF DATA INPUT"
330 REM CALL SUBROUTINE TO CHECK & EDIT DATA
340 GOSUB 1080
350 REM CHECK THAT NUMBER OF DATA PAIRS IS SENSIBLE
360 IF N >= 2 THEN 390
370 PRINT "NOT ENOUGH DATA PAIRS - RUN ON THIS DATA TERMINATED"
380 GOTO 910
390 IF N > 2 THEN 420
400 PRINT "BY DEFINITION A STRAIGHT LINE JOINS TWO POINTS, THUS"
410 REM SET INITIAL VALUES
420 READ X1, Y1, X2, Y2, C2, R
430 DATA 0, 0, 0, 0, 0, 1
440 REM CALCULATE THE MEAN VALUES
450 FOR I = 1 TO N
460    LET X1 = X1 + X(I)
470    LET Y1 = Y1 + Y(I)
480 NEXT I
490 LET X1 = X1 / N
500 LET Y1 = Y1 / N
510 REM CALCULATE SUMS
520 REM X2 IS N * VARIANCE OF THE X VALUES
530 REM Y2 IS N * VARIANCE OF THE Y VALUES
540 REM C2 IS N * COVARIANCE OF THE X & Y VALUES
550 FOR I = 1 TO N
560    LET X2 = X2 + (X(I) - X1) * (X(I) - X1)
570    LET Y2 = Y2 + (Y(I) - Y1) * (Y(I) - Y1)
580    LET C2 = C2 + (X(I) - X1) * (Y(I) - Y1)
590 NEXT I
600 IF X2 <> 0 THEN 630
610 PRINT "ALL THE X VALUES ARE THE SAME! ";
```

```
620 GOTO 670
630 IF Y2 <> 0 THEN 660
640 PRINT "ALL THE Y VALUES ARE THE SAME! ";
650 GOTO 670
660 LET R = C2 / SQR(X2 * Y2)
670 PRINT "CORRELATION COEFFICIENT ="; R
680 PRINT
690 IF X2 * Y2 = 0 THEN 910
700 REM CALCULATE PROBABILITY OF SUCH A CORRELATION BY CHANCE
710 GOSUB 1940
720 PRINT "THE ONE-TAILED PROBABILITY OF OBTAINING A CORRELATION AS"
730 PRINT "GOOD OR BETTER THAN THIS BY CHANCE FROM RANDOM RANKS IS";
740 LET F = 1
750 IF (P - 0.95) * (P - 0.05) <= 0 THEN 770
760 LET F = 2
770 PRINT INT(P * F * 100 + 0.5) / F; "%"
780 IF (P - 0.05) * (P - 0.95) > 0 THEN 810
790 PRINT "THERE IS NO EVIDENCE FOR A";
800 GOTO 890
810 IF (P - 0.01) * (P - 0.99) > 0 THEN 840
820 PRINT "THERE IS SOME";
830 GOTO 850
840 PRINT "THERE IS STRONG";
850 IF P > 0.5 THEN 880
860 PRINT " EVIDENCE FOR A DIRECT";
870 GOTO 890
880 PRINT " EVIDENCE FOR AN AN INVERSE";
890 PRINT " RELATION BETWEEN X & Y"
900 PRINT
910 PRINT "WOULD YOU LIKE ANOTHER RUN?"
920 GOSUB 1840
930 IF Q$ = "NO" THEN 1050
940 RESTORE
950 LET I$ = "NO"
960 PRINT "TYPE NEW FOR A RUN WITH COMPLETELY NEW DATA"
970 PRINT "   OR OLD TO EDIT AND RERUN THE EXISTING DATA"
980 INPUT Q$
990 IF Q$ = "NEW" THEN 100
1000 IF Q$ = "OLD" THEN 1030
1010 PRINT "REPLY '"; Q$; " NOT UNDERSTOOD"
1020 GOTO 960
1030 GOSUB 1130
1040 GOTO 360
1050 PRINT "JOB FINISHED"
1060 STOP
1070 REM SUBROUTINE TO CHECK THAT DATA ARE CORRECT & ALTER IF NECESSARY
1080 PRINT "ARE THE DATA VALUES ENTERED CORRECT?";
1090 REM A4 SHOULD BE SET TO THE NUMBER OF LINES ON THE VDU
1100 LET A4 = 20
1110 GOSUB 1840
1120 IF Q$ = "YES" THEN 1820
1130 PRINT "HERE IS A LIST OF THE CURRENT DATA"
1140 PRINT "LINE NUMBER","X","Y"
1150 FOR I = 1 TO N
1160    PRINT I, X(I), Y(I)
1170    IF INT(I / (A4 - 1)) * (A4 - 1) <> I THEN 1210
1180    PRINT "WOULD YOU LIKE TO CONTINUE LISTING";
1190    GOSUB 1840
1200    IF Q$ = "NO" THEN 1220
1210 NEXT I
1220 PRINT "TYPE R TO REPLACE";
```

```
1230 IF I$ = "NO" THEN 1250
1240 PRINT " AN EXISTING LINE OF DATA"
1250 IF N = 100 THEN 1300
1260 PRINT TAB(5); " A TO ADD";
1270 IF I$ = "NO" THEN 1290
1280 PRINT " AN EXTRA LINE"
1290 IF N = 1 THEN 1330
1300 PRINT TAB(5); " D TO DELETE";
1310 IF I$ = "NO" THEN 1330
1320 PRINT " AN EXISTING LINE"
1330 PRINT TAB(5); " L TO LIST";
1340 IF I$ = "NO" THEN 1360
1350 PRINT " THE DATA"
1360 PRINT "  OR C TO CONTINUE";
1370 IF I$ = "NO" THEN 1390
1380 PRINT " THE CALCULATION"
1390 INPUT Q$
1400 IF Q$ = "R" THEN 1500
1410 IF N = 100 THEN 1440
1420 IF Q$ = "A" THEN 1620
1430 IF N = 1 THEN 1450
1440 IF Q$ = "D" THEN 1670
1450 IF Q$ = "L" THEN 1130
1460 IF Q$ = "C" THEN 1820
1470 PRINT "REPLY '"; Q$; "' NOT UNDERSTOOD."
1480 GOTO 1220
1490 REM REPLACE LINE
1500 PRINT "TYPE THE LINENUMBER OF THE LINE TO BE REPLACED";
1510 INPUT I
1520 IF I <> INT(I) THEN 1540
1530 IF (I - 1) * (I - N) <= 0 THEN 1570
1540 PRINT "LINENUMBER MUST BE AN INTEGER IN THE RANGE 1 -"; N
1550 PRINT "RE-";
1560 GOTO 1500
1570 PRINT "TYPE THE CORRECT LINE TO REPLACE THE ONE WHICH IS WRONG:"
1580 PRINT "X, Y"
1590 INPUT X(I), Y(I)
1600 GOTO 1650
1610 REM ADD A NEW LINE
1620 LET N = N + 1
1630 PRINT "TYPE THE ADDITIONAL LINE OF DATA AS SHOWN:   X,Y"
1640 INPUT X(N), Y(N)
1650 PRINT "OK"
1660 GOTO 1220
1670 REM DELETE A LINE
1680 PRINT "TYPE THE LINENUMBER OF THE LINE TO BE DELETED"
1690 INPUT J
1700 IF (J - 1) * (J - N) > 0 THEN 1720
1710 IF J = INT(J) THEN 1740
1720 PRINT "LINENUMBER MUST BE AN INTEGER IN THE RANGE 1 -"; N
1730 GOTO 1680
1740 FOR I = J + 1 TO N
1750    LET X(I - 1) = X(I)
1760    LET Y(I - 1) = Y(I)
1770 NEXT I
1780 LET N = N - 1
1790 PRINT "OK"
1800 IF J > N THEN 1220
1810 GOTO 1130
1820 RETURN
1830 REM SUBROUTINE TO CHECK REPLIES
```

```
1840 IF I$ = "NO" THEN 1860
1850 PRINT " TYPE YES OR NO & PRESS RETURN."
1860 PRINT
1870 INPUT Q$
1880 IF Q$ = "YES" THEN 1920
1890 IF Q$ = "NO" THEN 1920
1900 PRINT "REPLY '"; Q$; "' NOT UNDERSTOOD.";
1910 GOTO 1850
1920 RETURN
1930 REM *** SUBROUTINE TO CALCULATE PROBABILITY
1940 LET N2 = N - 2
1950 READ B(1), B(2), B(3), B(4), P
1960 DATA 1.E+06, 10000, 1000, 100, 0
1970 REM AVOID CALCULATION IF R = 1 OR R = -1
1980 IF ABS(R) = 1 THEN 2240
1990 REM CONVERT PEARSON R TO STUDENT T VALUE
2000 LET T = ABS(R) * SQR(N2) / SQR(1 - R * R)
2010 IF N2 > 4 THEN 2040
2020 IF T > B(N2) THEN 2240
2030 GOTO 2050
2040 IF T > 50 THEN 2240
2050 LET A = T / SQR(N2)
2060 LET B = N2 / (N2 + T * T)
2070 LET J = N2 - 2
2080 LET K = N2 - INT(N2 / 2) * 2 +2
2090 LET S = 1
2100 IF J < 2 THEN 2180
2110 LET C = 1
2120 LET F2 = K
2130 FOR I = K TO J STEP 2
2140    LET C = C * B * (F2 - 1) / F2
2150    LET S = S + C
2160    LET F2 = F2 + 2
2170 NEXT I
2180 IF K > 2 THEN 2210
2190 LET P = 0.5 - 0.5 * A * SQR(B) * S
2200 GOTO 2240
2210 IF N2 > 1 THEN 2230
2220 LET S = 0
2230 LET P = 0.5 - (A * B * S + ATN(A)) / 3.14159
2240 IF R > 0 THEN 2260
2250 LET P = 1 - P
2260 RETURN
2270 END
```

used different ingredients to produce 10 different beers which are labelled A, B, C, D, E, F, G, H, I and J. Two different beer tasters tried all 10 samples, and arranged them in order of preference as shown in Table 7.3. The brewer would like to know how well the two tasters agree. If the tasters are unable to distinguish between the different beers then the orders they have chosen will be random, hence no significant correlation will exist. One could make the subjective judgement that since beer D is ranked first and second, and beer E is ranked ninth and tenth, the tasters clearly showed some preference. However, this result could have arisen by chance, and the brewer needs to know the probability that such a result could have arisen by chance. To achieve this the brewer must calculate a correlation coefficient and use statistical tables to find the probability of obtaining such a correlation value by chance.

Table 7.3

Rank	1st	2nd	3rd	4th	5th	6th	7th	8th	9th	10th
Beer taster 1	F	D	G	H	C	A	J	B	I	E
Beer taster 2	D	H	G	F	J	I	A	C	E	B

Spearman's Rank Correlation Coefficient ρ
(see Program 7.2)

Spearman's rank correlation coefficient (denoted by the Greek letter rho, ρ) is based on comparisons of the ranks given to each item by two different evaluators.

Spearman's rank correlation coefficient

$$\rho = 1 - \frac{6\Sigma D^2}{n(n^2-1)} \qquad (6)$$

where D is the difference between the ranks given for one item by the two judges, Σ is the summation of D^2 for all of the items, n is the number of items and ρ ranges from $+1$ for identical ranks to -1 for opposite ranks.

The method of calculating Spearman's correlation coefficient is illustrated in Table 7.4 by using the data on beer tasting mentioned previously.

Table 7.4

Beer	Beer taster 1 rank	Beer taster 2 rank	Rank difference D	D^2
A	6	7	-1	1
B	8	10	-2	4
C	5	8	-3	9
D	2	1	1	1
E	10	9	1	1
F	1	4	-3	9
G	3	3	0	0
H	4	2	2	4
I	9	6	3	9
J	7	5	2	4

$$\Sigma D = 0 \quad \Sigma D^2 = 42$$

Spearman's rank correlation coefficient

$$\rho = 1 - \frac{6 \times 42}{10(10^2-1)}$$

$$\rho = 0.745$$

The brewer's question still remains unanswered. How likely is it that a value of $\rho = 0.745$ from 10 readings could have arisen by chance? The question is answered indirectly by comparing the calculated value of ρ with the values from significance tables.

Table 7.5 gives the $2\frac{1}{2}\%$ significance values for varying numbers of items (beer samples in this case).

If 10 random ranks are taken then there is a $2\frac{1}{2}\%$ chance that the calculated value of ρ is greater than 0.6364. In the case with 10 different beer samples the calculated value of $\rho = 0.745$ lies outside this range. There is therefore less than a $2\frac{1}{2}\%$ chance that a correlation as good as this could have arisen by chance from random ranks. Since it is unlikely that this correlation has arisen by

Table 7.5

Number of items from which ρ is calculated n	$2\frac{1}{2}\%$ significance value for Spearman's ρ (one-tailed)
5	0.9000
6	0.8286
7	0.7450
8	0.7143
9	0.6833
10	0.6364
20	0.4451

A fuller significance table for ρ is given in Appendix 2.

chance, the brewer must assume that the tasters can distinguish between the different beers, and also that they have similar tastes.

The brewer is using a one-tailed test since he is only interested in agreement, that is direct correlation, between the two beer tasters. The brewer should not use a two-tailed test because this includes inverse correlation. The latter implies that the tasters can distinguish between the different beers and that they have opposite preferences, resulting in a negative value for ρ.

Equal ranks

It is possible that the beer taster may rank two or more beers equally, in which case they

Program 7.2 Trial run.

```
SPEARMAN'S RANK CORRELATION COEFFICIENT RHO
========== ==== =========== =========== ===

WOULD YOU LIKE FULL INSTRUCTIONS?
 TYPE YES OR NO & PRESS RETURN.

? YES


TEST TO COMPARE RANKS (IE. RELATIVE POSITIONS)
FOR TWO SETS OF EXPERIMENTAL DATA.  TYPE PAIRS OF RANKS
OR PAIRS OF DATA VALUES & THE PROGRAM SORTS OUT THE RANKS

TYPE THE NUMBER OF DATA PAIRS ? 10
TYPE A PAIR OF DATA VALUES SEPARATED BY A COMMA
THEN PRESS RETURN, TYPE NEXT PAIR OF DATA VALUES ETC
YOU WILL HAVE CHANCE TO CORRECT WRONGLY TYPED DATA LATER
INPUT DATA X,Y
? 6, 7
? 8, 10
? 5, 8
? 2, 1
? 10, 9
? 1, 4
? 3, 3
? 4, 2
? 9, 6
? 7, 5
END OF DATA INPUT
ARE THE DATA VALUES ENTERED CORRECT?  TYPE YES OR NO & PRESS RETURN.

? YES
WOULD YOU LIKE A LIST OF DATA VALUES & RANKS?
 TYPE YES OR NO & PRESS RETURN.

? NO

SPEARMAN'S RANK CORRELATION COEFFICIENT RHO = 0.745455
THE ONE-TAILED PROBABILITY OF OBTAINING A CORRELATION AS
GOOD OR BETTER THAN THIS BY CHANCE FROM RANDOM RANKS IS 0.7 %
THERE IS STRONG  EVIDENCE FOR A DIRECT  RELATION BETWEEN X & Y

WOULD YOU LIKE ANOTHER RUN?
 TYPE YES OR NO & PRESS RETURN.

? NO
END OF JOB
```

```
10 DIM X(100), Y(100), A(100), B(100), Q$(10), I$(3)
20 PRINT "SPEARMAN'S RANK CORRELATION COEFFICIENT RHO"
30 PRINT "========= ==== =========== =========== ==="
40 PRINT
50 PRINT "WOULD YOU LIKE FULL INSTRUCTIONS?"
60 GOSUB 1840
70 LET I$ = Q$
80 IF I$ = "NO" THEN 130
90 PRINT
100 PRINT "TEST TO COMPARE RANKS (IE. RELATIVE POSITIONS)"
110 PRINT "FOR TWO SETS OF EXPERIMENTAL DATA.  TYPE PAIRS OF RANKS"
120 PRINT "OR PAIRS OF DATA VALUES & THE PROGRAM SORTS OUT THE RANKS"
130 PRINT
140 PRINT "TYPE THE NUMBER OF DATA PAIRS";
150 INPUT N
160 IF N <> INT(N) THEN 180
170 IF (N - 2) * (N - 100) <= 0 THEN 200
180 PRINT "VALUE TYPED MUST BE A WHOLE NUMBER BETWEEN 2 AND 100"
190 GOTO 140
200 IF I$ = "NO" THEN 240
210 PRINT "TYPE A PAIR OF DATA VALUES SEPARATED BY A COMMA"
220 PRINT "THEN PRESS RETURN, TYPE NEXT PAIR OF DATA VALUES ETC"
230 PRINT "YOU WILL HAVE CHANCE TO CORRECT WRONGLY TYPED DATA LATER"
240 PRINT "INPUT DATA X,Y"
250 FOR I = 1 TO N
260    INPUT X(I), Y(I)
270 NEXT I
280 PRINT "END OF DATA INPUT"
290 REM CALL SUBROUTINE TO CHECK THAT DATA VALUES ARE CORRECT
300 GOSUB 1070
310 REM CHECK THAT THE NUMBER OF DATA PAIRS IS SENSIBLE
320 IF N >= 2 THEN 360
330 PRINT "NOT ENOUGH DATA PAIRS - RUN ABANDONED"
340 GOTO 910
350 REM CALCULATE RANKED A & B VALUES FROM RAW X & Y VALUES
360 FOR I = 1 TO N
370    LET A1 = 0.5
380    LET B1 = 0.5
390    FOR J = 1 TO N
400      IF X(J) < X(I) THEN 450
410      IF X(J) = X(I) THEN 440
420      LET A1 = A1 + 1
430      GOTO 450
440      LET A1 = A1 + 0.5
450      IF Y(J) < Y(I) THEN 500
460      IF Y(J) = Y(I) THEN 490
470      LET B1 = B1 + 1
480      GOTO 500
490      LET B1 = B1 + 0.5
500    NEXT J
510    LET A(I) = A1
520    LET B(I) = B1
530 NEXT I
540 PRINT "WOULD YOU LIKE A LIST OF DATA VALUES & RANKS?"
550 GOSUB 1830
560 IF Q$ = "NO" THEN 620
570 PRINT "X", "RANK X", "Y", "RANK Y"
580 FOR I = 1 TO N
590    PRINT X(I), A(I), Y(I), B(I)
600 NEXT I
610 REM CALCULATE SUM OF SQUARED RANK DIFFERENCES
```

```
620 LET R2 = 0
630 FOR I = 1 TO N
640    LET D = A(I) - B(I)
650    LET R2 = R2 + D * D
660 NEXT I
670 REM CALCULATE SPEARMANS RANK CORRELATION
680 LET R = 1 - R2 / (N / 6 * (N - 1) * (N + 1))
690 PRINT
700 PRINT "SPEARMAN'S RANK CORRELATION COEFFICIENT RHO ="; R
710 REM CALCULATE PROBABILITY OF SUCH A CORRELATION BY CHANCE
720 GOSUB 1930
730 PRINT "THE ONE-TAILED PROBABILITY OF OBTAINING A CORRELATION AS"
740 PRINT "GOOD OR BETTER THAN THIS BY CHANCE FROM RANDOM RANKS IS";
750 LET F = 1
760 IF (P - 0.95) * (P - 0.05) <=0 THEN 780
770 LET F = 10
780 PRINT INT(P * F * 100 + 0.5) / F; "%"
790 IF (P - 0.05) * (P - 0.95) > 0 THEN 820
800 PRINT "THERE IS NO EVIDENCE FOR A";
810 GOTO 900
820 IF (P - 0.01) * (P - 0.99) > 0 THEN 850
830 PRINT "THERE IS SOME";
840 GOTO 860
850 PRINT "THERE IS STRONG";
860 IF P > 0.5 THEN 890
870 PRINT " EVIDENCE FOR A DIRECT";
880 GOTO 900
890 PRINT " EVIDENCE FOR AN AN INVERSE";
900 PRINT " RELATION BETWEEN X & Y"
910 PRINT
920 PRINT "WOULD YOU LIKE ANOTHER RUN?"
930 GOSUB 1830
940 IF Q$ = "NO" THEN 2260
950 RESTORE
960 PRINT "TYPE NEW TO START AGAIN WITH NEW DATA"
970 PRINT "  OR OLD TO EDIT EXISTING DATA"
980 INPUT Q$
990 LET I$ = "NO"
1000 IF Q$ = "NEW" THEN 130
1010 IF Q$ = "OLD" THEN 1040
1020 PRINT "REPLY '"; Q$; "' NOT UNDERSTOOD."
1030 GOTO 960
1040 GOSUB 1120
1050 GOTO 320
1060 REM SUBROUTINE TO CHECK THAT DATA ARE CORRECT & ALTER IF NECESSARY
1070 PRINT "ARE THE DATA VALUES ENTERED CORRECT?";
1080 REM A4 SHOULD BE SET TO THE NUMBER OF LINES ON THE VDU
1090 LET A4 = 20
1100 GOSUB 1830
1110 IF Q$ = "YES" THEN 1810
1120 PRINT "HERE IS A LIST OF THE CURRENT DATA"
1130 PRINT "LINE NUMBER", "X", "Y"
1140 FOR I = 1 TO N
1150    PRINT I, X(I), Y(I)
1160    IF INT(I / (A4 - 1)) * (A4 - 1) <> I THEN 1200
1170    PRINT "WOULD YOU LIKE TO CONTINUE LISTING";
1180    GOSUB 1830
1190    IF Q$ = "NO" THEN 1210
1200 NEXT I
1210 PRINT "TYPE R TO REPLACE";
1220 IF I$ = "NO" THEN 1240
```

```
1230 PRINT " AN EXISTING LINE OF DATA"
1240 IF N = 100 THEN 1290
1250 PRINT TAB(5); " A TO ADD";
1260 IF I$ = "NO" THEN 1280
1270 PRINT " AN EXTRA LINE"
1280 IF N = 1 THEN 1320
1290 PRINT TAB(5); " D TO DELETE";
1300 IF I$ = "NO" THEN 1320
1310 PRINT " AN EXISTING LINE"
1320 PRINT TAB(5); " L TO LIST";
1330 IF I$ = "NO" THEN 1350
1340 PRINT " THE DATA"
1350 PRINT "  OR C TO CONTINUE";
1360 IF I$ = "NO" THEN 1380
1370 PRINT " THE CALCULATION"
1380 INPUT Q$
1390 IF Q$ = "R" THEN 1490
1400 IF N = 100 THEN 1430
1410 IF Q$ = "A" THEN 1610
1420 IF N = 1 THEN 1440
1430 IF Q$ = "D" THEN 1660
1440 IF Q$ = "L" THEN 1120
1450 IF Q$ = "C" THEN 1810
1460 PRINT "REPLY '"; Q$; "' NOT UNDERSTOOD."
1470 GOTO 1210
1480 REM REPLACE LINE
1490 PRINT "TYPE THE LINENUMBER OF THE LINE TO BE REPLACED";
1500 INPUT I
1510 IF I <> INT(I) THEN 1530
1520 IF (I - 1) * (I - N) <= 0 THEN 1560
1530 PRINT "LINENUMBER MUST BE AN INTEGER IN THE RANGE 1 -"; N
1540 PRINT "RE-";
1550 GOTO 1490
1560 PRINT "TYPE THE CORRECT LINE TO REPLACE THE ONE WHICH IS WRONG:"
1570 PRINT "X, Y"
1580 INPUT X(I), Y(I)
1590 GOTO 1640
1600 REM ADD A NEW LINE
1610 LET N = N + 1
1620 PRINT "TYPE THE ADDITIONAL LINE OF DATA AS SHOWN:   X,Y"
1630 INPUT X(N), Y(N)
1640 PRINT "OK"
1650 GOTO 1210
1660 REM DELETE A LINE
1670 PRINT "TYPE THE LINENUMBER OF THE LINE TO BE DELETED"
1680 INPUT J
1690 IF (J - 1) * (J - N) > 0 THEN 1710
1700 IF J = INT(J) THEN 1730
1710 PRINT "LINENUMBER MUST BE AN INTEGER IN THE RANGE 1 -"; N
1720 GOTO 1670
1730 FOR I = J + 1 TO N
1740    LET X(I - 1) = X(I)
1750    LET Y(I - 1) = Y(I)
1760 NEXT I
1770 LET N = N - 1
1780 PRINT "OK"
1790 IF J > N THEN 1210
1800 GOTO 1120
1810 RETURN
1820 REM SUBROUTINE TO CHECK REPLIES
1830 IF I$ = "NO" THEN 1850
```

```
1840 PRINT " TYPE YES OR NO & PRESS RETURN."
1850 PRINT
1860 INPUT Q$
1870 IF Q$ = "YES" THEN 1910
1880 IF Q$ = "NO" THEN 1910
1890 PRINT "REPLY '"; Q$; "' NOT UNDERSTOOD.";
1900 GOTO 1840
1910 RETURN
1920 REM *** SUBROUTINE TO CALCULATE PROBABILITY
1930 LET N2 = N - 2
1940 READ B(1), B(2), B(3), B(4), P
1950 DATA 1.E+06, 10000, 1000, 100, 0
1960 REM AVOID CALCULATION IF R = 1 OR R = -1
1970 IF ABS(R) = 1 THEN 2230
1980 REM CONVERT SPEARMAN RHO TO STUDENT T VALUE
1990 LET T = ABS(R) * SQR(N2) / SQR(1 - R * R)
2000 IF N2 > 4 THEN 2030
2010 IF T > B(N2) THEN 2230
2020 GOTO 2040
2030 IF T > 50 THEN 2230
2040 LET A = T / SQR(N2)
2050 LET B = N2 / (N2 + T * T)
2060 LET J = N2 - 2
2070 LET K = N2 - INT(N2 / 2) * 2 + 2
2080 LET S = 1
2090 IF J < 2 THEN 2170
2100 LET C = 1
2110 LET F2 = K
2120 FOR I = K TO J STEP 2
2130    LET C = C * B * (F2 - 1) / F2
2140    LET S = S + C
2150    LET F2 = F2 + 2
2160 NEXT I
2170 IF K > 2 THEN 2200
2180 LET P = 0.5 - 0.5 * A * SQR(B) * S
2190 GOTO 2230
2200 IF N2 > 1 THEN 2220
2210 LET S = 0
2220 LET P = 0.5 - (A * B * S + ATN(A)) / 3.14159
2230 IF R > 0 THEN 2250
2240 LET P = 1 - P
2250 RETURN
2260 PRINT "END OF JOB"
2270 END
```

should all be assigned their average rank. For example if beer taster 1 ranked G and H equally, they should both have the rank 3.5.

Description of Program to Calculate Spearman's Correlation Coefficient ρ

The program (Program 7.2) first prints a heading (lines 20–30) and then asks if full instructions are required (line 50). The answer, which must be either YES or NO, is checked in a subroutine (lines 1820–1910). Either full or abbreviated instructions are printed as appropriate in the first run, but abbreviated instructions are always given in subsequent runs.

The program then asks for the number of data pairs (line 140). The value typed is checked (lines 160–190) to ensure that it is an integer, and between 2 and 100 inclusive. The upper limit is imposed by the DIMension of the *X*, *Y*, *A* and *B* arrays in line 10, and the accuracy of the method used to calculate the significance of ρ is only guaranteed up to this limit.

A message (lines 210–240) then invites the user to type in pairs of data values. The data input loop extends from lines 250 to 270.

A subroutine (lines 1060–1810) is then called which asks if the data values are correct. The answer must be YES or NO, and is checked in a subroutine (lines 1820–1910). If the data are not correct, the values are listed and instructions are given to permit the addition, deletion or replacement of lines of data, re-listing the data, or continuing with the calculation. This subroutine is described in more detail in the write-up for Pearson's correlation coefficient.

Once the data are correct, a check is performed (lines 320–340) to ensure that at least two data pairs remain.

Next the data values which are stored in the X and Y arrays are converted into ranks and stored in the A and B arrays (lines 350–530). A message (line 540) asks if a list of the data values and ranks is required. If requested the data and ranks are printed (lines 570–600).

The sum of the squared rank differences is then calculated (lines 610–660). Using this, Spearman's rank correlation coefficient is evaluated (line 680) using Equation 6, and is printed out (line 700). A subroutine (lines 1920–2250) is then entered to work out the probability that a correlation as good or better than this could arise by chance. The subroutine is the same as that used in Pearson's correlation, where it is described more fully. The probability is then printed out (lines 730–780) together with one of five explanatory messages (lines 790–900).

Finally the user is offered another run (line 920). If another run is required, a choice is given between typing in a completely NEW set of data, or editing and re-running using the OLD (existing) data.

Kendall's Rank Correlation Coefficient τ

Kendall's rank correlation coefficient (denoted by the Greek letter tau τ) is based on whether two items out of the whole set, have been placed in the same relative position by the two ranking processes or judges. The coefficient ranges from $+1$ for identical ranks to -1 for opposite ranks. In the example about beer testing, this correlation coefficient is based on whether two different beers have been placed in the same relative positions by both beer tasters. If the two beers have been placed in the same relative position by both beer tasters, then this counts as 'agreement', whereas if their relative positions are reversed this counts as 'disagreement'.

This may be illustrated by first comparing beers A and B, then comparing beers A and C.

Beer taster 1 prefers beer A to beer B
Beer taster 2 prefers beer A to beer B
(this counts as an agreement)

Beer taster 1 prefers beer C to beer A
Beer taster 2 prefers beer A to beer C
(this counts as a disagreement)

If either taster prefers two beers equally then this counts as a tie. When all combinations of the beers have been compared (in this case after 45 comparisons), Kendall's rank correlation coefficient τ is calculated:

$$\tau = \frac{\text{number of agreements} - \text{number of disagreements}}{\text{number of comparisons}} \quad (7)$$

If n different samples are tested then the number of comparisons is $\frac{1}{2}n(n-1)$. Thus in the beer example where $n = 10$, the number of comparisons is 45. Equation 7 may therefore be re-written

$$\tau = \frac{\text{number of agreements} - \text{number of disagreements}}{\frac{1}{2}n(n-1)} \quad (8)$$

To calculate Kendall's rank correlation coefficient manually, it is easiest if the original data are sorted into the order chosen by one of the beer tasters as shown in Table 7.6

97

Table 7.6

Beer	F	D	G	H	C	A	J	B	I	E
Beer taster 1 ranks	1	2	3	4	5	6	7	8	9	10
Beer taster 2 ranks	4	1	3	2	8	7	5	10	6	9

Comparison of F with D, G, H, C, A, J, B, I, E gives	6 agreements and	3 disagreements
Comparison of D with G, H, C, A, J, B, I, E gives	8 agreements and	0 disagreements
Comparison of G with H, C, A, J, B, I, E gives	6 agreements and	1 disagreements
Comparison of H with C, A, J, B, I, E gives	6 agreements and	0 disagreements
Comparison of C with A, J, B, I, E gives	2 agreements and	3 disagreements
Comparison of A with J, B, I, E gives	2 agreements and	2 disagreements
Comparison of J with B, I, E gives	3 agreements and	0 disagreements
Comparison of B with I, E gives	0 agreements and	2 disagreements
Comparison of I with E gives	1 agreements and	0 disagreements
TOTAL	34 agreements	11 disagreements

Since this manual comparison is laborious and may be error prone, it is worth checking that the number of agreements plus ties plus disagreements is equal to the total number of comparisons which should have been performed, i.e. $34 + 0 + 11 = 45$.

Kendall's rank correlation coefficient is evaluated using Equation 8.

$$\tau = \frac{34 - 11}{45} = 0.511$$

In a similar way to the other correlations, the value of $\tau = 0.511$ is looked up in a significance table (see Table 7.7).

The calculated value for τ is just on the $2\frac{1}{2}\%$ significance value, hence there is a $2\frac{1}{2}\%$ chance that a correlation as good as this could have arisen from random ranks. This provides some evidence of correlation between the ranks assigned by the two beer tasters. Clearly a larger calculated value of τ might lie within the 1% significance level, and there would then be only a 1 in 100 chance of such good correlation occurring from random ranks. This would strengthen the evidence for agreement between the two beer tasters.

A relationship between Spearman's ρ and Kendall's τ was shown by H.E. Daniels in 1950. This is

$$-1 \leqslant 3\tau - 2\rho \leqslant +1$$

In the beer tasting example
$$(3 \times 0.511) - (2 \times 0.745) = 0.043$$

Description of Program to Calculate Kendall's Correlation Coefficient τ

The program (Program 7.3) first prints a heading, and then asks if full instructions are required. The answer which must be YES or NO is checked in a subroutine (lines

Table 7.7

Number of items from which τ is calculated n	$2\frac{1}{2}\%$ significance value for Kendall's τ (one-tailed)
5	1
6	0.87
7	0.71
8	0.64
9	0.56
10	0.51
20	0.33

A fuller significance table for τ is given in Appendix 3.

1380–1470). If the answer is YES then full instructions are given throughout the first run.

Next the program asks for the number of data pairs and performs a number of checks on the value typed in (lines 80–140). The value must be an integer and lie in the range 2–100 inclusive. The test is meaningless on less than two values, and array sizes $X(100)$ and $Y(100)$ impose the upper limit. Any unacceptable value is rejected, and the user is prompted with a message to re-type the value correctly.

Following this the user is invited to type in the pairs of data values (lines 150–210). These data values will generally be the ranks from the two judges, but the program will also work if numerical scores awarded by the judges are entered instead of ranks. Examples of numeri-

cal scores include the judging of gymnastics, ice skating and diving, and typing in the numeric data saves the user the effort of ranking the scores. A consequence of this feature is that the program cannot check that the ranks are sensible values. (Ranks must be either whole numbers, e.g. 1, 2, 3 or halves, e.g. 4.5 as a result of a tie for fourth and fifth places. Furthermore ranks must be in the range one to the number of points.)

A subroutine (lines 620–1370) is then called to permit the verification and alteration of the data pairs. This allows listing, deletion, addition or replacement of data, and is fully described in the description of the program for Pearson's correlation coefficient.

The number of 'agreements' and 'disagree-

Program 7.3   Trial run.

```
KENDALL'S RANK CORRELATION COEFFICIENT
======= = ==== =========== ===========

WOULD YOU LIKE FULL INSTRUCTIONS?
 TYPE YES OR NO & PRESS RETURN.

? YES
TYPE THE NUMBER OF DATA PAIRS
? 10
TYPE DATA PAIRS ONE AT A TIME SEPARATED BY A COMMA
THEN PRESS RETURN, TYPE THE NEXT PAIR OF VALUES, RETURN ETC
YOU WILL HAVE THE CHANCE TO CORRECT TYPING ERRORS LATER
? 1, 4
? 2, 1
? 3, 3
? 4, 2
? 5, 8
? 6, 7
? 7, 5
? 8, 10
? 9, 6
? 10, 9
ARE THE DATA VALUES ENTERED CORRECT?   TYPE YES OR NO & PRESS RETURN.

? YES

KENDALL'S RANK CORRELATION COEFFICIENT = 0.511111

THE ONE TAILED PROBABILITY OF A BETTER CORRELATION ARISING
BY CHANCE FROM RANDOM RANKS = 2 %

WOULD YOU LIKE ANOTHER RUN?
 TYPE YES OR NO & PRESS RETURN.

? NO
END OF JOB
```

```
10 DIM X(100), Y(100), Q$(10), I$(3)
20 PRINT "KENDALL'S RANK CORRELATION COEFFICIENT"
30 PRINT "======= = ==== ========== =========="
40 PRINT
50 PRINT "WOULD YOU LIKE FULL INSTRUCTIONS?"
60 GOSUB 1400
70 LET I$ = Q$
80 PRINT "TYPE THE NUMBER OF DATA PAIRS"
90 INPUT N
100 IF N <> INT(N) THEN 120
110 IF (N - 2) * (N - 100) <= 0 THEN 150
120 PRINT "THERE MUST BE A WHOLE NUMBER OF PAIRS BETWEEN 2 & 100"
130 PRINT "RE-";
140 GOTO 80
150 PRINT "TYPE DATA PAIRS ONE AT A TIME SEPARATED BY A COMMA"
160 IF I$ = "NO" THEN 190
170 PRINT "THEN PRESS RETURN, TYPE THE NEXT PAIR OF VALUES, RETURN ETC"
180 PRINT "YOU WILL HAVE THE CHANCE TO CORRECT TYPING ERRORS LATER"
190 FOR I = 1 TO N
200   INPUT X(I), Y(I)
210 NEXT I
220 REM *** CHECK THAT DATA ARE CORRECT
230 GOSUB 630
240 REM COUNT NUMBER OF AGREEMENTS & NUMBER OF DISAGREEMENTS
250 LET A = 0
260 FOR I = 1 TO N - 1
270   FOR J = I + 1 TO N
280     LET A = A + SGN(X(I) - X(J)) * SGN(Y(I) - Y(J))
290   NEXT J
300 NEXT I
310 REM *** CALCULATE NUMBER OF COMPARISONS
320 LET C = N * (N - 1) / 2
330 PRINT
340 LET K = A / C
350 PRINT "KENDALL'S RANK CORRELATION COEFFICIENT ="; K
360 PRINT
370 REM CONVERT K INTO  NO. OF STANDARD DEVIATIONS ON NORMAL CURVE
380 LET S = ABS(K) * SQR(4.5 * N * (N - 1) / (2 * N + 5))
390 REM CALC AREA UNDER NORMAL CURVE
400 GOSUB 1500
410 PRINT "THE ONE TAILED PROBABILITY OF A BETTER CORRELATION ARISING"
420 LET P = 1
430 IF (F - 0.05) * (F - 0.95) <= 0 THEN 450
440 LET P = 10
450 PRINT "BY CHANCE FROM RANDOM RANKS ="; INT((1-F)*P*100+0.5)/P; "%"
460 PRINT
470 PRINT "WOULD YOU LIKE ANOTHER RUN?"
480 GOSUB 1390
490 IF Q$ = "NO" THEN 600
500 LET I$ = "NO"
510 PRINT "TYPE NEW FOR A RUN WITH COMPLETELY NEW DATA"
520 PRINT "  OR OLD TO EDIT AND RERUN THE EXISTING DATA"
530 INPUT Q$
540 IF Q$ = "NEW" THEN 80
550 IF Q$ = "OLD" THEN 580
560 PRINT "REPLY '"; Q$; "' NOT UNDERSTOOD"
570 GOTO 510
580 GOSUB 680
590 GOTO 250
600 PRINT "END OF JOB"
610 STOP
```

```
620 REM SUBROUTINE TO CHECK THAT DATA ARE CORRECT & ALTER IF NECESSARY
630 PRINT "ARE THE DATA VALUES ENTERED CORRECT?";
640 REM A4 SHOULD BE SET TO THE NUMBER OF LINES ON THE VDU
650 LET A4 = 20
660 GOSUB 1390
670 IF Q$ = "YES" THEN 1370
680 PRINT "HERE IS A LIST OF THE CURRENT DATA"
690 PRINT "LINE NUMBER", "X", "Y"
700 FOR I = 1 TO N
710    PRINT I, X(I), Y(I)
720    IF INT(I / (A4 - 1)) * (A4 - 1) <> I THEN 760
730    PRINT "WOULD YOU LIKE TO CONTINUE LISTING";
740    GOSUB 1390
750    IF Q$ = "NO" THEN 770
760 NEXT I
770 PRINT "TYPE R TO REPLACE";
780 IF I$ = "NO" THEN 800
790 PRINT " AN EXISTING LINE OF DATA"
800 IF N = 100 THEN 850
810 PRINT TAB(5);" A TO ADD";
820 IF I$ = "NO" THEN 840
830 PRINT " AN EXTRA LINE"
840 IF N = 1 THEN 880
850 PRINT TAB(5); " D TO DELETE";
860 IF I$ = "NO" THEN 880
870 PRINT " AN EXISTING LINE"
880 PRINT TAB(5); " L TO LIST";
890 IF I$ = "NO" THEN 910
900 PRINT " THE DATA"
910 PRINT "  OR C TO CONTINUE";
920 IF I$ = "NO" THEN 940
930 PRINT " THE CALCULATION"
940 INPUT Q$
950 IF Q$ = "R" THEN 1050
960 IF N = 100 THEN 990
970 IF Q$ = "A" THEN 1170
980 IF N = 1 THEN 1000
990 IF Q$ = "D" THEN 1220
1000 IF Q$ = "L" THEN 680
1010 IF Q$ = "C" THEN 1370
1020 PRINT "REPLY '"; Q$; "' NOT UNDERSTOOD."
1030 GOTO 770
1040 REM REPLACE LINE
1050 PRINT "TYPE THE LINENUMBER OF THE LINE TO BE REPLACED";
1060 INPUT I
1070 IF I <> INT(I) THEN 1090
1080 IF (I - 1) * (I - N) <= 0 THEN 1120
1090 PRINT "LINENUMBER MUST BE AN INTEGER IN THE RANGE 1 -"; N
1100 PRINT "RE-";
1110 GOTO 1050
1120 PRINT "TYPE THE CORRECT LINE TO REPLACE THE ONE WHICH IS WRONG:"
1130 PRINT "X, Y"
1140 INPUT X(I), Y(I)
1150 GOTO 1200
1160 REM ADD A NEW LINE
1170 LET N = N + 1
1180 PRINT "TYPE THE ADDITIONAL LINE OF DATA AS SHOWN:   X,Y"
1190 INPUT X(N), Y(N)
1200 PRINT "OK"
1210 GOTO 770
1220 REM DELETE A LINE
```

```
1230 PRINT "TYPE THE LINENUMBER OF THE LINE TO BE DELETED"
1240 INPUT J
1250 IF (J - 1) * (J - N) > 0 THEN 1270
1260 IF J = INT(J) THEN 1290
1270 PRINT "LINENUMBER MUST BE AN INTEGER IN THE RANGE 1 -"; N
1280 GOTO 1230
1290 FOR I = J + 1 TO N
1300    LET X(I - 1) = X(I)
1310    LET Y(I - 1) = Y(I)
1320 NEXT I
1330 LET N = N - 1
1340 PRINT "OK"
1350 IF J > N THEN 770
1360 GOTO 680
1370 RETURN
1380 REM SUBROUTINE TO CHECK REPLIES
1390 IF I$ = "NO" THEN 1410
1400 PRINT " TYPE YES OR NO & PRESS RETURN."
1410 PRINT
1420 INPUT Q$
1430 IF Q$ = "YES" THEN 1470
1440 IF Q$ = "NO" THEN 1470
1450 PRINT "REPLY '"; Q$; "' NOT UNDERSTOOD.";
1460 GOTO 1400
1470 RETURN
1480 REM CALC CUMULATIVE AREA UNDER NORMAL CURVE
1490 REM CONSTANTS SET FOR 8 FIGURE ACCURACY
1500 LET X9 = -S * 7.0710678E-1
1510 LET F = 0
1520 IF X9 >= 9.5 THEN 1680
1530 LET F = 1
1540 IF X9 <= -4.5 THEN 1680
1550 LET T = 1 - 7.5 / (ABS(X9) + 3.75)
1560 LET Y = 0
1570 FOR I = 1 TO 12
1580    READ C
1590    LET Y = Y * T + C
1600 NEXT I
1610 RESTORE
1620 DATA 3.14753E-05, -0.000138746, -6.41279E-06, 0.00178663
1630 DATA -0.00823169, 0.0241519, -0.0547992, 0.102602
1640 DATA -0.163572, 0.226008, -0.273422, 0.14559
1650 LET F = 0.5 * EXP(-X9 * X9) * Y
1660 IF X9 >= 0 THEN 1680
1670 LET F = 1 - F
1680 RETURN
1690 END
```

ments' in the data are then calculated (lines 240–300) as the first step in calculating τ. The method of evaluation is different from that used in the manual calculation. Each combination of two data pairs is compared in turn. Consider the comparison of the Ith and Jth pairs. If the difference in the Ith and Jth ranks or score from judge X has the same sign as the equivalent difference for judge Y then the two judges agree about the relative positions of I and J, and $+1$ is added to the agreement total A. If the differences are of opposite sign then the two judges disagree and -1 is added to A. If there is a tie then zero is added to A.

The number of comparisons required is calculated (lines 310–320) using $\frac{1}{2}n(n-1)$, and τ is calculated (line 340) using Equation 8, and printed (line 350).

The significance of τ is calculated using the slight approximation that τ is normally distributed with a mean of zero and a standard deviation of $\sqrt{[(2n+5)/(4.5n(n-1))]}$. The τ value is thus converted (line 380) into a number of standard deviations from the mean on a standardised normal curve. The area under the normal curve up to this number of standard deviations is then calculated using an order 11 empirical polynomial in a subroutine (lines 1480–1680). The area thus obtained is the probability of obtaining a worse correlation by chance. By subtraction from one the probability of obtaining a better correlation by chance is obtained. The probability is printed (lines 410–450) rounded to give a whole number if it is in the range 5%–95%, or with one decimal figure if it is outside this range. This method of calculating the area is based on that used by the Numerical Algorithms Group (NAG). (This subroutine is also used by the program which generates a table of areas under a normal curve given in Appendix 4.)

The program then asks if another run is required (line 470), and if so the option is offered of editing the existing data and re-running, or alternatively typing in a completely new set of data.

Exercises

7.1 Plot scatter diagrams for the following sets of data, and state whether the data appear to be approximately linearly related. Calculate Pearson's r to check this.

(a) x 0   0   1   1
    y 0   1   0   1
(b) x 0   1   2   3   4   5
    y 5.4   6.6   9.1   10.4   12.6   13.8

7.2 The examination marks of 10 students in mathematics and physics are:

Mathematics   69   74   88   47   66
               41   95   55   50   47
Physics   66   69   71   48   63
               60   85   45   51   32

Calculate Pearson's r and check whether the correlation is significant at the 1% level.

7.3 The times in minutes taken by each of eight people to perform the same routine job on an assembly line were recorded early in the morning and again later in the afternoon.

Early morning   10.0   8.0   9.1   7.5
                 8.6   9.2   11.3   15.1
Late afternoon   11.5   8.7   9.9   11.1
                 9.9   9.1   13.6   13.2

Calculate Pearson's r, and state whether it is significant at the 5% level.

7.4 Two observers ranked the same five samples of eau-de-Cologne into order based on the strength of the perfume, on two different occasions. Their results are shown below:

	Observer 1				
First testing	1	5	4	3	2
Second testing	2	3	5	4	1
	Observer 2				
First testing	2	1	5	4	3
Second testing	3	2	5	4	1

Use Spearman's correlation coefficient on the replicate results from each observer to determine which of the two observers was the most self-consistent.

Table 7.8

Program	Ranks from critic 1	Ranks from critic 2
A	1	2
B	2	3
C	3	1
D	4	5
E	5	4
F	6	6
G	7	8
H	8	7

7.5 Use the data from Question 7.4 to see how well the two observers agreed on their second testing. Is the result significant at the 5% level?

7.6 Two TV critics were each asked to rank eight television programs. Use Kendall's rank correlation to establish whether their assessments (Table 7.8) agree significantly.

8

Straight Line Fitting (Least Squares)

Many practical problems yield a series of pairs of data values. It is usual for each data pair that one value x is chosen by the experimenter while the other value y is obtained experimentally. A new value of x is then chosen and the appropriate value of y measured. Some examples include:

(i) Selecting the temperature x, and measuring the length y of a bar of metal.

(ii) Fixing the length x of a simple pendulum and measuring its periodic time y (time for one complete oscillation).

(iii) Driving a car at a constant speed x and measuring the fuel consumption as the number of miles per gallon y.

(iv) Treating equivalent plots of land with a given weight of fertilizer x and measuring the crop yield y.

(v) Measuring the results from a new analytical method x against results from a standard method y.

In such cases, the value which is chosen is always given the letter x, and is often referred to as the independent variable. The value which is measured is given the letter y, and is called the dependent variable since its value depends on x. The objective is to establish what, if any, relationship exists between the x and y values so obtained. Two methods of establishing if a relationship exists are plotting a scatter diagram, or calculating Pearson's correlation coefficient.

Scatter Diagram

A graph is plotted with each (x, y) pair represented by a point. This is called a scatter diagram. If the graph points lie within a narrow band, the variables x and y are said to be correlated, and a relationship exists between them. If no band exists there is an absence of correlation between x and y, and no relationship exists between them. The scatter diagrams (Fig. 8.1) are typical of results from (i), (ii), (iii) and (iv) above. Fig. 8.1 shows four examples of correlation between x and y. In Examples (i), (ii) and (iv) the value of y *increases* as x increases and the correlation is said to be 'direct'. In Example (iii) the value of y *decreases* as x increases, and the correlation is said to be 'inverse'.

Example (i) (Fig. 8.1) indicates a linear (straight line) relationship between x and y. Straight lines are easy to recognise and simple to express mathematically:

$$y = mx + c$$

where m is the slope of the line and c is the intercept on the y axis (see Fig. 8.2). The experimental points in Example (i) do not lie exactly on a straight line for several reasons. These may include: (a) human observational errors, for example parallax or carelessness; (b) random errors because of environmental changes; and (c) errors inherent in the apparatus for example play in mechanical parts, the stray inductance or capacitance of connecting leads in electrical apparatus. Fitting a straight line through the points has the advantage that it tends to remove errors of this sort. It should be noted that systematic errors are not removed in this way. Common systematic errors include balances or meters not correctly

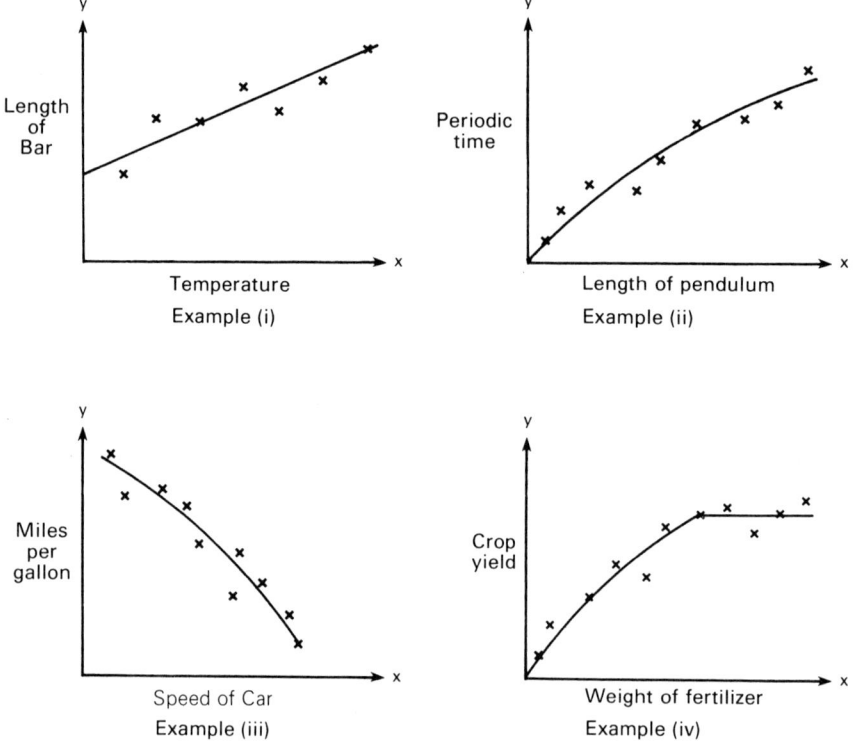

Fig. 8.1   Scatter diagrams.

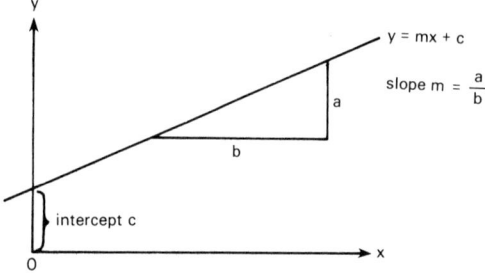

Fig. 8.2

zeroed, thermometers, pipettes and burettes incorrectly calibrated. The method by which the best values for the slope m and the intercept c are chosen is given in a later section.

The scatter diagram in Example (ii) (Fig. 8.1) suggests a curve rather than a straight line. The theoretical equation for a simple pendulum is:

$$T = 2\pi\sqrt{\frac{l}{g}}$$

where T is the periodic time, l is the length of the pendulum and g is the acceleration due to gravity (9.8 m s^{-2} or 32 ft s^{-2}). Using x and y for l and T respectively.

$$y = \frac{2\pi}{\sqrt{g}} \cdot \sqrt{x}$$

Comparing this with the straight line equation $y = mx + c$ it can be seen that by plotting a graph of y against $\sqrt{x}$ should give a line of slope $m = 2\pi/\sqrt{g}$ and intercept $c = 0$ (see Fig. 8.3).

There are no theoretical equations for Examples (iii) and (iv) (Fig. 8.1). In such cases one might obtain a straight line by changing the data before plotting, for example by plotting logarithms of one or both axes, by squaring or cubing one of the axes or by plotting reciprocals for one of the axes. If a straight line is not obtained it could be that the interrelation between x and y cannot be rearranged into a straight line form. Fitting a quadratic or a higher order polynomial to the

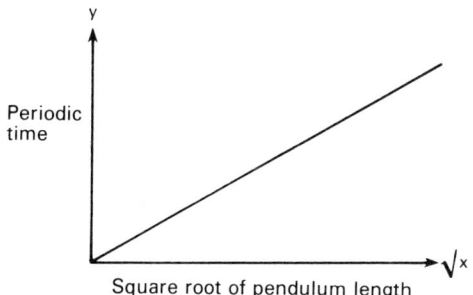

Fig. 8.3

y

Periodic time

Square root of pendulum length

$\sqrt{x}$

curve may be sufficient for smoothing or interpolation. This is discussed and a program provided in Chapter 9.

Pearson's Correlation Coefficient

This is fully described in Chapter 7 on correlations. Pearson's coefficient r lies in the range $+1$ (perfect direct linear correlation), through zero (no linear correlation), to -1 (perfect inverse linear correlation). As a rule of thumb, a fairly good straight line is indicated by values above 0.95 or below -0.95.

Derivation of Least-Squares Equations

It is quite possible to use the equations at the end of this section without following their derivation. For those interested and for completeness, the derivation is given below.

Consider n points on a graph (x_1, y_1), (x_2, y_2), ..., (x_n, y_n). The x_i values have been chosen by the experimenter (independent variable) while the y_i values have been measured (dependent variable) and are thus subject to errors. The 'best' straight line through these points has the equation

$$y = mx + c$$

The objective is to determine the values for slope m and intercept c. For a given values x_i the corresponding y value on the 'best' straight line is $mx_i + c$. The difference Δ between this calculated y value and the experi-

mentally observed y_i value is called the error in y_i (or the y residual), and has the value difference

$$\Delta_i = y_i - (mx_i + c)$$

The least-squares criterion used to determine the 'best' straight line is to make the sum of the differences squared as small as possible, i.e. minimise the expression E

$$E = \sum_{i=1}^{i=n} \Delta_i^2 = \sum_{i=1}^{i=n} (y_i - mx_i - c)^2 \qquad (1)$$

The standard way of obtaining the maxima and minima of an expression is to differentiate the expression and solve it for the case(s) where the derived function equals zero. Equation 1 contains two variables m and c, hence it is necessary to minimise E with respect to m, and also with respect to c. To do this requires the simultaneous solution of both partial derivatives $\partial E/\partial m$ and $\partial E/\partial c$ equal to zero. The partial derivative $\partial E/\partial m$ is obtained by differentiating the expression for E with respect to m and assuming that c is a constant. Similarly the partial derivative $\partial E/\partial c$ is obtained by differentiating E with respect to c and assuming that m is a constant.

Equation 1 may be expanded

$$E = \sum y_i^2 + m^2 \sum x_i^2 + nc^2 - $$
$$- 2m \sum x_i y_i - 2c \sum y_i + 2mc \sum x_i$$

partially differentiating with respect to m gives:

$$\frac{\partial E}{\partial m} = 0 + 2m \sum x_i^2 + 0 - $$
$$- 2 \sum x_i y_i - 0 + 2c \sum x_i \qquad (2)$$

similarly differentiating with respect to c gives:

$$\frac{\partial E}{\partial c} = 0 + 0 + 2nc - $$
$$- 0 - 2 \sum y_i + 2m \sum x_i \qquad (3)$$

Equating 2 to zero and rearranging

$$\sum x_i y_i = c \sum x_i + m \sum x_i^2 \qquad (4)$$

Equating 3 to zero and rearranging

$$\sum y_i = nc + m \sum x_i \qquad (5)$$

107

Equations 4 and 5 give two linearly independent equations in two unknowns. There are many ways of solving them to obtain m and c. One simple approach is:

(a) multiply each term in Equation 4 by n;
(b) multiply each term in Equation 5 by Σx_i;
(c) subtract these two equations from each other thus eliminating the c terms—the resulting equation involves only m;
(d) Substitute the equation for m back in Equation 4 to obtain an equation involving only c.

The correct solutions are

$$\text{Slope } m = \frac{n\Sigma x_i y_i - \Sigma x_i \cdot \Sigma y_i}{n\Sigma x_i^2 - (\Sigma x_i)^2} \qquad (6)$$

and

$$\text{Intercept } c = \frac{\Sigma x_i^2 \cdot \Sigma y_i - \Sigma x_i \cdot \Sigma x_i y_i}{n\Sigma x_i^2 - (\Sigma x_i)^2} \qquad (7)$$

The above equations for slope and intercept are widely used. It is worth noting that the denominators of both equations 6 and 7 involve the subtraction of two large positive quantities from each other. These equations are therefore potentially inaccurate if only a limited number of significant figures are carried as on calculators and computers. Any subtraction between two numbers which are almost equal results in a reduction in the number of significant figures of accuracy which may be claimed. This is further discussed in the section on finding the roots of an equation (Chapter 10).

The way to reduce this problem of loss of accuracy is to take advantage of the fact that the least-squares line must pass through the point $(\bar{x}, \bar{y})$ where $\bar{x}$ and $\bar{y}$ are the mean values, i.e. $\Sigma x_i/n$ and $\Sigma y_i/n$. This can be seen from Equation 5 divided throughout by n

$$\frac{\Sigma y_i}{n} = c + \frac{m\Sigma x_i}{n}$$

thus

$$\bar{y} = c + m\bar{x}$$

i.e.

$$\bar{y} = m\bar{x} + c \qquad (8)$$

More accuracy will be retained by reducing the magnitude of terms which are summed. This may be achieved by subtracting $\bar{x}$ from all the x values and $\bar{y}$ from all the y values. This is equivalent to moving the origin of the graph from the point $(0, 0)$ to the point $(\bar{x}, \bar{y})$. This change has no effect on the slope but allows it to be calculated more accurately. The change makes the intercept zero, but the original intercept is readily calculated from Equation 8 as

$$c = \bar{y} - m\bar{x} \qquad (9)$$

The equation for the improved accuracy for the slope is

$$m = \frac{\Sigma X_i Y_i}{\Sigma X_i^2} \qquad (10)$$

where

$$X_i = (x_i - \bar{x}) \text{ and } Y_i = (y_i - \bar{y}).$$

Equation 10 can easily be obtained from Equation 6 by shifting the origin, i.e replacing x and y by X and Y, and remembering that ΣX_i must be zero.

A further marginal improvement to the accuracy of the intercept can be obtained by re-writing Equation 9

$$c = \frac{\Sigma Y_i}{n} - \frac{\Sigma X_i Y_i}{\Sigma X_i^2} \cdot \frac{\Sigma X_i}{n}$$

$$c = \frac{\Sigma X_i^2 \cdot \Sigma Y_i - \Sigma X_i \cdot \Sigma X_i Y_i}{n\Sigma X_i^2} \qquad (11)$$

Equation 11 is slightly superior to Equation 9 particularly when c is close to zero.

Equations 10 and 11 should always be used on a computer in preference to Equations 6 and 7. The more accurate equations require that all of the x and y values are stored in arrays, the values for $\bar{x}$ and $\bar{y}$ calculated, and then the sums of ΣX_i, ΣY_i, ΣX_i^2 and $\Sigma X_i Y_i$ collected. This involves slightly more arithmetic and appreciably more memory which is usually available on a computer but it is not available on a calculator. The improvement in accuracy is illustrated in the next section.

A Numerical Example of the Accuracy of the Different Methods

The object of this section is to illustrate the improved accuracy of Equations 10 and 11 over Equations 6 and 7 (see Table 8.1). The data have deliberately been chosen to give inaccurate values for the intercept with Equation 7.

Data	x	y
	10 000	10 001
	11 001	11 002
	12 002	12 003

Clearly the best straight line has $m = 1$ and $c = 1$. On a computer carrying six significant figures, Equation 7 yields a meaningless and incorrect value for the intercept while Equation 11 gives an intercept which is wrong by less than 1 in 999. With a computer carrying 12 significant figures, both methods yield the exact answer.

How Good a Fit is the Best Straight Line?

A problem with an automatic (computerised) method of fitting a straight line is that it will ALWAYS give a best line, even if the fit is totally unreasonable. If a graph or scatter diagram is plotted then wildly erroneous points will be readily detected and either re-measured or disregarded. The method of least squares uses all of the data, and the calculated values are affected by the erroneous value(s). Furthermore no reasonable human being would attempt to fit a straight line to a circle, to four points at the corners of a square, to a cosine wave and numerous other cases which are non-linear. The computer has no sense of what is unreasonable, and will produce a solution if so instructed. Some warning is needed that the computer is carrying out an unreasonable task. The program described next reports the following indicators:

(i) Pearson's correlation coefficient r;
(ii) Standard deviation of the points from the least-squares line;
(iii) The individual errors Δ_i between each observed y value and corresponding point on the straight line;
(iv) The sum of the errors squared $\Sigma\Delta_i^2$.

Pearson's correlation coefficient should be close to $+1$ or -1 for a reasonable straight line. This is mentioned earlier in this chapter, and is more fully described in Chapter 7. It will detect the totally unreasonable cases mentioned above giving a value of r close to or equal to zero. It is less good at detecting a gentle curve and little use at detecting erroneous points.

A low standard deviation corresponds to a good fit. A high value is caused by a poor fit, and may be due to a bad scatter of points, an

Table 8.1

	Calculated value for m	Calculated value for c
Equations 6 and 7		
Computer carrying 6 significant figures	1.000 00	0.613 170
Computer carrying 12 significant figures	1.000 000 000 00	1.000 000 000 00
Equations 10 and 11		
Computer carrying 6 significant figures	1.000 00	0.999 004
Computer carrying 12 significant figures	1.000 000 000 00	1.000 000 000 00

unreasonable case as described above, or by one or more erroneous values. Unfortunately the magnitude of the standard deviation is directly proportional to the magnitude of the y_i values (i.e. doubling all of the y_i values gives double the standard deviation). Interpretation of the value of the standard deviation is therefore subjective.

The individual errors are invaluable in detecting wildly erroneous points, since these points have disproportionately large errors. If a poor fit is obtained then the individual errors should be examined to see if they follow some pattern. For example if the points actually followed a curve (see Fig. 8.4).

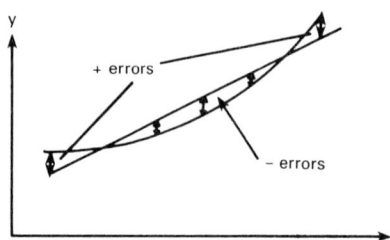

Fig. 8.4

If the list of individual errors suggests that an occasional point is erroneous, then this should be remeasured if possible or alternatively deleted. The program should then be re-run on the amended data. Discarding points should always be undertaken with care.

Confidence Limits for the Slope

It is often important to known how reliably the slope has been calculated, that is to quote a range of values within which the true slope is 95% likely to lie. Thus the slope should be quoted as:

$$\text{Slope} \pm t \cdot \text{Standard error of the slope} \quad (12)$$

where t is the 95% Student's t value (Appendix 6) with $(n-2)$ degrees of freedom. (The number of degrees of freedom is the number of points n less one for the slope and less

110

another since the straight line must pass through the point $(\bar{x}, \bar{y})$.)

First the standard deviation of the points from the least-squares line is calculated in the same same way as the standard deviation of y except that for each point $\bar{y}$ is replaced by the corresponding point on the straight line, which is $mx+c$.

Standard deviation of points from least-squares line

$$= \sqrt{\frac{[\Sigma[y_i - (mx_i + c)]^2]}{n-2}} \quad (13)$$

The standard error of the slope can be derived from first principles and is:

Standard error of slope

$$= \frac{\text{Standard deviation of points from line}}{\sqrt{[\Sigma(x_i - \bar{x})^2]}} \quad (14)$$

Using the values derived from Equations 13 and 14 in Equation 12, limits of accuracy may be placed on the slope. These are shown graphically in Fig. 8.5.

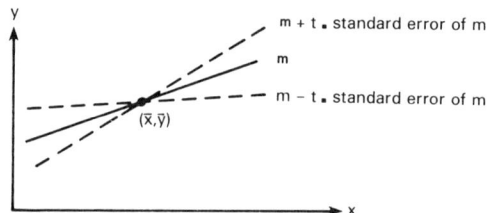

Fig. 8.5

Confidence Limits for a y Value Derived from the Line

In addition to the error in the slope discussed previously, there is also some additional error in the height of the line up the y axis. By definition the least-squares line must pass through $(\bar{x}, \bar{y})$ which is the mean of the observed data points. However $\bar{y}$ may differ from the true value because of errors in the individual y_i values.

From the central limit theorem, the standard error of $\bar{y}$ is

$$\frac{\text{Standard deviation of points from least-squares line}}{\sqrt{n}}$$

$$=\frac{\sqrt{\{\Sigma[y_i-(mx_i+c)]^2/(n-2)\}}}{\sqrt{n}} \qquad (15)$$

In an analogous manner to Equation 12 the true mean y value is 95% certain to lie in the range

$$\bar{y}\pm t\cdot\text{Standard error of }\bar{y} \qquad (16)$$

This is shown graphically in Fig. 8.6.

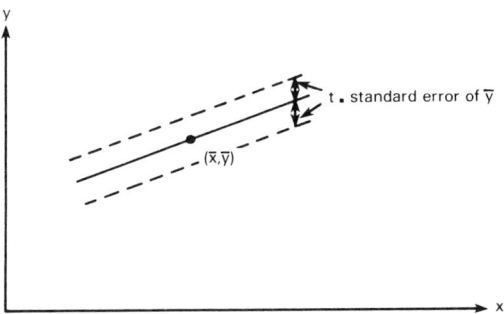

Fig. 8.6

From the error in the slope, and the error in $\bar{y}$, the standard error of a y value derived from the least-squares line at x may be expressed:

$$\text{Standard error of calculated } y \text{ value} =$$

$$\begin{array}{c}\text{Standard error of points} \\ \text{from least-squares line}\end{array} \times \sqrt{\left[\frac{1}{n}+\frac{(x-\bar{x})^2}{\Sigma(x_i-\bar{x})^2}\right]}$$

Hence the confidence limits for the calculated y value are

$$y\pm t\cdot\text{Standard error of calculated } y \text{ value}$$

In particular the confidence limits for the

intercept of the least-squares line on the y axis may be calculated by setting $x=0$. The value of t should have $(n-2)$ degrees of freedom, and should be chosen for the required probability level (usually 95%).

It is apparent from Equation 17 that the most reliable estimates of y are obtained for x values close to $\bar{x}$, and further x is from $\bar{x}$ the larger the possible error. This is shown in the graph (Fig. 8.7).

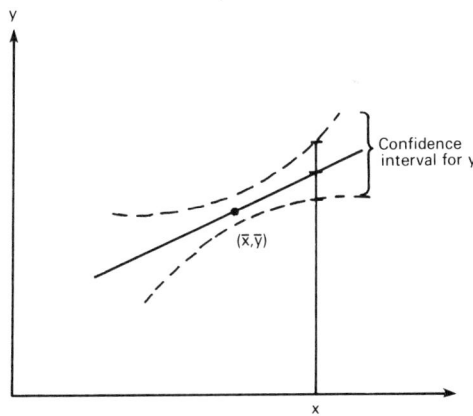

Fig. 8.7

Confidence Limits for an x Value Derived from the Line

In a number of methods of instrumental analysis such as a flame photometer or an absorption spectrophotometer, a number of solutions of known concentration of the material to be analysed are first used to obtain instrumental readings. A least-squares line is then fitted to these data to calibrate the instrument. A solution of unknown concentration is then introduced into the instrument giving a reading, which is converted into a concentration using the least-squares calibration graph. The problem of producing confidence limits is one of producing confidence limits for an x value from the least-squares line and a y value.

The standard error of x can be derived from first principles:

111

Standard error of calculated x value $=$

$$= \left[\frac{\begin{array}{c}\text{Standard error of points} \\ \text{from least-squares line}\end{array}}{\text{Slope}}\right]$$

$$\cdot \sqrt{\left[1 + \frac{1}{n} + \frac{(y - \bar{y})^2}{\text{slope}^2 \cdot \Sigma(x_i - \bar{x})^2}\right]} \quad (18)$$

Provided that ($t \times$ standard error of points from line/slope) is small, i.e. less than about 0.3, the confidence limits for the calculated x values are estimated as:

$$x \pm t \cdot \text{Standard error of calculated } x \text{ value} \quad (19)$$

Closer confidence limits may be obtained by taking l instrumental readings on the unknown solution. If the average of these is used instead of the y value then Equation 18 becomes:

Standard error of calculated x value $=$

$$= \left[\frac{\begin{array}{c}\text{Standard error of points} \\ \text{from least-squares line}\end{array}}{\text{Slope}}\right]$$

$$\cdot \sqrt{\frac{1}{l} + \frac{1}{n} + \frac{(y - \bar{y})^2}{\text{slope}^2 \cdot \Sigma(x_i - \bar{x})^2}} \quad (20)$$

Example

In the analysis of iron(III), ammonium thiocyanate is added and the intensity of colour produced is measured by a spectrophotometer. Four standard solutions containing 0.20, 0.40, 0.60 and 0.80 mg l^{-1} gave absorbances of 0.238, 0.506, 0.782 and 0.978 respectively. Calculate the average x and y values and the slope of the calibration curve, and use this to estimate the concentration of an iron(III) solution which gave an absorbance of 0.582. Calculate the standard deviation of points from the least-squares line and use this to estimate the standard error of the slope and $\bar{y}$. Finally calculate the confidence limits for the concentration of the solution whose absorbance was 0.582.

112

Calculation of Slope

Sum of x values	$= 2.00$
Mean x	$= 0.50$
Sum of y values	$= 2.504$
Mean y	$= 0.626$
Sum of $(x - x \text{ mean})^2$	$= 0.20$
Sum of $(y - y \text{ mean})^2$	$= 0.3132$
Sum of $(x - x \text{ mean}) \cdot (y - y \text{ mean})$	$= 0.2496$
Slope	$= 0.2496/0.20 = 1.248$

Correlation coefficient r

$$= 0.2496 \left/ \sqrt{(0.20 \times 0.3132)} \right. = 0.997$$

Calculation of Concentration

For a straight line $y = mx + c$. Since we have not calculated the intercept c, but have calculated the means $\bar{x}, \bar{y}$ (the centroidal point), the alternative straight line equation may be used:

$$y - \bar{y} = m(x - \bar{x})$$

$$\text{hence } x = \bar{x} + (y - \bar{y})/m$$

$$= 0.50 + (0.582 - 0.626)/1.248$$

$$= 0.4647$$

Concentration of unknown $= 0.465$ mg l^{-1} iron(III)

Calculation of the Standard Deviation of the Points from the Line

x	y	y calculated from line	$(y - y_{\text{calc}})^2$
0.20	0.238	0.2516	0.000 185 0
0.40	0.506	0.5012	0.000 023 0
0.60	0.782	0.7508	0.000 973 4
0.80	0.978	1.0004	0.000 501 8
			$\Sigma 0.001\ 683\ 2$

Using Equation 13

Standard deviation of points from least-squares line

$$= \sqrt{\frac{0.001\,683}{4-2}} = 0.029\,01$$

Using Equation 14 standard error of the slope

$$= \frac{0.029\,01}{\sqrt{0.2}} = 0.064\,87$$

Using Equation 15

Standard error of $\bar{y}$

$$= \frac{0.029\,01}{\sqrt{4}} = 0.014\,5$$

Using Appendix 6 the 95% confidence t value for two degrees of freedom is 4.303

Hence using Equation 12

95% confidence limits for slope

$$= 1.248 \pm 4.303 \times 0.064\,87$$

$$= 1.248 \pm 0.279$$

It is worth noting that the confidence limits on the slope are very wide even though the correlation coefficient is very close to 1. The reason for the wide confidence limits is the small number of points on the calibration curve.

Using Equation 16

95% confidence limits for $\bar{y}$

$$= 0.626 \pm 4.303 \times 0.0145$$

$$= 0.626 \pm 0.062$$

Confidence Limits for Concentration of Solution

Using Equation 18

Standard error of calculated x value

$$= \frac{0.029\,01}{1.248} \cdot \sqrt{\left[1 + \frac{1}{4} + \frac{(0.582 - 0.626)^2}{1.248^2 \times 0.20}\right]}$$

$$= 0.029\,20$$

Using Equation 19, confidence limit for calculated x value

$$= 0.0465 \pm 4.303 \times 0.029\,20$$

$$= 0.465 \pm 0.126$$

$$= 0.47 \pm 0.13$$

The limits of accuracy are so bad that the analysis is useless since the result is subject to about 27% error. Any self-respecting analyst would repeat the experiment with more points on the calibration curve. This has a big effect on the value of t, as well as the n that appears in the equations. Several measurements on the unknown solution should be made, and their average value used as y. This means that Equation 20 should be used instead of Equation 18.

How to Apply Least Squares when both x and y are Equally Prone to Error

At the beginning of this chapter it was assumed that the x values were *chosen* by the experimenter and considered to be free from error, hence x is called the independent variable. The corresponding y values are *measured*, making y the dependent variable. The y measurements are subject to errors. The method of least squares assumes that all of the error is associated with the y values.

In some circumstances it is not obvious which variable is dependent and which is independent since both are measured, and both are subject to errors. Some simple examples are:

(i) The relationship between the intelligence quotient IQ (x) of an individual and the weight of his brain (y).
(ii) The relationship between the height (x) and weight (y) of human beings.
(iii) The relationship between liver weight (x) and kidney weight (y) of guinea pigs.

Plainly one cannot take an individual, adjust his IQ to a certain value, and then measure his brain weight, whereas one can adjust the

113

length of a pendulum and measure its corresponding periodic time. In examples (i), (ii) and (iii) above both the x and y values are subject to errors

The conventional way of dealing with data of this sort is as follows:

1. Assume that all of the error is in the y terms (and none in the x), and fit the least-squares line. The graph (Fig. 8.8) shows the errors in the y values making this assumption, i.e. the least-squares line of regression of y on x.

2. Assume that all of the error occurs in the x terms (and none in the y terms), and fit the least-squares line. This can be done using the program for least squares by exchanging the x and y values that are typed in. The graph (Fig. 8.9) shows the errors in the x values for the least squares.

3. The two lines of regression are then compared. There are three possible cases:

(a) The slopes of both lines are identical. Both lines pass exactly through all of the points and consequently Pearson's correlation coefficient is $+1$ or -1.

(b) One line is horizontal and the other is vertical—that is the angle between the two lines is 90°. Pearson's correlation coefficient is zero, and there is no relationship whatsoever between x and y.

(c) The more usual case lies between these two extremes. If the angle between the two regression lines is small then x and y are related, and for example when estimating brain weight (y) from IQ (x) the first regression line (y on x) should be used. Conversely when estimating IQ (x) from brain weight (y) the second regression line (x on y) should be used.

Pearson's Correlation Coefficient

It should be noted that the value of Pearson's correlation coefficient is the same for regression of y on x and x on y. This property makes Pearson's correlation coefficient useful for determining whether a linear relationship exists between x and y. The program for Pearson's correlation given in Chapter 7 determines whether the calculated value is significant, i.e. whether a linear relationship between x and y exists at the 5% significance level.

The slope of x on y can be calculated from the slope of y on x and Pearson's correlation coefficient as shown below.

Slope of y on x

$$= \frac{\Sigma X_i Y_i}{\Sigma X_i^2} \text{ where } X_i = (x_i - \bar{x})$$
$$\text{and } Y_i = (y_i - \bar{y})$$

Slope of x on y

$$= \frac{\Sigma X_i Y_i}{\Sigma Y_i^2}$$

Pearson's r

$$= \frac{\Sigma X_i Y_i}{\sqrt{\Sigma X_i^2 \cdot \Sigma Y_i^2}}$$

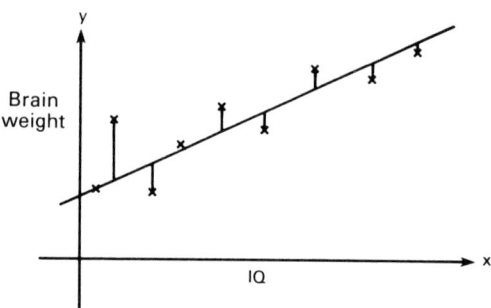

Fig. 8.8

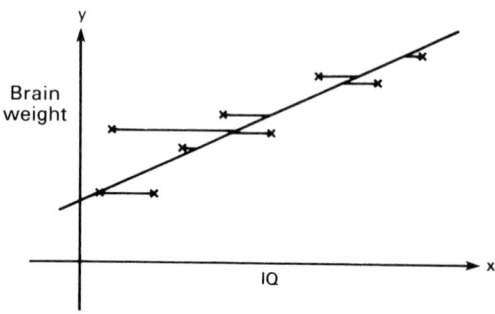

Fig. 8.9

this is equivalent to Equation 5 Chapter 7

114

$$r^2 = \frac{\Sigma X_i\,Y_i \cdot \Sigma X_i\,Y_i}{\Sigma X_i^2 \cdot \Sigma Y_i^2}$$

$$= (\text{slope of } y \text{ on } x) \cdot (\text{slope of } x \text{ on } y)$$

Hence slope of x on y

$$= \frac{r^2}{\text{slope of } y \text{ on } x}$$

Description of the Least-Squares Program (See Program 8.1)

First the program prints a title, and asks if full instructions are required. The reply is checked by a subroutine (lines 1230–1320) and must be either YES or NO. Any other reply is rejected. Full instructions or shortened ones are

Program 8.1   Trial run.

```
PROGRAM TO FIT A STRAIGHT LINE THROUGH A SET OF POINTS
======= == === = ======== ==== ======= = === == ======

WOULD YOU LIKE FULL INSTRUCTIONS?   TYPE YES OR NO & PRESS RETURN.

? YES
TYPE IN X & Y VALUES SEPARATED BY A COMMA
THEN PRESS RETURN AND TYPE THE NEXT PAIR OF VALUES
YOU WILL BE GIVEN THE CHANCE TO EDIT INCORRECT DATA LATER

INPUT DATA
TERMINATE DATA WITH BOTH X & Y EQUAL TO 999999
 X,Y
? 10000, 10001
? 11001, 11002
? 12002, 12003
? 999999, 999999
ARE THE DATA VALUES ENTERED CORRECT?   TYPE YES OR NO & PRESS RETURN.

? YES

RESULTS OF CALCULATION:
------- -- ------------
SLOPE  = 1

INTERCEPT ON Y AXIS  = 0.999004

PEARSON'S CORRELATION COEFFICIENT  = 1

STANDARD DEVIATION OF POINTS FROM THE LINE  = 0

WOULD YOU LIKE A LIST OF ERRORS?   TYPE YES OR NO & PRESS RETURN.

? YES

ERROR IN Y VALUE FOR EACH DATA POINT
X               Y OBS         Y CALC        ERROR
10000           10001         10001         0
11001           11002         11002         0
12002           12003         12003         0

SUM OF ERRORS SQUARED  = 0

WOULD YOU LIKE ANOTHER RUN?   TYPE YES OR NO & PRESS RETURN.

? NO
END OF JOB

10 DIM Q$(10), I$(3), X(100), Y(100)
20 PRINT "PROGRAM TO FIT A STRAIGHT LINE THROUGH A SET OF POINTS"
30 PRINT "======= == === = ======== ==== ======= = === == ======"
```

```
40  PRINT
50  PRINT "WOULD YOU LIKE FULL INSTRUCTIONS?";
60  GOSUB 1250
70  LET I$ = Q$
80  IF Q$ = "NO" THEN 130
90  PRINT "TYPE IN X & Y VALUES SEPARATED BY A COMMA"
100 PRINT "THEN PRESS RETURN AND TYPE THE NEXT PAIR OF VALUES"
110 PRINT "YOU WILL BE GIVEN THE CHANCE TO EDIT INCORRECT DATA LATER"
120 PRINT
130 PRINT "INPUT DATA"
140 PRINT "TERMINATE DATA WITH BOTH X & Y EQUAL TO 999999"
150 PRINT " X,Y"
160 REM SET INITIAL VALUES TO ZERO
170 READ C, S2, S3, X2, Y2, S4, E2, N
180 DATA 1, 0, 0, 0, 0, 0, 0, 0
190 REM READ IN X & Y FOR EACH DATA POINT & STORE IN ARRAYS
200 FOR I = 1 TO 100
210   INPUT X(I), Y(I)
220   IF ABS(X(I) - 999999) + ABS(Y(I) - 999999) = 0 THEN 260
230   LET N = N + 1
240 NEXT I
250 PRINT "PROGRAM CAN ONLY HANDLE A MAXIMUM OF 100 VALUES"
260 IF N > 0 THEN 300
270 PRINT "PLEASE TYPE IN SOME DATA VALUES"
280 GOTO 200
290 REM CALL SUBROUTINE TO CHECK AND ALTER DATA IF NECESSARY
300 GOSUB 1340
310 PRINT
320 IF N > 2 THEN 380
330 PRINT
340 PRINT "RUN ON THIS DATA ABANDONED BECAUSE THERE ARE"
350 PRINT "NOT ENOUGH DATA POINTS"
360 GOTO 620
370 REM CALL SUBROUTINE TO WORK OUT LEAST-SQUARES FIT ETC.
380 GOSUB 870
390 PRINT "RESULTS OF CALCULATION;"
400 PRINT "------- -- ------------"
410 PRINT "SLOPE  ="; S
420 PRINT
430 PRINT "INTERCEPT ON Y AXIS  ="; Y1
440 PRINT
450 PRINT "PEARSON'S CORRELATION COEFFICIENT  ="; C
460 PRINT
470 PRINT "STANDARD DEVIATION OF POINTS FROM THE LINE  ="; S1
480 PRINT
490 PRINT "WOULD YOU LIKE A LIST OF ERRORS?";
500 GOSUB 1240
510 IF Q$ = "NO" THEN 620
520 REM CALCULATE & PRINT ERROR FOR EACH DATA POINT
530 PRINT
540 PRINT "ERROR IN Y VALUE FOR EACH DATA POINT"
550 PRINT "X", "Y OBS", "Y CALC", "ERROR"
560 FOR I = 1 TO N
570   PRINT X(I), Y(I), A2 + S * (X(I)-A1), (Y(I)-A2) - S * (X(I)-A1)
580 NEXT I
590 PRINT
600 PRINT "SUM OF ERRORS SQUARED  ="; E2
610 REM DECIDE WHETHER TO FINISH OR HAVE ANOTHER RUN
620 PRINT
630 PRINT "WOULD YOU LIKE ANOTHER RUN?";
```

```
640 GOSUB 1240
650 IF Q$ = "NO" THEN 820
660 LET I$ = "NO"
670 RESTORE
680 PRINT "TYPE NEW FOR A RUN WITH COMPLETELY NEW DATA"
690 PRINT "  OR OLD TO EDIT AND RERUN THE EXISTING DATA"
700 INPUT Q$
710 IF Q$ = "NEW" THEN 780
720 IF Q$ = "OLD" THEN 750
730 PRINT "REPLY '"; Q$; "' NOT UNDERSTOOD"
740 GOTO 680
750 READ C, S2, S3, X2, Y2, S4, E2
760 GOSUB 1390
770 GOTO 320
780 PRINT "TYPE IN A NEW SET OF DATA"
790 PRINT "==== == = === === == ===="
800 GOTO 120
810 REM TERMINATE JOB
820 PRINT "END OF JOB"
830 STOP
840 REM ***** SUBROUTINE TO CALCULATE LEAST SQUARES FIT, ETC. *****
850 REM ARRAYS X & Y CONTAIN N DATA POINTS
860 REM CALCULATE SUMS OF X & Y VALUES
870 FOR I = 1 TO N
880    LET S2 = S2 + X(I)
890    LET S3 = S3 + Y(I)
900 NEXT I
910 REM CALCULATE THE AVERAGE X & Y VALUES
920 LET A1 = S2 / N
930 LET A2 = S3 / N
940 FOR I = 1 TO N
950    LET X9 = X(I) - A1
960    LET Y9 = Y(I) - A2
970    LET X2 = X2 + X9 * X9
980    LET Y2 = Y2 + Y9 * Y9
990    LET S4 = S4 + X9 * Y9
1000 NEXT I
1010 PRINT
1020 IF X2 <> 0 THEN 1070
1030 PRINT "RUN TERMINATED BY THE PROGRAM BECAUSE ALL"
1040 PRINT "THE X-COORDINATES ARE THE SAME."
1050 GOTO 620
1060 REM CALCULATE SLOPE
1070 LET S = S4 / X2
1080 REM CALCULATE INTERCEPT ON Y AXIS
1090 LET Y1 = (X2 * S3 - S2 * S4) / (N * X2)
1100 IF Y2 = 0 THEN 1140
1110 REM CALCULATE CORRELATION COEFFICIENT
1120 LET C = S4 / SQR(X2 * Y2)
1130 REM CALCULATE SUM OF ERRORS SQUARED
1140 FOR I = 1 TO N
1150    LET E1 = (Y(I) - A2) - S * (X(I) - A1)
1160    LET E2 = E2 + E1 * E1
1170 NEXT I
1180 REM CALCULATE STANDARD DEVIATION
1190 LET S1 = SQR(E2 / (N - 2))
1200 IF N < 30 THEN 1220
1210 LET S1 = SQR(E2 / N)
1220 RETURN
1230 REM ***** SUBROUTINE TO CHECK REPLIES *****
```

```
1240 IF I$ - "NO" THEN 1260
1250 PRINT " TYPE YES OR NO & PRESS RETURN."
1260 PRINT
1270 INPUT Q$
1280 IF Q$ = "YES" THEN 1320
1290 IF Q$ = "NO" THEN 1320
1300 PRINT "REPLY '"; Q$; "' NOT UNDERSTOOD.";
1310 GOTO 1250
1320 RETURN
1330 REM ****SUBROUTINE TO CHECK DATA ARE CORRECT & ALTER IF NECESSARY
1340 PRINT "ARE THE DATA VALUES ENTERED CORRECT?";
1350 REM A4 SHOULD BE SET TO THE NUMBER OF LINES ON THE VDU
1360 LET A4 = 20
1370 GOSUB 1240
1380 IF Q$ = "YES" THEN 2080
1390 PRINT "HERE IS A LIST OF THE CURRENT DATA"
1400 PRINT "LINE NUMBER", "X", "Y"
1410 FOR I = 1 TO N
1420    PRINT I, X(I), Y(I)
1430    IF INT(I / (A4 - 1)) * (A4 - 1) <> I THEN 1470
1440    PRINT "WOULD YOU LIKE TO CONTINUE LISTING?";
1450    GOSUB 1240
1460    IF Q$ = "NO" THEN 1480
1470 NEXT I
1480 PRINT "TYPE R TO REPLACE";
1490 IF I$ = "NO" THEN 1510
1500 PRINT " AN EXISTING LINE OF DATA"
1510 IF N = 100 THEN 1560
1520 PRINT TAB(5); " A TO ADD";
1530 IF I$ = "NO" THEN 1550
1540 PRINT " AN EXTRA LINE"
1550 IF N = 1 THEN 1590
1560 PRINT TAB(5); " D TO DELETE";
1570 IF I$ = "NO" THEN 1590
1580 PRINT " AN EXISTING LINE"
1590 PRINT TAB(5); " L TO LIST";
1600 IF I$ = "NO" THEN 1620
1610 PRINT " THE DATA"
1620 PRINT "   OR C TO CONTINUE";
1630 IF I$ = "NO" THEN 1650
1640 PRINT " THE CALCULATION"
1650 INPUT Q$
1660 IF Q$ = "R" THEN 1760
1670 IF N = 100 THEN 1700
1680 IF Q$ = "A" THEN 1880
1690 IF N = 1 THEN 1710
1700 IF Q$ = "D" THEN 1930
1710 IF Q$ = "L" THEN 1390
1720 IF Q$ = "C" THEN 2080
1730 PRINT "REPLY '"; Q$; "' NOT UNDERSTOOD."
1740 GOTO 1480
1750 REM REPLACE LINE
1760 PRINT "TYPE THE LINENUMBER OF THE LINE TO BE REPLACED";
1770 INPUT I
1780 IF I <> INT(I) THEN 1800
1790 IF (I - 1) * (I - N) <= 0 THEN 1830
1800 PRINT "LINENUMBER MUST BE AN INTEGER IN THE RANGE 1 -"; N
1810 PRINT "RE-";
1820 GOTO 1760
1830 PRINT "TYPE THE CORRECT LINE TO REPLACE THE ONE WHICH IS WRONG"
```

```
1840 PRINT "X, Y"
1850 INPUT X(I), Y(I)
1860 GOTO 1910
1870 REM ADD A NEW LINE
1880 LET N = N + 1
1890 PRINT "TYPE THE ADDITIONAL LINE OF DATA AS SHOWN:   X,Y"
1900 INPUT X(N), Y(N)
1910 PRINT "OK"
1920 GOTO 1480
1930 REM DELETE A LINE
1940 PRINT "TYPE THE LINENUMBER OF THE LINE TO BE DELETED"
1950 INPUT J
1960 IF (J - 1) * (J - N) > 0 THEN 1980
1970 IF J = INT(J) THEN 2000
1980 PRINT "LINENUMBER MUST BE AN INTEGER IN THE RANGE 1 -"; N
1990 GOTO 1940
2000 FOR I = J + 1 TO N
2010   LET X(I - 1) = X(I)
2020   LET Y(I - 1) = Y(I)
2030 NEXT I
2040 LET N = N - 1
2050 PRINT "OK"
2060 IF J > N THEN 1480
2070 GOTO 1390
2080 RETURN
2090 END
```

printed in the first run, but only shortened instructions are printed in subsequent runs.

The data input loop extends from lines 200–240. A pair of x and y values is typed on a line, and the RETURN key pressed. Further lines are typed in a similar way, and the end of data input is indicated by typing the dummy line 999999,999999 and RETURN. The X and Y arrays are dimensioned as 100 in the first line of the program, and limit the number of (x, y) points to a maximum of 100.

After the data input is complete a check is performed (lines 260–280) to ensure that at least one valid (x, y) value has been typed. Then a subroutine is entered (lines 1330–2080) which asks if the data entered are correct. If the answer is YES the subroutine is skipped, but if the answer is NO the current data are listed and instructions given explaining how to replace or delete existing lines, add new lines, re-list the data or continue the calculation. This subroutine is described in more detail in Chapter 7. When the data are correct a check is made to ensure that there are at least two data points (lines 320–360) since an infinite number of straight lines can be fitted through a single point.

The least-squares fitting is performed in a subroutine (lines 840–1220). This has deliberately been coded as a subroutine to allow it to be easily implemented in other programs. Equations 10 and 11 are used to prevent loss of accuracy as discussed earlier.

The results: slope, intercept, Pearson's correlation coefficient and the standard deviation of the points from the line are then printed in lines 390–470. The user is given the option of printing a table showing the 'error' in the y coordinate of each term (that is the difference between each input y coordinate and the straight line). The sum of the errors squared is also printed.

Finally the user is offered another run. If this is required then either a completely NEW set of data may be input, or the OLD (existing) data may be edited and re-run.

Exercises

8.1 Given 20 pairs of $(x_i \ y_i)$ values, the following quantities were calculated: $\Sigma x_i = 200$, $\Sigma y_i = 110$, $\Sigma x_i^2 = 2200$, $\Sigma y_i^2 = 655$, and $\Sigma x_i \ y_i = 1075$. Find the linear regression equations of x on y, and of y on x. Which would be more useful in the following cases?

(a) x is the telephone bill and y the number of employees for each of 20 companies.

(b) x is the age and y the reaction times of 20 children.

8.2 The amount of pocket money received by four school children from each of the classes aged 11, 12, 13, 14, 15 and 16 are given in Table 8.2.

(a) Plot these data on a scatter diagram.

(b) Calculate the mean pocket money for each age.

(c) Find the slope and intercept for the appropriate least-squares line (age/mean pocket money).

8.3 From a survey of 10 hospitals, the data in Table 8.3 were collected. Fit a least-squares line to the data, and estimate the cost per patient per day in a 500 bed hospital.

8.4 The monthly electricity bills (y) of 20 families of size (x) are given in Table 8.4. By fitting a least-squares line, estimate the mean monthly electricity bill for a family of size 3. Calculate the average bill for households of 3 people, and explain which gives the better estimate.

8.5 The age at which people get married was studied by considering a sample of 24 couples. The age of the wife (x) and husband (y) are given in Table 8.5. Calculate the regression lines of x on y and of y on x. Use these to predict the age of the spouse of a man a woman aged 25.

8.6 The number of Civil Servants required to collect Value Added Tax in 10 towns of different sizes is given below

Population of town (thousands):
6, 8, 9, 12, 17, 19, 21, 23, 25, 26
Number of Civil Servants:
9, 12, 14, 19, 25, 27, 32, 33, 35, 35

Calculate the regression line for predicting the number of Civil Servants needed for different town, and use this to predict the number required for a town of 15 000 inhabitants.

Table 8.2

Age (years)	Pocket money (pence)
11	20, 35, 40, 70
12	30, 50, 60, 70
13	35, 40, 70, 80
14	35, 50, 90, 100
15	50, 85, 110, 150
16	50, 75, 100, 200

Table 8.3

Hospital	Number of beds	Cost per patient per day (£)
1	810	39
2	190	54
3	310	46
4	1100	40
5	230	51
6	400	45
7	760	37
8	240	51
9	610	42
10	400	46

Table 8.4

x	y	x	y	x	y	x	y	x	y
1	6	2	6	3	10	4	9	5	10
1	6	2	8	3	10	4	11	5	15
1	8	2	9	3	12	4	13	5	18
1	8	2	9	3	16	4	19	5	21

Table 8.5

x	y	x	y	x	y	x	y
17	20	19	25	18	20	21	26
22	23	16	26	25	27	17	26
19	21	28	23	25	28	21	32
21	29	20	43	26	28	26	29
54	58	29	33	21	25	29	28
27	29	25	25	23	25	23	20

9

Curve Fitting (Polynomials)

Polynomials are often fitted to experimental data either to smooth the data or to allow interpolation. A polynomial equation has the form

$$y = a+bx+cx^2+dx^3+ \ldots \qquad (1)$$

where $a, b, c, d \ldots$ are constants and are called the coefficients of the polynomial. The 'order' of the polynomial is the largest power of x in the equation. Thus for a quadratic equation $y=a+bx+cx^2$ the order is 2, and for a straight line $y=a+bx$ the order is 1.

When fitting a polynomial to n data points $(x_1 y_1), (x_2 y_2), (x_3 y_3), \ldots, (x_n, y_n)$ it is assumed that all of the errors occur in the measured y values and that there are no errors in the measured x values. For each value of x_r (with $r = 1, 2, \ldots, n$) there will be a calculated y value from the polynomial, and the difference between this and the observed y_r value is called the residual Δ_r in y_r. Thus

$$\Delta_r = y_r-(a+bx_r+cx_r^2+dx_r^3+ \ldots)$$

The principle underlying the fitting of the polynomial is to make the sum of the residuals squared as small as possible by choosing appropriate values for $a, b, c, d \ldots$

$$\text{Sum of residuals squared} = E = \sum_{r=1}^{r=n} \Delta_r^2$$

The 'best' polynomial of a given order is that which minimises E. Increasing the order of the polynomial can only decrease the minimum value of E, but may result in less smoothing of the data. In the extreme case the order is equal to $n-1$, and the polynomial passes exactly through each point in a general set of data.

This is called the interpolating polynomial, for which $E=0$ and there is no smoothing of the data.

The method for minimising E is to partially differentiate E with respect to each of the coefficients in turn, and equate each of the partial derivatives to zero. Since the order of the polynomial is m, this will result in $m+1$ simultaneous equations, which are called the normal equations. Solving the normal equations yields the required coefficients $a, b, c, d, \ldots$ This approach is identical to that used in the previous chapter for fitting a straight line—that is a polynomial of order 1—except that some symbols are different:

$$y = mx+c \text{ becomes } y = a+bx$$

since the slope m becomes b and the intercept c becomes a. Re-writing Equations 2 and 3 from the previous chapter for the partial derivatives gives:

$$\frac{\partial E}{\partial a} = 2na-2\Sigma y_r+2b\Sigma x_r \qquad (2)$$

and

$$\frac{\partial E}{\partial b} = 2b\Sigma x_r^2-2\Sigma x_r y_r+2a\Sigma x_r \qquad (3)$$

Equating the partial derivatives to zero and rearranging

$$an +b\Sigma x_r = \Sigma y_r$$
$$a\Sigma x_r+b\Sigma x_r^2 = \Sigma x_r y_r$$

The normal equations above can be written in matrix form:

$$\begin{pmatrix} n & \Sigma x_r \\ \Sigma x_r & \Sigma x_r^2 \end{pmatrix} \begin{pmatrix} a \\ b \end{pmatrix} = \begin{pmatrix} \Sigma y_r \\ \Sigma x_r y_r \end{pmatrix} \qquad (4)$$

One method of calculating the coefficients a and b is to evaluate the inverse of the 2×2 matrix

$$\text{inverse of} \begin{pmatrix} n & \Sigma x_r \\ \Sigma x_r & \Sigma x_r^2 \end{pmatrix} = \begin{pmatrix} n & \Sigma x_r \\ \Sigma x_r & \Sigma x_r^2 \end{pmatrix}$$

and then premultiplying both sides of Equation 4 by the inverse matrix to give

$$\begin{pmatrix} a \\ b \end{pmatrix} = \begin{pmatrix} n & \Sigma x_r \\ \Sigma x_r & \Sigma x_r^2 \end{pmatrix}^{-1} \begin{pmatrix} \Sigma y_r \\ \Sigma x_r y_r \end{pmatrix}$$

Fitting a polynomial of order 2, that is a quadratic equation $y = a + bx + cx^2$ yields the following normal equations:

$$an \quad + b\Sigma x_r + c\Sigma x_r^2 = \Sigma y_r$$

$$a\Sigma x_r + b\Sigma x_r^2 + c\Sigma x_r^3 = \Sigma x_r y_r$$

$$a\Sigma x_r^2 + b\Sigma x_r^3 + c\Sigma x_r^4 = \Sigma x_r^2 y_r$$

hence in matrix form

$$\begin{pmatrix} n & \Sigma x_r & \Sigma x_r^2 \\ \Sigma x_r & \Sigma x_r^2 & \Sigma x_r^3 \\ \Sigma x_r^2 & \Sigma x_r^3 & \Sigma x_r^4 \end{pmatrix} \begin{pmatrix} a \\ b \\ c \end{pmatrix} = \begin{pmatrix} \Sigma y_r \\ \Sigma x_r y_r \\ \Sigma x_r^2 y_r \end{pmatrix}$$

Premultiplying both sides of this equation by the inverse matrix gives

$$\begin{pmatrix} a \\ b \\ c \end{pmatrix} = \begin{pmatrix} n & \Sigma x_r & \Sigma x_r^2 \\ \Sigma x_r & \Sigma x_r^2 & \Sigma x_r^3 \\ \Sigma x_r^2 & \Sigma x_r^3 & \Sigma x_r^4 \end{pmatrix}^{-1} \begin{pmatrix} \Sigma y_r \\ \Sigma x_r y_r \\ \Sigma x_r^2 y_r \end{pmatrix}$$

In an analogous way a polynomial of order m yields an $m+1$ by $m+1$ matrix, and the coefficients may be obtained by

$$\begin{bmatrix} a \\ b \\ \cdot \\ \cdot \\ \cdot \\ \cdot \end{bmatrix} = \begin{bmatrix} n & \Sigma x_r & \ldots & \Sigma x_r^m \\ \Sigma x_r & \Sigma x_r^2 & \ldots & \Sigma x_r^{m+1} \\ \cdot & \cdot & & \cdot \\ \cdot & \cdot & & \cdot \\ \cdot & \cdot & & \cdot \\ \Sigma x_r^m & \Sigma x_r^{m+1} & \ldots & \Sigma x_r^{2m} \end{bmatrix}^{-1} \begin{bmatrix} \Sigma x_r \\ \Sigma x_r y_r \\ \cdot \\ \cdot \\ \cdot \\ \Sigma x_r^m y_r \end{bmatrix}$$

Polynomials of order 1 or 2 (straight line or quadratic fits) can be obtained by manually building the matrix and solving the matrix equation. Though in theory it is possible to fit higher order polynomials in this way, the time taken to perform the calculations renders this impracticable. Furthermore, unless a large number of significant figures are carried throughout the calculation then the result may be wildly inaccurate.

The speed of a computer overcomes the excessive time taken for manual calculation of higher order polynomials. However, since a computer only carries a limited number of significant figures, the problems of accuracy remain. Even using double precision where the computer carries double the usual number of significant figures only allows reliable answers up to about an order of six on most computers.

It is important to identify the sources of inaccuracy as a first step towards overcoming the problem of loss of accuracy. It has been found that the major cause of inaccuracy is ill-conditioning of the solution of the normal equations with respect to the coefficients of the matrix. More simply a small change in the value of a particular term or terms in the matrix drastically changes the coefficients of the polynomial obtained as the solution. Ill-conditioning does not always occur, and is a property of the way in which the problem has been formulated. It follows that by formulating the problem in a different way it may be possible to avoid the difficulties of ill-conditioning.

A second smaller source of inaccuracy is termed instability, and is caused by the accumulation of rounding errors in performing the calculations. Instability is a direct result of the method of calculation.

Method of Reducing Loss in Accuracy

1. The accuracy of the coefficients is likely to be improved by performing the calculations carrying a larger number of significant figures.

122

Table 9.1 Equation 7

$$
\begin{bmatrix} c_0 \\ c_1 \\ c_2 \\ \cdot \\ \cdot \\ \cdot \\ c_m \end{bmatrix} = \begin{bmatrix} \Sigma p_0(x_r)p_0(x_r) & \Sigma p_0(x_r)p_1(x_r) & \Sigma p_0(x_r)p_2(x_r) \ldots \\ \Sigma p_1(x_r)p_0(x_r) & \Sigma p_1(x_r)p_1(x_r) & \Sigma p_1(x_r)p_2(x_r) \ldots \\ \Sigma p_2(x_r)p_0(x_r) & \Sigma p_2(x_r)p_1(x_r) & \Sigma p_2(x_r)p_2(x_r) \ldots \\ \cdot \\ \cdot \\ \cdot \\ \Sigma p_m(x_r)p_0(x_r) & \Sigma p_m(x_r)p_1(x_r) & \Sigma p_m(x_r)p_2(x_r) \ldots \end{bmatrix}^{-1} \begin{bmatrix} \Sigma p_0(x_r)y_r \\ \Sigma p_1(x_r)y_r \\ \Sigma p_2(x_r)y_r \\ \cdot \\ \cdot \\ \cdot \\ \Sigma p_m(x_r)y_r \end{bmatrix} \qquad (7)
$$

2. The magnitude of the x, y data may affect the accuracy of the coefficients, particularly if the mean of the x values is a long way from zero. This can be overcome by scaling the data into a small range close to zero—for example into the range $+2$ to -2, before building and solving the matrix. The resulting coefficients refer to the scaled data, but may be appropriately converted back to refer to the original unscaled data.

3. Results which are unreliable will be produced if the problem is 'ill-conditioned'. This is generally associated with values off the leading diagonal which are large relative to the values on the leading diagonal. Better results will be obtained if a method is found which keeps the off-diagonal terms small, and the ideal case is to have all off-diagonal terms zero. A method of achieving this was devised by G. E. Forsythe (*Journal of the Society for Industrial and Applied Mathematics*, 1957, **5**, 74) which has revolutionised the whole subject of polynomial curve fitting.

Orthogonal Polynomials

It is possible to re-write Equation 1 in terms of a set of polynomials p_i, where p_i is an arbitrary polynomial of order i. Thus

$$y = c_0p_0(x) + c_1p_1(x) + c_2p_2(x) + \\ + c_3p_3(x) + \ldots + c_mp_m(x) \quad (6)$$

The polynomials $p_0, p_1, p_2, \ldots, p_m$ are derived directly from the x_r data and are thus known. The problem of fitting the best curve to the data becomes one of choosing the best coeffi-

cients $c_0, c_1, c_2, \ldots, c_m$ and from the values of these deriving the values of the coefficients a, b, c, d ... used in Equation 1.

It might at first sight seem that there is considerably more work in evaluating the coeffients c_0, c_1, c_2, c_3 ... than in evaluating the coefficients a, b, c, d ... directly for no apparent benefit. Furthermore the relatively simple normal equations given in Equation 5 are replaced by the more complicated ones in Table 9.1.

The objective is to choose the polynomials p_i such that all terms which are off the leading diagonal in the matrix above will evaluate to zero. The matrix can then be inverted accurately in one line thus eliminating problems from ill-conditioning. This is clearly a major benefit. For example

$$
\begin{bmatrix} 2 & 0 & 0 & 0 \\ 0 & 5 & 0 & 0 \\ 0 & 0 & 4 & 0 \\ 0 & 0 & 0 & 8 \end{bmatrix}^{-1} = \begin{bmatrix} \frac{1}{2} & 0 & 0 & 0 \\ 0 & \frac{1}{5} & 0 & 0 \\ 0 & 0 & \frac{1}{4} & 0 \\ 0 & 0 & 0 & \frac{1}{8} \end{bmatrix}
$$

exactly

Polynomials with these properties are orthogonal over the data.

Equation 1 may be considered as a special case of Equation 6 where $p_0(x) = 1$, $p_1(x) = x$, $p_2(x) = x^2$, $p_3(x) = x^3, \ldots$, $p_i(x) = x^i, \ldots$, $p_m(x) = x^m$. This special case is not orthogonal, and ill-conditioning of the problem can and frequently does occur.

Forsythe's Orthogonal Polynomials

Forsythe showed that it was always possible to derive an orthogonal set of polynomials p_i

from the x_r data provided, and he gave a set of rules for doing this. The use of these orthogonal polynomials has revolutionised the whole subject of polynomial curve fitting, and has made it possible to fit much higher orders than hitherto.

The polynomials p_i are derived from each other, and are defined

$$p_0(x) = 1$$

$$p_1(x) = 2\,(x-\alpha_1)p_0(x)$$

$$p_2(x) = 2(x-\alpha_2)p_1(x) - \beta_1 p_0(x)$$

$$p_3(x) = 2(x-\alpha_3)p_2(x) - \beta_2 p_1(x)$$

.

.

.

$$p_{i+1}(x) = 2(x-\alpha_{i+1})p_i(x) - \beta_i p_{i-1}(x)$$

where

$$\alpha_{i+1} = \frac{\sum_{r=1}^{r=n} x_r p_i^2(x_r)}{\sum_{r=1}^{r=n} p_i^2(x_r)}$$

and

$$\beta_i = \frac{\sum_{r=1}^{r=n} p_i^2(x_r)}{\sum_{r=1}^{r=n} p_{i-1}^2(x_r)}$$

Use of the above procedure overcomes the problem of loss of accuracy due to ill-conditioning when solving the matrix equation. The orthogonal polynomials and the coefficients $c_0, c_1, c_2 \ldots c_m$ can be used to evaluate the polynomial fitted to the original data. It is often required to express the fitted polynomial in terms of a power series as in Equation 1. It is possible to convert the coefficients $c_0, c_1, c_2, \ldots, c_m$ back into the coefficients a, b, c, $d, \ldots$ used in Equation 1. Though a power series may be a more convenient expression, the conversion process may introduce arithmetic rounding errors.

The use of orthogonal polynomials has cured the problem of ill-conditioning, but instability due to accumulation of rounding errors remains. Instability is reduced by carrying more significant figures in the calculation.

A polynomial in the form of a power series may be evaluated in an elegant way. Consider the polynomial

$$y = 2x^4 - 4x^3 + 6x^2 - 3x + 15 \qquad (8)$$

The correct way to evaluate this is

$$y = \{[(2x-4)x+6]x-3\}x+15$$

This is known as Horner's rule, although the method was first given by Isaac Newton in 1711. The principle is to start with the coefficient of the highest order term, multiply by x, add in the next coefficient, multiply by x, add the next coefficient, and continue multiplying by x and adding coefficients until all the coefficients have been used. Whether the calculation is performed by hand, or by computer, the calculation is faster and is likely to produce a more accurate answer than evaluating Equation 8 as it is written.

If further accuracy is required in evaluating the polynomial then the power series given in Equation 1 must be abandoned. The value of the polynomial at a point can be evaluated directly from Forsythe's α and β values, avoiding the necessity of converting α and β into a power series form. A further slight improvement in accuracy can be obtained by representing the fitting polynomial in the form of a series of Chebyshev polynomials. It is necessary to use the Chebyshev polynomial directly to evaluate the function, since conversion of Chebyshev polynomials into power series coefficients generally destroys the extra accuracy just gained. This technique is discussed in G. J. Hayes's book *Numerical Approximation to Functions and Data*, Athlone Press 1970.

Finally it should be noted that high order polynomials may produce unwanted spikes between data points and hence interpolation should be performed with care. Furthermore, polynomials other than order zero tend to plus or minus infinity for large plus or minus values of x, hence extrapolation beyond the range of data values supplied should not be undertaken.

Description of the Program to Fit Polynomials
(see Program 9.1)

Accuracy

It is strongly recommended that this program is only run on computers which support a version of BASIC which carries 12 or more significant decimal figures. Loss of accuracy will probably be significant—particularly with high order polynomials, if fewer figures are carried. On a number of mainframes this is accomplished by using a double precision version of BASIC. On microcomputers some versions of BASIC including CBASIC, Cromenco disc BASIC and Xitan disc BASIC (as used on the 380-Z), automatically carry sufficient significant figures. Some other versions allow double precision to be specified in the program. Microsoft BASIC-80 and TRS level II BASIC achieve this by adding the line:

5 DEFDBL A-Z

The results obtained from BASIC's carrying only six or eight figures may be erroneous.

Memory Requirements

The arrays DIMensioned at 100 in line 10 use a considerable amount of memory. The value of 100 permits up to 100 (x, y) data pairs to be stored. If memory is restricted, the value of 100 may be reduced to a smaller value in all of these arrays, but a few additional changes are also required: the value of 100 must be changed to the new value in lines 210, 290, 2940 and 3100.

The Program

First the program prints a heading (lines 70–80), and a message (line 100) asks if full instructions are required. The answer which must be YES or NO is input and checked in a subroutine (lines 3580–3670). Full or abbreviated instructions are printed as appropriate

throughout the program on the first run, but only abbreviated instructions are given on a second or subsequent run.

Instructions for inputing the data are given (lines 140–190), and the data are input in a loop from lines 210 to 280. The data are entered as an (x, y) pair and the appropriate weight on one line. For many purposes the weights are chosen as 1, but different weights may be chosen for individual points based on the reliability of the particular point. Weights are checked to ensure that they are greater than zero (lines 240–260).

If the maximum number of points which the arrays can hold have been entered then a message (line 290) is printed before the calculation proceeds.

A check is performed (lines 300–310) to ensure that at least two acceptable data pairs have been provided. If they have not, then the run is abandoned with a message (line 1070), and the user is asked if another run is required. Provided that sufficient data have been input, a subroutine (lines 2760–3570) is entered to check that the data are correct. If the data are correct then the subroutine is exited, but otherwise the data are listed and instructions are printed explaining how to replace or delete an existing line, or alternatively to add a new line. The operation of this subroutine is fully described in Chapter 7. When the data are correct, the calculation continues.

The maximum order of polynomial which the program tests for is set to 9 in line 370, and this value is re-set (lines 380–390) to the number of points minus two if there are 10 or fewer points. A message (lines 410–470) requests the order of the polynomial to be fitted, or zero if the program is to choose the 'best' polynomial based on the goodness of fit. The value typed is checked (lines 490–530) to ensure

(i) that it is an integer,
(ii) that it is not negative, and
(iii) that it does not exceed the maximum order.

If the value typed is rejected, a message requests the user to re-type the correct value,

125

Program 9.1 Trial run.

```
PROGRAM TO FIT A POLYNOMIAL TO A SET OF POINTS
======= == === = ========== == = === == ======

WOULD YOU LIKE FULL INSTRUCTIONS.  TYPE YES OR NO & PRESS RETURN.

? YES
TYPE IN A PAIR OF X & Y VALUES & WEIGHT SEPARATED BY COMMAS
THEN PRESS RETURN, TYPE THE NEXT PAIR OF VALUES ETC
TERMINATE DATA WITH  999999, 999999, 999999

STARTING DATA
 X, Y, WEIGHT
? 1, 10, 1
? 2, 49, 1
? 3, 142, 1
? 4, 313, 1
? 5, 586, 1
? 6, 985, 1
? 7, 1534, 1
? 8, 2257, 1
? 9, 3178, 1
? 999999, 999999, 999999

ARE THE DATA VALUES ENTERED CORRECT?  TYPE YES OR NO & PRESS RETURN.

? YES

TYPE IN THE ORDER REQUIRED IN THE RANGE 1 - 7  OF THE
ONE SPECIFIC POLYNOMIAL REQUIRED.
OR TYPE 0 IF ALL THE POLYNOMIALS FROM ORDER 0 - 7 ARE TO
BE EXAMINED, AND THE ONE WHICH FITS BEST REPORTED,
THEN PRESS RETURN.
? 0

MAXIMUM ORDER OF POLYNOMIAL TESTED FOR = 7
ORDER OF BEST POLYNOMIAL FOUND = 3

POLYNOMIAL ORDER     GOODNESS OF FIT
0          0.4918592889118
1          0.070900097402596
2          0.0015151515515145
3          1.465494392505E-14
4          1.831867990632E-14
5          2.442490654179E-14
6          3.663735981269E-14
7          7.327471962657E-14

COEFFICIENTS OF THE BEST OR SPECIFIED ORDER POLYNOMIAL
(Y = A + B*X + C*X^2 + D*X^3 +...)
A=  0.9999999993597
B=  2.000000000512
C=  2.999999999878
D=  4.000000000008

WOULD YOU LIKE A TABLE OF RESIDUALS
 TYPE YES OR NO & PRESS RETURN.

? NO
WOULD YOU LIKE ANOTHER RUN  TYPE YES OR NO & PRESS RETURN.
```

126

REMEMBER THAT YOU MUST NOT EXTRAPOLATE BEYOND THE
DATA POINTS, AND ALSO THAT INTERPOLATION BETWEEN
POINTS IS DANGEROUS WITH HIGH ORDER POLYNOMIALS.
END OF JOB

```
10 DIM P(100),R(100),T(100),U(100),V(100),W(100),X(100),Y(100),Z(100)
20 DIM A(10),B(10),C(10),D(11),F(10),G(10),L(10),Q(10),S(10)
30 DIM A$(2),I$(3),Q$(10)
40 REM ARRAY SIZES LIMIT PROGRAM TO A MAXIMUM OF 100 DATA POINTS.
50 REM THE NUMBER OF DATA POINTS SHOULD BE AT LEAST 2 GREATER THAN THE
60 REM MAXIMUM ORDER OF THE POLYNOMIAL.
70 PRINT "PROGRAM TO FIT A POLYNOMIAL TO A SET OF POINTS"
80 PRINT "======= == === = ========= == = === == ======"
90 PRINT
100 PRINT "WOULD YOU LIKE FULL INSTRUCTIONS.";
110 GOSUB 3600
120 LET I$ = Q$
130 IF I$ = "NO" THEN 160
140 PRINT "TYPE IN A PAIR OF X & Y VALUES & WEIGHT SEPARATED BY COMMAS"
150 PRINT "THEN PRESS RETURN, TYPE THE NEXT PAIR OF VALUES ETC"
160 PRINT "TERMINATE DATA WITH  999999, 999999, 999999"
170 PRINT
180 PRINT "STARTING DATA"
190 PRINT " X, Y, WEIGHT"
200 LET N = 0
210 FOR I = 1 TO 100
220    INPUT X(I), Y(I), W(I)
230    IF ABS(X(I) - 999999) + ABS(Y(I) - 999999) = 0 THEN 310
240    IF W(I) >= 0 THEN 270
250    PRINT "NEGATIVE WEIGHTS ARE IMPOSSIBLE - RETYPE LAST LINE"
260    GOTO 220
270    LET N = N + 1
280 NEXT I
290 PRINT "PROGRAM CAN ONLY HANDLE MAXIMUM OF 100 VALUES"
300 REM CHECK THAT THERE ARE AT LEAST 2 POINTS
310 IF N < 2 THEN 1070
320 PRINT
330 REM CALL SUBROUTINE TO CHECK THAT DATA ARE CORRECT
340 GOSUB 2770
350 PRINT
360 REM CALCULATE MAXIMUM ORDER BASED ON NUMBER OF DATA POINTS
370 LET N9 = 9
380 IF N - 2 >= 9 THEN 400
390 LET N9 = N - 2
400 IF I$ = "YES" THEN 430
410 PRINT "TYPE ORDER REQUIRED"
420 GOTO 480
430 PRINT "TYPE IN THE ORDER REQUIRED IN THE RANGE 1 -"; N9; " OF THE"
440 PRINT "ONE SPECIFIC POLYNOMIAL REQUIRED."
450 PRINT "OR TYPE 0 IF ALL THE POLYNOMIALS FROM ORDER 0 -";N9;"ARE TO"
460 PRINT "BE EXAMINED, AND THE ONE WHICH FITS BEST REPORTED,"
470 PRINT "THEN PRESS RETURN."
480 INPUT L
490 IF L <> INT(L) THEN 520
500 IF L < 0 THEN 520
510 IF L <= N9 THEN 550
520 PRINT "INCORRECT VALUE TYPED"
530 GOTO 430
```

```
540 REM SET THE MAXIMUM ORDER TO 9, IE M1 (MAXORDER+1) TO 10
550 LET M1 = 10
560 IF L <= 0 THEN 580
570 LET M1 = L + 1
580 LET I = N - 1
590 IF M1 <= I THEN 620
600 LET M1 = I
610 REM CALL SUBROUTINE TO FIT THE POLYNOMIAL
620 GOSUB 1180
630 LET M2 = M1 - 1
640 PRINT
650 IF L = 0 THEN 680
660 PRINT "ORDER OF POLYNOMIAL SPECIFIED ="; N2
670 GOTO 710
680 PRINT "MAXIMUM ORDER OF POLYNOMIAL TESTED FOR ="; M2
690 PRINT "ORDER OF BEST POLYNOMIAL FOUND ="; N2
700 PRINT
710 PRINT "POLYNOMIAL ORDER    GOODNESS OF FIT"
720 FOR I = 1 TO M1
730    PRINT I - 1; TAB(10); G(I)
740 NEXT I
750 PRINT
760 PRINT "COEFFICIENTS OF THE BEST OR SPECIFIED ORDER POLYNOMIAL"
770 PRINT "(Y = A + B*X + C*X^2 + D*X^3 +...)"
780 LET N3 = N2 + 1
790 FOR I = 1 TO N3
800    READ A$
810    PRINT A$; TAB(5); F(I)
820 NEXT I
830 DATA "A=", "B=", "C=", "D=", "E=", "F=", "G=", "H=", "I=", "J="
840 RESTORE
850 PRINT
860 PRINT "WOULD YOU LIKE A TABLE OF RESIDUALS"
870 GOSUB 3590
880 IF Q$ = "NO" THEN 980
890 PRINT "X              Y              Y(CALC)        DIFF"
900 LET R2 = 0
910 FOR I = 1 TO N
920    PRINT X(I), Y(I), Z(I), R(I)
930    LET R2 = R2 + R(I) ^ 2
940 NEXT I
950 PRINT
960 PRINT "SUM OF ERRORS SQUARED ="; R2
970 PRINT
980 PRINT "WOULD YOU LIKE ANOTHER RUN";
990 GOSUB 3590
1000 IF Q$ = "NO" THEN 1100
1010 LET I$ = "NO"
1020 PRINT "WOULD YOU LIKE TO TRY ANOTHER ORDER WITH THE SAME DATA"
1030 GOSUB 3590
1040 IF Q$ = "YES" THEN 310
1050 GOTO 160
1060 REM ENTER IF THERE ARE NOT ENOUGH POINTS
1070 PRINT "RUN TERMINATED - NOT ENOUGH DATA POINTS"
1080 GOTO 980
1090 REM TERMINATE JOB
1100 IF I$ = "NO" THEN 1140
1110 PRINT "REMEMBER THAT YOU MUST NOT EXTRAPOLATE BEYOND THE"
1120 PRINT "DATA POINTS, AND ALSO THAT INTERPOLATION BETWEEN"
1130 PRINT "POINTS IS DANGEROUS WITH HIGH ORDER POLYNOMIALS."
1140 PRINT "END OF JOB"
```

```
1150 STOP
1160 REM SUBROUTINE TO CALCULATE A WEIGHTED LEAST SQUARES POLYNOMIAL
1170 REM BY FORSYTHE"S METHOD USING ORTHOGONAL POLYNOMIALS.
1180 LET M3 = M1 - 1
1190 LET N2 = M3
1200 FOR I = 1 TO M1
1210    LET C(I) = 0
1220 NEXT I
1230 LET Q(1) = 0
1240 LET D(1) = 0
1250 LET D(2) = 0
1260 LET A(1) = 1
1270 LET D2 = 0
1280 LET P1 = 0
1290 LET S1 = 0
1300 LET G1 = 0
1310 LET I1 = 0
1320 LET S2 = W(1)
1330 REM FIND THE MAXIMUM AND MINIMUM X & Y
1340 LET X9 = X(1)
1350 LET X1 = X(1)
1360 LET Y9 = Y(1)
1370 LET Y1 = Y(1)
1380 FOR I = 2 TO N
1390    IF X(I) <= X9 THEN 1410
1400    LET X9 = X(I)
1410    IF X(I) >= X1 THEN 1430
1420    LET X1 = X(I)
1430    IF Y(I) <= Y9 THEN 1450
1440    LET Y9 = Y(I)
1450    IF Y(I) >= Y1 THEN 1470
1460    LET Y1 = Y(I)
1470    LET S2 = S2 + W(I)
1480 NEXT I
1490 REM CHECK THAT SUM OF WEIGHTS IS NOT ZERO
1500 IF S2 = 0 THEN 2740
1510 LET Y3 = (Y9 + Y1) / 2
1520 LET Y4 = (Y9 - Y1) / 2
1530 IF Y4 > 0 THEN 1580
1540 LET F(1) = Y(1)
1550 LET N2 = 0
1560 GOTO 2720
1570 REM SCALE Y TERMS INTO THE RANGE +1 TO -1
1580 FOR I = 1 TO N
1590    LET V(I) = (Y(I) - Y3) / Y4
1600    LET D2 = D2 + W(I) * V(I) ^ 2
1610    LET P(I) = 1
1620    LET T(I) = 0
1630    LET P1 = P1 + W(I) * V(I)
1640    LET S1 = S1 + W(I)
1650 NEXT I
1660 LET S(1) = P1 / S1
1670 LET C(1) = S(1)
1680 LET D2 = D2 - S(1) * P1
1690 LET G(1) = ABS(D2 / (N - 1))
1700 LET A1 = 4 / (X9 - X1)
1710 LET B1 = -2 - A1 * X1
1720 REM SCALE X TERMS INTO THE RANGE +2 TO -2
1730 FOR I = 1 TO N
1740    LET U(I) = A1 * X(I) + B1
1750 NEXT I
```

```
1760 REM START LOOP FOR EACH ORDER
1770 FOR I = 1 TO M3
1780    LET D1 = 0
1790    FOR J = 1 TO N
1800       LET D1 = D1 + W(J) * U(J) * P(J) ^ 2
1810    NEXT J
1820    REM L IS FORSYTHES ALPHA
1830    LET L(I + 1) = D1 / S1
1840    LET W2 = S1
1850    LET S1 = 0
1860    LET P1 = 0
1870    REM STORE VALUE OF CURRENT ORTHOGONAL POLYNOMIAL IN P( )
1880    REM AND OF PREVIOUS ORTHOGONAL POLYNOMIAL IN T( )
1890    FOR J = 1 TO N
1900       LET D1 = Q(I) * T(J)
1910       LET T(J) = P(J)
1920       LET P(J) = (U(J) - L(I + 1)) * P(J) - D1
1930       LET S1 = S1 + W(J) * P(J) ^ 2
1940       LET P1 = P1 + W(J) * V(J) * P(J)
1950    NEXT J
1960    REM Q IS FORSYTHES BETA
1970    LET Q(I + 1) = S1 / W2
1980    LET S(I + 1) = P1 / S1
1990    LET D2 = D2 - S(I + 1) * P1
2000    LET G(I + 1) = ABS(D2 / (N - I - 1))
2010    IF L > 0 THEN 2180
2020    REM ENTER IF PROGRAM HAS TO DECIDE ON BEST ORDER (L = 0)
2030    IF I1 = 1 THEN 2130
2040    IF G(I + 1) < G(I) THEN 2180
2050    REM ENTER IF A MINIMUM DETECTED
2060    LET N2 = I - 1
2070    LET I1 = 1
2080    LET G1 = G(I)
2090    FOR J = 1 TO M1
2100       LET B(J) = C(J)
2110    NEXT J
2120    GOTO 2180
2130    IF G(I + 1) >= 0.6 * G1 THEN 2180
2140    LET I1 = 0
2150    LET N2 = M3
2160    REM BUILD COEFFICIENTS OF J TH ORDER TERM IN A( ) & SUM TO FORM
2170    REM EXPLICIT POWER SERIES IN C( )
2180    FOR J = 1 TO I
2190       LET D1 = D(J + 1) * Q(I)
2200       LET D(J + 1) = A(J)
2210       LET A(J) = D(J) - L(I + 1) * A(J) - D1
2220       LET C(J) = C(J) + S(I + 1) * A(J)
2230    NEXT J
2240    LET C(I + 1) = S(I + 1)
2250    LET A(I + 1) = 1
2260    LET D(I + 2) = 0
2270    IF I1 = 0 THEN 2320
2280    IF I <> M3 THEN 2320
2290    FOR J = 1 TO M1
2300       LET C(J) = B(J)
2310    NEXT J
2320 NEXT I
2330 LET D(1) = 1
2340 LET B(1) = 1
2350 LET F(1) = C(1)
2360 FOR I = 2 TO M1
```

```
2370    LET D(I) = 1
2380    LET B(I) = B1 * B(I - 1)
2390    LET F(1) = F(1) + C(I) * B(I)
2400  REM WORK OUT EXPLICIT POWER SERIES IN UNSCALED X, & ADD
2410    REM INTO THE COEFFICIENTS F( ) THE RELEVANT CONTRIBUTIONS
2420 NEXT I
2430 FOR J = 2 TO M1
2440    LET D(1) = D(1) * A1
2450    LET F(J) = C(J) * D(1)
2460    LET K1 = 2.
2470    LET J1 = J + 1
2480    IF J1 > M1 THEN 2560
2490    FOR I = J1 TO M1
2500      LET D(K1) = A1 * D(K1) + D(K1 - 1)
2510      LET F(J) = F(J) + C(I) * D(K1) * B(K1)
2520      LET K1 = K1 + 1
2530    NEXT I
2540 NEXT J
2550 REM CALCULATE YCALC & RESIDUAL FOR EACH POINT (ON ORIGINAL SCALE).
2560 FOR I = 1 TO N
2570    LET J = N2 + 1
2580    LET Y5 = F(J)
2590    IF N2 = 0 THEN 2630
2600    FOR K = 1 TO N2
2610      LET Y5 = F(J - 1) + (X(I) * Y5)
2620      LET J = J - 1
2630    NEXT K
2640    LET Z(I) = Y5 * Y4 + Y3
2650    LET R(I) = (V(I) - Y5) * Y4
2660 NEXT I
2670 REM CONVERT COEFF ARRAY F( ) BACK TO ORIGINAL SCALE
2680 LET F(1) = (F(1) * Y4) + Y3
2690 FOR I = 2 TO M1
2700    LET F(I) = F(I) * Y4
2710 NEXT I
2720 RETURN
2730 REM ENTER IF ERRORS DETECTED
2740 PRINT "JOB TERMINATED BY PROGRAM BECAUSE SUM OF WEIGHTS = 0"
2750 STOP
2760 REM SUBROUTINE TO CHECK THAT DATA ARE CORRECT & ALTER IF NECESSARY
2770 PRINT "ARE THE DATA VALUES ENTERED CORRECT?";
2780 REM A4 SHOULD BE SET TO THE NUMBER OF LINES ON THE VDU
2790 LET A4 = 20
2800 GOSUB 3590
2810 IF Q$ = "YES" THEN 3570
2820 PRINT "HERE IS A LIST OF THE CURRENT DATA"
2830 PRINT "LINE NUMBER", "X", "Y", "WEIGHT"
2840 FOR I = 1 TO N
2850    PRINT I, X(I), Y(I), W(I)
2860    IF INT(I / (A4 - 1)) * (A4 - 1) <> I THEN 2900
2870    PRINT "WOULD YOU LIKE TO CONTINUE LISTING";
2880    GOSUB 3590
2890    IF Q$ = "NO" THEN 2910
2900 NEXT I
2910 PRINT "TYPE R TO REPLACE";
2920 IF I$ = "NO" THEN 2940
2930 PRINT " AN EXISTING LINE OF DATA"
2940 IF N = 100 THEN 2990
2950 PRINT TAB(5); " A TO ADD";
2960 IF I$ = "NO" THEN 2980
2970 PRINT " AN EXTRA LINE"
```

```
2980 IF N = 1 THEN 3020
2990 PRINT TAB(5); " D TO DELETE";
3000 IF I$ = "NO" THEN 3020
3010 PRINT " AN EXISTING LINE"
3020 PRINT TAB(5); " L TO LIST";
3030 IF I$ = "NO" THEN 3050
3040 PRINT " THE DATA"
3050 PRINT "  OR C TO CONTINUE";
3060 IF I$ = "NO" THEN 3080
3070 PRINT " THE CALCULATION"
3080 INPUT Q$
3090 IF Q$ = "R" THEN 3190
3100 IF N = 100 THEN 3130
3110 IF Q$ = "A" THEN 3330
3120 IF N = 1 THEN 3140
3130 IF Q$ = "D" THEN 3430
3140 IF Q$ = "L" THEN 2820
3150 IF Q$ = "C" THEN 3570
3160 PRINT "REPLY '"; Q$; "' NOT UNDERSTOOD."
3170 GOTO 2910
3180 REM REPLACE LINE
3190 PRINT "TYPE THE LINENUMBER OF THE LINE TO BE REPLACED";
3200 INPUT I
3210 IF I <> INT(I) THEN 3230
3220 IF (I - 1) * (I - N) < = 0 THEN 3260
3230 PRINT "LINENUMBER MUST BE AN INTEGER IN THE RANGE 1 -"; N
3240 PRINT "RE-";
3250 GOTO 3190
3260 PRINT "TYPE THE CORRECT LINE TO REPLACE THE ONE WHICH IS WRONG:"
3270 PRINT "X, Y, WEIGHT"
3280 INPUT X(I), Y(I), W(I)
3290 IF W(I) >= 0 THEN 3400
3300 PRINT "NEGATIVE WEIGHTS ARE IMPOSSIBLE - LAST LINE REJECTED"
3310 GOTO 3260
3320 REM ADD A NEW LINE
3330 LET N = N + 1
3340 PRINT "TYPE THE ADDITIONAL LINE OF DATA AS SHOWN:"
3350 PRINT "X, Y, WEIGHT"
3360 INPUT X(N), Y(N), W(N)
3370 IF W(N) >= 0 THEN 3400
3380 PRINT "NEGATIVE WEIGHTS ARE IMPOSSIBLE - LAST LINE REJECTED"
3390 GOTO 3340
3400 PRINT "OK"
3410 GOTO 2910
3420 REM DELETE A LINE
3430 PRINT "TYPE THE LINENUMBER OF THE LINE TO BE DELETED"
3440 INPUT J
3450 IF (J - 1) * (J - N) >0 THEN 3470
3460 IF J = INT(J) THEN 3490
3470 PRINT "LINENUMBER MUST BE AN INTEGER IN THE RANGE 1 -"; N
3480 GOTO 3430
3490 FOR I = J + 1 TO N
3500    LET X(I - 1) = X(I)
3510    LET Y(I - 1) = Y(I)
3520 NEXT I
3530 LET N = N - 1
3540 PRINT "OK"
3550 IF J > N THEN 2910
3560 GOTO 2820
3570 RETURN
3580 REM SUBROUTINE TO CHECK REPLIES
```

```
3590 IF I$ = "NO" THEN 3610
3600 PRINT " TYPE YES OR NO & PRESS RETURN."
3610 PRINT
3620 INPUT Q$
3630 IF Q$ = "YES" THEN 3670
3640 IF Q$ = "NO" THEN 3670
3650 PRINT "REPLY '"; Q$; "' NOT UNDERSTOOD.";
3660 GOTO 3600
3670 RETURN
3680 END
```

but otherwise a subroutine (lines 1160–2720) is called (line 620) to fit the polynomial.

The polynomial fitting subroutine is based of Forsythe's method of orthogonal polynomials using α and β. The main steps are as follows:

(i) A number of initial values are set (lines 1180–1320).

(ii) The maximum and minimum values of x and y are found (lines 1330–1480).

(iii) A check is performed to make sure that all of the weights are not zero (lines 1490–1500).

(iv) If all of the y values are the same, a zero order polynomial is returned (lines 1530–1560).

(v) The y values are scaled to lie in the range $+1$ to -1 (lines 1570–1650), and the x values are scaled into the range $+2$ to -2 (lines 1700–1750).

(vi) A loop (lines 1760–2320) performs a number of calculations for each order of polynomial tested:

    (a) Forsythe's α values are calculated (lines 1780–1830).

    (b) The current orthogonal polynomial is calculated (lines 1870–1950) and the previous orthogonal polynomial is stored.

    (c) Forsythe's β values are calculated (lines 1960–1970).

    (d) The sum of the residuals squared and the goodness of fit are calculated (lines 1990–2000).

    (e) If the program is selecting the 'best' polynomial the lines from 2010 to 2150 are used. (The method used is a development from Algorithm 296 by G. J. Makinson in *Communications of the ACM 1967*, **10**, 2, 87–88 with slight improvement.) This calculates the goodness of fit for each of the polynomials from zero order to the maximum order, and selects the order for which the goodness of fit is a local minimum. If there is more than one local minimum, then the later one (higher order) must be better than the first by an empirical factor of 0.6 for it to be selected.

    (f) The coefficients c_0, c_1, $c_2, \ldots, c_m$ for the orthogonal polynomials are evaluated (lines 2160–2230) for the current order of polynomial being calculated by the main loop (lines 1770–2320). If the program is choosing the best order, the coefficients for the orthogonal polynomials corresponding to the best polynomial fit are stored in the C array (lines 2270–2310).

The sequence of operations (a), (b), (c), (d), (e) and (f) is repeated for each order of the curve fitting polynomial up to the order specified by the user, or up to the maximum order if the computer is choosing the best polynomial.

(vii) The coefficients $c_0, c_1, c_2, \ldots, c_m$ for the othogonal polynomials are used to calculate the coefficients for the polynomial through the scaled data (lines 2360–2540).

(viii) The scaled residuals are calculated for each data point using the scaled data and the scaled polynomial coefficients. These residuals are then scaled to match the original data (lines 2550–2660).

(ix) Finally the coefficients for the power series polynomial through the scaled data values are converted to give the coefficients $a, b, c, d, \ldots$ for the polynomial through the original (unscaled) data points (lines 2670–2710).

On returning to the main part of the program from the polynomial fitting subroutine, a message is printed either giving the order of the polynomial specified (line 660) or the maximum order tested for and the best order found (lines 680–690). A table is then printed (lines 710–740) showing the goodness of fit of each of the polynomials from order zero up to either the order specified or the maximum order tested.

The coefficients of the best order polynomial (chosen by the computer) or of the order specified by the user are then printed (lines 760–830). A table of residuals may optionally be printed (lines 860–960).

Finally, the user is asked if another run is required (line 980). The answer which must be YES or NO is checked in a subroutine (lines 3580–3670). Should another run be required, the option is given of re-running with the data values already entered (when the data may be edited or a different order polynomial specified) or alternatively to enter a completely new set of data.

10

Solving Equations

In many areas of scientific work a mathematical model is used to describe the scientific observations. Examples include the rate of a chemical reaction, the rate of growth of a bacterial colony, the degree of ionisation of a compound in solution and many others. Given an equation which adequately describes the observations, it is usually possible to obtain mathematical solutions to the equations, and these may then be interpreted in terms of the original experiment.

Frequently these equations are non-linear. If they are linear, they can be solved exactly in one line. If they are quadratic or cubic they should be solved exactly using the algebraic methods given in subsequent sections. In other cases a graph should be plotted, and approximate solutions obtained. The accuracy of these solutions may be considerably improved using iterative numerical methods. Two such methods: the Newton–Raphson method and the method of bisection are given. Before using approximate methods, a preliminary investigation of the function should be underaken to find if it may be simplified to a quadratic or a cubic, and also to check that the function is continuous. For example:

$$x^4 + 3x^2 - 1 = 0$$

and

$$\tan^2 x + 3 \tan x - 1 = 0$$

can both be solved from the solutions to the quadratic

$$x^2 + 3x - 1 = 0$$

If the solutions to the last equation are r_1 and r_2 then the solutions to the first equation are $\pm\sqrt{r_1}$, and $\pm\sqrt{r_2}$ and the solutions to the second equation are arctan (r_1), and arctan (r_2).

Alternatively an expression such as:

$$x \cos x - \cos x - \tfrac{1}{2} x + \tfrac{1}{2} = 0$$

may be factorised to:

$$(x-1)(\cos x - \tfrac{1}{2}) = 0$$

hence

$$x = 1 \text{ or } \cos x = \tfrac{1}{2}$$

Quadratic Equations

A quadratic equation has the form

$$ax^2 + bx + c = 0 \qquad (1)$$

where b and c can take any value and a is non-zero. Many scientific and mathematical applications involve solving this equation, this is finding the values of x which satisfy Equation 1. This corresponds to finding the points where the graph of $y = ax^2 + bx + c$ cuts the x axis. Three cases are possible as shown in Fig. 10.1. It can be seen that the curve may cut the x axis in two places, touch the axis in one place, or not reach the x axis, giving two real roots, two coincident real roots or no real roots respectively. The word 'real' is used in the mathematical sense to distinguish from 'complex' roots which involve $\sqrt{-1} = i$.

The next section gives the derivation of the equation to solve quadratics. It is not necessary to follow this, but Equation 4 should be remembered.

Derivation of Equation to Solve Quadratic Equations

$$ax^2 + bx + c = 0$$

135

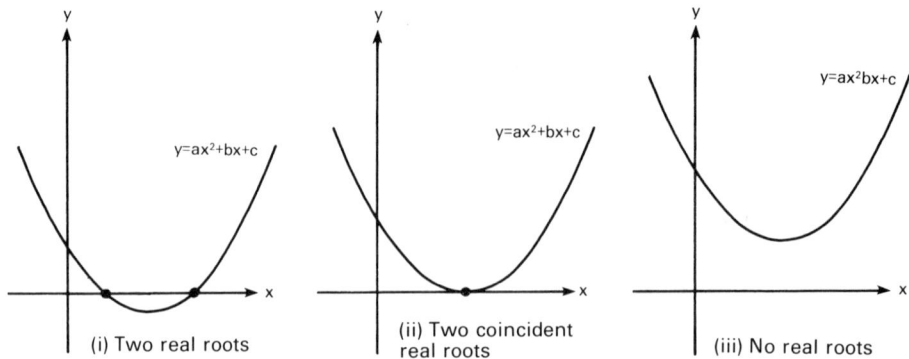

Fig. 10.1

Dividing throughout by a gives:

$$x^2 + \frac{b}{a}x + \frac{c}{a} = 0 \qquad (2)$$

Completing the square, or by inspection, it can be seen that

$$\left(x + \frac{b}{2a}\right)^2 = x^2 + \frac{b}{a}x + \frac{b^2}{4a^2}$$

hence

$$x^2 + \frac{b}{a}x = \left(x + \frac{b}{2a}\right)^2 - \frac{b^2}{4a^2} \qquad (3)$$

Substituting Equation 3 into Equation 2

$$\left(x + \frac{b}{2a}\right)^2 - \frac{b^2}{4a^2} + \frac{c}{a} = 0$$

rearranging

$$\left(x + \frac{b}{2a}\right)^2 = \frac{b^2}{4a^2} - \frac{c}{a} = \frac{b^2 - 4ac}{4a^2}$$

taking the square root of both sides

$$x + \frac{b}{2a} = \pm\frac{\sqrt{(b^2 - 4ac)}}{2a}$$

rearranging

$$x = \frac{-b \pm \sqrt{(b^2 - 4ac)}}{2a} \qquad (4)$$

The term $b^2 - 4ac$ is called the discriminant. Three cases are possible:

(i) if $b^2 - 4ac$ is greater than zero then two different solutions for x are obtained.

(ii) if $b^2 - 4ac$ is equal to zero both solutions for x have the same numerical value. The two roots (solutions) are said to be coincident.

(iii) if $b^2 - 4ac$ is less than zero then no real roots exist. This is because it is not permissible to take the square root of a negative number without introducing the complex mathematical number $i = \sqrt{-1}$. Using i two complex solutions may be obtained:

$$x = -\frac{b}{2a} \pm \frac{\sqrt{4ac - b^2}}{2a} \cdot i$$

Complex roots do not physically exist, and should only be used with care and understanding.

The three cases for the discriminant outlined above, correspond directly with the three graphs drawn in Fig. 10.1.

Accuracy of the Solutions

Though solutions from Equation 4 are mathematically correct, they may be subject to numerical errors when a limited number of significant figures are carried. This is particularly acute when one root is close to zero because b is approximately equal to $\sqrt{(b^2 - 4ac)}$. When only a limited number of significant figures are carried then the subtraction of two almost equal numbers results in loss of accuracy.

A simple illustration of the loss of accuracy when *subtracting* two numbers of almost equal magnitude and the *same sign* is given by evaluating $\sqrt{9236} - \sqrt{9235}$ working to six significant figures.

$\sqrt{9236} = 96.104\ 1$

$\sqrt{9235} = 96.098\ 9$

difference $= 0.005\ 2$

Calculation to six significant figures accuracy has given an answer with only two figures accuracy. In such cases one tries to improve the method of calculation. In this case

$$\sqrt{9326} - \sqrt{9235} =$$

$$= \frac{(\sqrt{9236} - \sqrt{9235})\,(\sqrt{9236} + \sqrt{9235})}{(\sqrt{9236} + \sqrt{9235})}$$

$$= \frac{1}{\sqrt{9236} + \sqrt{9235}}$$

Using the latter equation the calculated answer is $5.202\ 83 \times 10^{-3} = 0.005\ 202\ 83$, which is correct to six figures. It should be noted that loss of accuracy can also occur when two numbers of almost equal magnitude, but *opposite signs*, are *added* together. This problem does not occur with multiplication or division.

The problem of loss of accuracy when solving a quadratic for which a root is almost zero can be overcome in the following manner:

(i) The product of the two roots is c/a.

(ii) If one root can be solved accurately then the second root can be obtained as $c/(a \cdot \text{accurate root})$.

This avoids the inherent loss of accuracy for one of the roots from Equation 4 if one of the roots is close to zero.

(iii) If b is positive, the more accurate root obtained from Equation 4 is

$$x = \frac{(-b) - \sqrt{(b^2 - 4ac)}}{2a}$$

It should be noted that loss of accuracy is avoided by subtracting two terms of *opposite* sign: the $(-b)$ term is negative and the square root term is positive.

(iv) If b is negative, the more accurate root obtained is

$$x = \frac{(-b) + \sqrt{(b^2 - 4ac)}}{2a}$$

This is because $(-b)$ is positive and the square root term is positive, making the numerator the sum of two numbers of the same sign.

Description of the Program to Solve Quadratic Equations (see Program 10.1)

A title is printed and the user is asked to type in the three coefficients a, b and c for the equation

$$ax^2 + bx + c = 0$$

A check is performed (line 90) to ensure that the value of a is not zero. If it is zero then a warning message (line 110) explains that this is not a quadratic equation, and the user is offered another run. This check is necessary to avoid division by zero in Equation 4.

Next the discriminant $b^2 - 4ac$ is calculated. Should it be a zero, then both roots are equal, and their value is printed (line 150). If the discriminant is negative then the equation has complex roots, and these are calculated and printed (lines 190–230). Otherwise the 'more accurate root' r_1 is calculated in line 270 or 290 as appropriate. The second root r_2 is calculated in line 300 using the relationship: 'product of the two roots $= c/a$'. Both roots are printed (line 310), and a message is printed asking if another run is required (line 330). The answer is checked to ensure that it is YES or NO.

Cubic Equations

A cubic equation has the form

$$ax^3 + bx^2 + cx + d = 0 \qquad (5)$$

The problem is to solve this equation, that is given the values of a, b, c and d to find the values of x for which the left-hand side of the equation is zero. This is analogous to finding the places where the graph of $y = ax^3 + bx^2 + cx + d$ cuts the x axis. There are three possible cases (Fig. 10.2).

Program 10.1   Trial run.

```
PROGRAM TO SOLVE QUADRATIC EQUATIONS
======= == ===== ========= =========
EG.   A*X^2 + B*X + C = 0

TYPE IN THE THREE COEFFICIENTS A,B,C
WITH A COMMA BETWEEN TERMS.   THEN PRESS RETURN
? 1, 1, -2

THE TWO ROOTS ARE   -2 AND   1

WOULD YOU LIKE ANOTHER RUN? (YES/NO)
? YES

TYPE IN THE THREE COEFFICIENTS A,B,C
WITH A COMMA BETWEEN TERMS.   THEN PRESS RETURN
? 2, 4, 2
BOTH ROOTS ARE EQUAL, AND HAVE THE VALUE: -1

WOULD YOU LIKE ANOTHER RUN? (YES/NO)
? YES

TYPE IN THE THREE COEFFICIENTS A,B,C
WITH A COMMA BETWEEN TERMS.   THEN PRESS RETURN
? 1, 2, 3

THIS EQUATION DOES NOT HAVE REAL ROOTS
THE TWO COMPLEX ROOTS ARE:
      -1 + 1.41421 * I
AND   -1 - 1.41421 * I
WHERE I IS THE SQUARE ROOT OF -1

WOULD YOU LIKE ANOTHER RUN? (YES/NO)
? NO
END OF JOB
```

The first step in the solution of Equation 5 is to divide throughout by a, thus reducing the number of constants to three:

$$x^3 + \frac{b}{a}x^2 + \frac{c}{a}x + \frac{d}{a} = 0$$

or

$$x + b_1 x^2 + c_1 x + d_1 = 0$$

Next the cube is completed by substituting $y - b_1/3$ for x, i.e.

$$x = y - b_1/3 \tag{6}$$

giving

$$\left(y - \frac{b_1}{3}\right)^3 + b_1\left(y - \frac{b_1}{3}\right)^2 +$$

$$+ c_1\left(y - \frac{b_1}{3}\right) + d_1 = 0$$

which reduces to

$$y^3 + \left(c_1 - \frac{b_1^2}{3}\right)y +$$

$$+ \left(\frac{2b_1^3}{27} - \frac{b_1 c_1}{3} + d_1\right) = 0$$

Although superficially this appears to be a more complicated expression, it is in fact a simplification since the squared term y^2 has vanished. The equation may be re-written

$$y^3 + c_2 y + d_2 = 0 \tag{7}$$

Equation 7 can be solved using the following substitution

$$y = k \cos \theta \tag{8}$$

where

$$k^2 = -4c_2/3 \tag{9}$$

```
10  DIM Q$(8)
20  PRINT "PROGRAM TO SOLVE QUADRATIC EQUATIONS"
30  PRINT "======= == ===== ========= ========="
40  PRINT "EG.   A*X^2 + B*X + C = 0"
50  PRINT
60  PRINT "TYPE IN THE THREE COEFFICIENTS A,B,C"
70  PRINT "WITH A COMMA BETWEEN TERMS.  THEN PRESS RETURN"
80  INPUT A, B, C
90  IF A <> 0 THEN 130
100 PRINT
110 PRINT "THIS IS NOT A QUADRATIC EQUATION."
120 GOTO 320
130 LET D = B * B - 4 * A * C
140 IF D <> 0 THEN 170
150 PRINT "BOTH ROOTS ARE EQUAL, AND HAVE THE VALUE:"; -B / (2 * A)
160 GOTO 320
170 PRINT
180 IF D > 0 THEN 250
190 PRINT "THIS EQUATION DOES NOT HAVE REAL ROOTS"
200 PRINT "THE TWO COMPLEX ROOTS ARE:"
210 PRINT TAB(6); -B / (2 * A); "+"; SQR(-D) / (2 * ABS(A)); "* I"
220 PRINT "AND "; -B / (2 * A); "-"; SQR(-D) / (2 * ABS(A)); "* I"
230 PRINT "WHERE I IS THE SQUARE ROOT OF -1"
240 GOTO 320
250 LET D = SQR(D)
260 IF B >= 0 THEN 290
270 LET R1 = (-B + D) / (2 * A)
280 GOTO 300
290 LET R1 = (-B -D) / (2 * A)
300 LET R2 = C / (A * R1)
310 PRINT "THE TWO ROOTS ARE "; R1; "AND ";R2
320 PRINT
330 PRINT "WOULD YOU LIKE ANOTHER RUN? (YES/NO)"
340 INPUT Q$
350 IF Q$ = "YES" THEN 50
360 IF Q$ = "NO" THEN 390
370 PRINT "REPLY '"; Q$; "' NOT UNDERSTOOD. PLEASE ANSWER YES OR NO"
380 GOTO 320
390 PRINT "END OF JOB"
400 END
```

Substituting Equation 8 in 7

$$k^3 \cos^3 \theta + c_2 k \cos \theta + d_2 = 0 \qquad (10)$$

But

$$\cos^3 \theta = \tfrac{1}{4} \cos 3\theta + \tfrac{3}{4} \cos \theta \qquad (11)$$

Substituting Equation 11 into 10:

$$\tfrac{1}{4} k^3 \cos 3\theta + \tfrac{3}{4} k^3 \cos \theta + c_2 k \cos \theta + d_2 = 0$$

Rearranging

$$\tfrac{1}{4} k^3 \cos 3\theta + \tfrac{3}{4} k \cos \theta (k^2 + \tfrac{4}{3} c_2) + d_2 = 0$$

Comparison with Equation 9 shows that the term in brackets is zero hence

$$\tfrac{1}{4} k^3 \cos 3\theta + d_2 = 0$$

Rearranging

$$\cos 3\theta = -4d_2/k^3$$

Thus one solution for θ is

$$\theta_1 = \tfrac{1}{3} \text{arc cos} (-4d_2/k^3) \qquad (12)$$

and two other solutions are

$$\theta_2 = \theta_1 + 2\pi/3$$

and

$$\theta_3 = \theta_1 - 2\pi/3$$

(Note that $2\pi/3$ radians $= 120°$.)

The three roots to the cubic equation can now be obtained from the three solutions for θ.

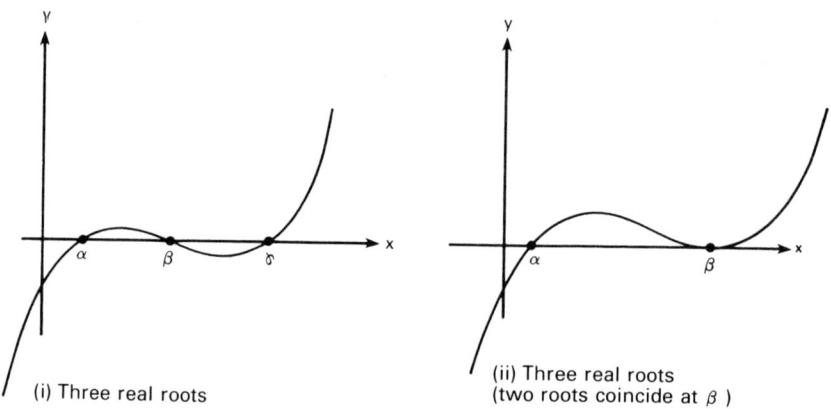

(i) Three real roots

(ii) Three real roots
(two roots coincide at β)

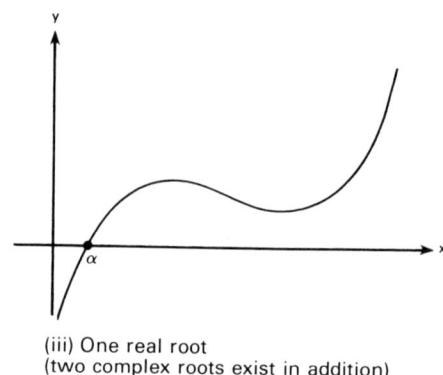

(iii) One real root
(two complex roots exist in addition)

Fig. 10.2

Starting with equation 6

$$x = y - b_1/3$$

and using Equation 8

$$x = k \cos \theta - b_1/3$$

and three solutions (roots) of x are

$$x_1 = k \cos \theta_1 - b_1/3 \qquad (13)$$

$$x_2 = k \cos \theta_2 - b_1/3$$
$$= -\tfrac{1}{2} k \, (\cos \theta_1 + \sqrt{3} \cdot \sin \theta_1) - b_1/3 \qquad (14)$$

$$x_3 = k \cos \theta_3 - b_1/3$$
$$= -\tfrac{1}{2} k \, (\cos \theta_1 - \sqrt{3} \cdot \sin \theta_1) - b_1/3 \qquad (15)$$

The above three solutions are useful for cases where the equation yields three real roots. When there are complex roots, solution by hand is even harder, and a different method is normally adopted. Experienced mathemati-

cians may accept the challenge of deriving a solution which handles complex roots. One satisfactory solution is coded in the following computer program (Program 10.2). If a computer is available, the program is recommended since it is faster, more reliable and requires no mathematical aptitude.

Description of the Program to Solve Cubic Equations (see Program 10.2)

The program prints a heading (lines 20–30) and then asks the user to type in the coefficients a, b, c and d. The value of a is checked (lines 110–140) to ensure that it is not zero, since if it is zero the equation is not a cubic and the method would fail subsequently through dividing by zero (line 150). Four terms are

140

evaluated for subsequent use (lines 150–180) including the terms c_2 and d_2 first used in Equation 7. The cubic equation which is being solved is then printed out.

One of two different methods of calculation is then employed depending on whether the equation has one real root and two complex roots or alternatively three real roots. If there are three real roots then the section from lines 240–370 is skipped.

If there are complex roots then the section lines 240–370 is used. Lines 260 and 270 which calculate the cube root of P and Q respectively are worthy of comment. Cube roots may be evaluated by raising to the power of 1/3. The user may be unaware of the fact that raising to the power is often calculated internally by the computer using logarithms. Since the logarithm of a negative number does not exist, cube roots of negative numbers cannot be evaluated directly by this method even though the roots exist. This is overcome in the program by raising the modulus of the number to the power 1/3 and giving the answer the sign of the original. The one real root is printed (lines 290–300) and the two complex roots are evaluated and printed (lines 310–360). The section for three real roots is then skipped, and the user asked if another run is required (line 520).

Program 10.2   Trial run.

```
PROGRAM TO SOLVE CUBIC EQUATIONS
======= == ===== ===== =========

TYPE THE COEFFICIENTS OF THE GENERAL CUBIC EQUATION:

    A * X*X*X + B * X*X + C * X + D = 0

TYPE A, B, C & D SEPARATED BY COMMAS, THEN PRESS RETURN
? 1, -6, 11, -6

            3           2
1          X    +  -6 X    +  11 X   +   -6
THREE REAL ROOTS
1
3
2

WOULD YOU LIKE ANOTHER RUN? TYPE YES OR NO AND PRESS RETURN
? YES

TYPE THE COEFFICIENTS OF THE GENERAL CUBIC EQUATION:

    A * X*X*X + B * X*X + C * X + D = 0

TYPE A, B, C & D SEPARATED BY COMMAS, THEN PRESS RETURN
? 1, 2, 4, 8

            3           2
1          X    +  2 X    +  4 X   +   8
ONE REAL ROOT
-2
AND TWO COMPLEX ROOTS
-2.38419E-07   +   2   * I
-2.38419E-07   -   2   * I
WHERE I IS THE SQUARE ROOT OF -1

WOULD YOU LIKE ANOTHER RUN? TYPE YES OR NO AND PRESS RETURN
? NO
END OF JOB
```

```
10  DIM Q$(9)
20  PRINT "PROGRAM TO SOLVE CUBIC EQUATIONS"
30  PRINT "======= == ===== ===== ========="
40  PRINT
50  PRINT "TYPE THE COEFFICIENTS OF THE GENERAL CUBIC EQUATION:"
60  PRINT
70  PRINT TAB(5); "A * X*X*X + B * X*X + C * X + D = 0"
80  PRINT
90  PRINT "TYPE A, B, C & D SEPARATED BY COMMAS, THEN PRESS RETURN"
100 INPUT A, B, C, D
110 IF A <> 0 THEN 150
120 PRINT "THIS IS NOT A CUBIC EQUATION"
130 PRINT "RE-";
140 GOTO 90
150 LET F = B / (3 * A)
160 LET C2 = (3 * A * C - B * B) / (3 * A * A)
170 LET D2 = ((2 * B * F / 3 - C) * F + D) / A
180 LET H = D2 * D2 + C2 * C2 * C2 * 4 / 27
190 PRINT
200 PRINT TAB(10); "3"; TAB(20); "2"
210 PRINT A;TAB(9);"X   + ";B;TAB(19);"X   + ";C;TAB(29);"X   + ";D
220 REM JUMP IF THERE ARE THREE REAL ROOTS
230 IF H <= 0 THEN 390
240 LET P = (D2 + SQR(H)) / 2
250 LET Q = (D2 - SQR(H)) / 2
260 LET P3 = ABS(P) ^ (1 / 3) * SGN(P)
270 LET Q3 = ABS(Q) ^ (1 / 3) * SGN(Q)
280 LET R = -P3 - Q3 - F
290 PRINT "ONE REAL ROOT"
300 PRINT R
310 LET R1 = P3 / 2 + Q3 / 2 - F
320 LET R2 = SQR(3) / 2 * (P3 - Q3)
330 PRINT "AND TWO COMPLEX ROOTS"
340 PRINT R1; " + "; R2; " * I"
350 PRINT R1; " - "; R2; " * I"
360 PRINT "WHERE I IS THE SQUARE ROOT OF -1"
370 GOTO 510
380 REM PREVENT DIVISION BY ZERO IF P = PI/2 OR 3*PI/2
390 IF ABS(D2) >= 1.0E-06 THEN 430
400 LET T = 1.5708
410 GOTO 440
420 REM WORK OUT USING FROM ARC TAN RATHER THAN ARC COS
430 LET T = ATN(SQR(-H) / D2)
440 IF T >= 0 THEN 460
450 LET T = T + 3.14159
460 LET T = T / 3
470 PRINT "THREE REAL ROOTS"
480 PRINT -SQR(-4 * C2 / 3) * COS(T) - F
490 PRINT 0.5 * SQR(-4 * C2 / 3) * (COS(T) + SQR(3) * SIN(T)) - F
500 PRINT 0.5 * SQR(-4 * C2 / 3) * (COS(T) - SQR(3) * SIN(T)) - F
510 PRINT
520 PRINT "WOULD YOU LIKE ANOTHER RUN? TYPE YES OR NO AND PRESS RETURN"
530 INPUT Q$
540 IF Q$ = "YES" THEN 40
550 IF Q$ = "NO" THEN 580
560 PRINT "REPLY '"; Q$; "' NOT UNDERSTOOD. PLEASE ANSWER YES OR NO."
570 GOTO 530
580 PRINT "END OF JOB"
590 END
```

If there are three real roots then the section from lines 240 to 370 is skipped, and the section from lines 380 to 500 is used for the calculation. In the derivation of equations, arc cosines were used in Equation 12 to produce equations 13, 14 and 15 for the three roots. The arc cos function is not generally available in BASIC on computers. However, the program uses a modified equation using the arc tangent function. The arc tangent function ATN is fairly widely available in full implementations of BASIC. Should this function not be available then arc tangents may be evaluated using the following polynomial (Gregory's series), taking sufficient terms to provide the accuracy required:

$$\text{arc tangent } (x) = x - \frac{x^3}{3} + \frac{x^5}{5} - \frac{x^7}{7} + \dots$$

This equation holds only when x is in the range $+1$ to -1. Should x be outside this range the arc tangent may be calculated using

$$\text{arc tangent } (x) = \frac{\pi}{2} - \text{arc tangent} \left(\frac{1}{x} \right)$$

and Gregory's series for $\frac{1}{x}$.

The three real roots are calculated and printed (lines 480–500), and the user is then asked if another run is required. The answer is checked to ensure that it is either YES or NO.

Newton–Raphson Method

In contrast to the previous algebraic solutions for quadratic and cubic equations, the Newton–Raphson procedure is a numerical method for obtaining an approximate solution to functions. The method is iterative, and requires an initial estimate for x that is close to the root. This is shown as point P in Fig. 10.3. R is the root of $f(x)=0$, and P is the initial estimate for the root.

An improved estimate B for the root is obtained in the following manner:

(i) The point on the graph of the function $y=f(x)$ which corresponds to the

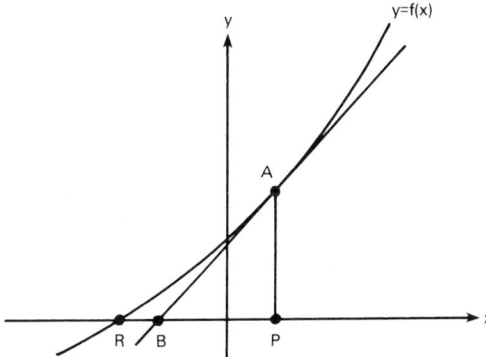

Fig. 10.3

initial estimate P is obtained. This is point A.

(ii) The tangent to the curve at point A is drawn.

(iii) The point at which the tangent cuts the x axis is marked point B. This is generally a better estimate of the root than P.

The value of B is taken as the improved estimate for the root, and the steps (i), (ii) and (iii) repeated a number of times. It can be seen that B closes in on R.

The value of B may be obtained numerically using the following equation

$$B = P - \frac{f(P)}{f'(P)} \qquad (16)$$

where P is the estimated value for the root,

$f(P)$ is the value of the function at P,

and $f'(P)$ is the value of the derivative (tangent) of the function at P.

Derivation of Newton–Raphson Equation

By definition the value of the derivative of the function at A yields the slope of line AB. The slope may also be expressed as the length of line AP divided by the length of line BP.

$$f'(P) = \frac{\text{Length of } AP}{\text{Length of } BP} \qquad (17)$$

The length of AP is the value of the function at

143

P, i.e. $f(P)$ and the length of BP is $P-B$. Substituting these values into Equation 17 gives:

$$f'(P) = \frac{f(P)}{P-B}$$

Rearranging

$$P-B = \frac{f(P)}{f'(P)}$$

$$B = P - \frac{f(P)}{f'(P)}$$

This equation is identical to equation 16. Expressed in words the equation means that the new estimate for the root equals the old estimate minus the ratio of the function to its derivative.

Limitations of the Method

The Newton–Raphson method requires the derivative of the function. Differentiating some functions to obtain the derivative may be difficult, and iteration, that is repeating the cycle of calculations, is time consuming and tedious. A computer program is provided which will perform 50 iterative cycles on a polynomial. (For simplicity and ease of use, the program automatically differentiates the polynomial function.) Experience suggests that on most computers 50 cycles is generous, and the machine accuracy is likely to be the limiting factor in the accuracy of the root.

This method will fail to produce a sensible solution if there are no roots or will fail completely if the derivative calculates to zero. This corresponds to a horizontal tangent which cannot cut the x axis.

Description of Newton–Raphson Program Applied to Polynomials (see Program 10.3)

The program first prints a heading (lines 20–30), and then asks if full instructions are required (lines 50–60). Any answer other than

YES or NO is rejected (lines 80–110). If requested, instructions are printed (lines 120–190).

A message (line 210) requests the user to type in the order of the polynomial. The value typed is checked (lines 230–260) to ensure that it is an integer and in the range 1 to 20. The upper limit of 20 is imposed by the DIMension of the C array in line 10, but it must be remembered that the limited number of figures carried by the computer may produce significant errors when evaluating high order polynomials. In practice, the latter is the most restrictive.

Next the user is invited to type in the coefficients a, b, c, . . . one at a time, starting with the highest order coefficient (lines 270–310). Finally the starting value for x is requested (lines 320–330).

The program then executes a loop (lines 340–520) up to a maximum of 50 times. Within the loop the value of the function at x is calculated (lines 350–390). If the value of the function is zero, then an exact root has been found, iteration stops, and the root is printed out (line 540). Usually the value of the function is not zero, and the program evaluates the first derivative of the function at x (lines 410–450). Should the derivative be zero, which corresponds to a horizontal part on the graph of the function, then the Newton–Raphson method fails and an error message is printed (lines 460–480). Usually the derivative is not zero. A check is made to find if the estimate for x has changed by more than 10, and if so a warning message is printed (lines 490–500). This message is often an indication that the original estimate for x was a long way from any root, that the iteration may be closing in on a root other than the one expected, or that there is no root in the neighbourhood of the starting value or no root at all. The next estimate for x is then calculated (line 510) and the iterative cycle repeated. After 50 iterations the current value for x is printed. This is usually an estimate for a root. However, if there is no root the answer will be meaningless, but this will usually be indicated by a large number of warning

Program 10.3 Trial run.

```
NEWTON-RAPHSON METHOD FOR FINDING ROOTS OF POLYNOMIALS
====== ======= ====== === ======= ===== == ===========
WOULD YOU LIKE INSTRUCTIONS?
TYPE YES OR NO AND PRESS RETURN
? YES
THIS PROGRAM ITERATIVELY SOLVES POLYNOMIAL EQUATIONS
EQUAL TO ZERO BY THE NEWTON RAPHSON METHOD
EG.  AX^5 + BX^4 + CX^3 + DX^2 + EX + F = 0
THE PROGRAM REQUIRES FIRST THE ORDER OF THE POLYNOMIAL
(5 IN THIS CASE), AND THEN THE COEFFICIENTS A FIRST,
THEN B, THEN C ETC.

FINALLY THE PROGRAM NEEDS THE STARTING VALUE FOR X

TYPE THE ORDER OF THE POLYNOMIAL AND PRESS RETURN
? 3
TYPE IN THE COEFFICIENTS, THE HIGHEST ORDER FIRST
PRESS RETURN AFTER EACH VALUE
? 2
? -12
? 22
? -12
TYPE THE STARTING VALUE FOR X
? 5
THE ROOT IS 3

WOULD YOU LIKE ANOTHER RUN (YES/NO)
? YES

TYPE THE ORDER OF THE POLYNOMIAL AND PRESS RETURN
? 3
TYPE IN THE COEFFICIENTS, THE HIGHEST ORDER FIRST
PRESS RETURN AFTER EACH VALUE
? 2
? -12
? 22
? -12
TYPE THE STARTING VALUE FOR X
? -5
AFTER 50 ITERATIONS THE BEST ESTIMATE FOR  THE ROOT IS 1

WOULD YOU LIKE ANOTHER RUN (YES/NO)
? YES

TYPE THE ORDER OF THE POLYNOMIAL AND PRESS RETURN
? 3
TYPE IN THE COEFFICIENTS, THE HIGHEST ORDER FIRST
PRESS RETURN AFTER EACH VALUE
? 2
? -12
? 22
? -12
TYPE THE STARTING VALUE FOR X
? 1.7
THE ROOT IS 2

WOULD YOU LIKE ANOTHER RUN (YES/NO)
? NO
END OF JOB

10 DIM C(21), Q$(10)
20 PRINT "NEWTON-RAPHSON METHOD FOR FINDING ROOTS OF POLYNOMIALS"
```

```
30  PRINT "====== ======= ====== === ======= ===== == =========="
40  PRINT
50  PRINT "WOULD YOU LIKE INSTRUCTIONS?"
60  PRINT "TYPE YES OR NO AND PRESS RETURN"
70  INPUT Q$
80  IF Q$ = "YES" THEN 120
90  IF Q$ = "NO" THEN 200
100 PRINT "REPLY '"; Q$; "' NOT UNDERSTOOD.   PLEASE ANSWER YES OR NO"
110 GOTO 70
120 PRINT "THIS PROGRAM ITERATIVELY SOLVES POLYNOMIAL EQUATIONS"
130 PRINT "EQUAL TO ZERO BY THE NEWTON RAPHSON METHOD"
140 PRINT "EG.   AX^5 + BX^4 + CX^3 + DX^2 + EX + F = 0"
150 PRINT "THE PROGRAM REQUIRES FIRST THE ORDER OF THE POLYNOMIAL"
160 PRINT "(5 IN THIS CASE), AND THEN THE COEFFICIENTS A FIRST,"
170 PRINT "THEN B, THEN C ETC."
180 PRINT
190 PRINT "FINALLY THE PROGRAM NEEDS THE STARTING VALUE FOR X"
200 PRINT
210 PRINT "TYPE THE ORDER OF THE POLYNOMIAL AND PRESS RETURN"
220 INPUT P
230 IF P <> INT (P) THEN 250
240 IF (P - 1) * (P - 20) <= 0 THEN 270
250 PRINT "RETYPE AN INTEGER IN THE RANGE 1 TO 20"
260 GOTO 220
270 PRINT "TYPE IN THE COEFFICIENTS, THE HIGHEST ORDER FIRST"
280 PRINT "PRESS RETURN AFTER EACH VALUE"
290 FOR I = 1 TO P + 1
300   INPUT C(I)
310 NEXT I
320 PRINT "TYPE THE STARTING VALUE FOR X"
330 INPUT X
340 FOR L = 1 TO 50
350   REM CALCULATE F(X)
360   LET F = 0
370   FOR I = 1 TO P + 1
380     LET F = F * X + C(I)
390   NEXT I
400   IF F = 0 THEN 540
410   REM CALCULATE FIRST DERIVATIVE OF F(X)
420   LET F1 = 0
430   FOR I = 1 TO P
440     LET F1 = F1 * X + (P + 1 - I) * C(I)
450   NEXT I
460   IF F1 <> 0 THEN 490
470   PRINT "NEWTON-RAPHSON METHOD FAILS - DERIVATIVE = 0 AT X="; X
480   GOTO 550
490   IF ABS(F / F1) < 10 THEN 510
500   PRINT "WARNING - X ESTIMATE CHANGED APPRECIABLY"
510   LET X = X - F / F1
520 NEXT L
530 PRINT "AFTER 50 ITERATIONS THE BEST ESTIMATE FOR ";
540 PRINT "THE ROOT IS"; X
550 PRINT
560 PRINT "WOULD YOU LIKE ANOTHER RUN (YES/NO)"
570 INPUT Q$
580 IF Q$ = "YES" THEN 200
590 IF Q$ = "NO" THEN 620
600 PRINT "REPLY '";Q$;"' NOT UNDERSTOOD TYPE YES OR NO & PRESS RETURN"
610 GOTO 560
620 PRINT "END OF JOB"
630 END
```

146

messages that the estimate of x has changed appreciably.

Finally the user is offered another run (lines 560–610).

Method of Bisection

This is a simple iterative procedure for finding a root of an equation. The method is based on the point at which the function changes sign. The only two occasions when the sign of a function can change are:

(i) When the function cuts the x axis— which corresponds to a root of the equation.
(ii) Where a discontinuity occurs in the function. (Not all discontinuities cause sign changes, e.g. $y = 1/(x-2)^2$ is discontinuous at $x = 2$ but is always positive.)

These two cases are illustrated in Figs. 10.4 and 10.5.

The method requires two starting values for x. The lower value is called L and the upper value is called U. These must be chosen such that the sign of the function at L is opposite to the sign of the function at U. The algorithm for the method of bisection closes in on a sign change between L and U. This will either be a root or a discontinuity. The working of the algorithm is outlined below:

(a) The mid-point M between L and U is calculated.
(b) The value of the function at M is calculated.
(c) The value of the function at L is calculated.
(d) If the values of the function at M and L have opposite signs then the value of U is re-set to the value of M, and the procedure is repeated from (a) onwards.
(e) If the values of the function at M and L have identical signs then the value of L is re-set to the value of M, and the procedure is repeated from (a) onwards.

(f) Otherwise the value of the function is zero at M, and M is a root.

If the function is continuous over the range from L to U then the algorithm must close in on a root. Should the function be discontinuous with a discontinuity between L and U then two different cases might arise (Figs. 10.6 and 10.7).

If the discontinuity does not cause a sign change then the algorithm will usually close in on a root. It is, however, remotely possible that the algorithm will fail if it attempts to evaluate the function at the discontinuity. Should this occur the root can often be found

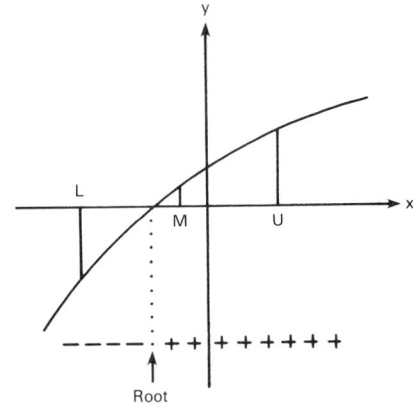

Fig. 10.4

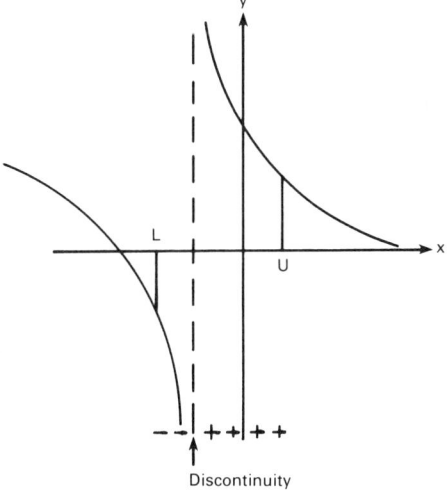

Fig. 10.5

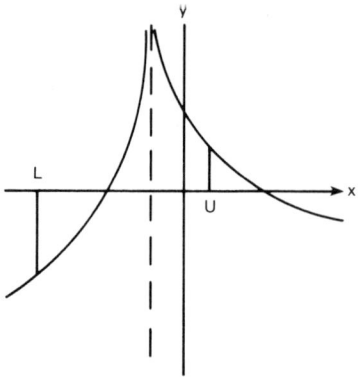

Fig. 10.6 The discontinuity does not cause a sign change.

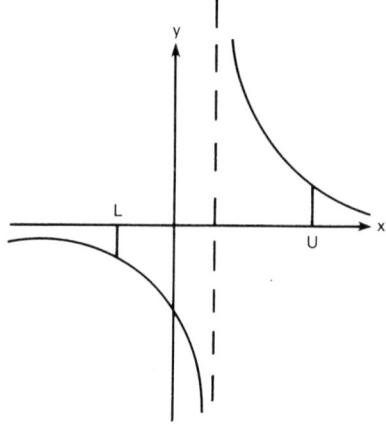

Fig. 10.7 The discontinuity does cause a sign change.

by repeating the procedure with slightly different values for L and/or U.

If the discontinuity causes the sign change the algorithm closes in on the discontinuity. The algorithm will therefore fail.

On a computer, 'failing' by the algorithm will produce a computer error which will be reported. The precise error reported will depend on the function used, and also on the computer. The following are typical errors:

    arithmetic overflow
    division by zero error
    invalid argument errors, e.g. tan (90°),
        log (0).

Since digital computers may round the last

digit it is possible that the algorithm closes in on but does not quite find the root or discontinuity. For the root, this means that the value of the function at M is very close but not exactly equal to zero. Similarly the value of M may be very close to the discontinuity but still not produce a computer error. In both of these cases the iterative procedure is unable to find a root or discontinuity. The value of the function at M is close to zero for a root, and is a large number (either positive or negative) for a discontinuity.

Because of the possible difficulties with discontinuous functions, the program provided is *not* robust.

Description of Bisection Program (see Program 10.4)

This program is different from the others in this book in that it is intended that users will modify it for themselves to solve a function of their own choice. To help initial understanding the function $y = \cos(x) - x$ has been built in at line 1000. As written, the program will attempt to solve $y = \cos(x) - x = 0$.

First the program prints a heading (lines 10–20). Next the program tests (lines 40–80) to see whether the function at line 1000 has been changed by the user. (This is accomplished by evaluating the function at $X = 1.2345$, and comparing the result with COS (1.2345) − 1.2345.) If the function has not been changed then the program prints instructions (lines 90–190) explaining how to do this in a subsequent run. If the function has been changed then these instructions are omitted.

A message then asks the user to type in the lower and upper limits L and U to be used for the bisection process (lines 210–230). These limits are described earlier—see Fig. 10.4. Two checks are performed on the values typed. First the value of L must be smaller than the value of U—that is the lower limit must be smaller than the upper limit. If the values fail this test, an explanatory message is printed (line 250) and the user is requested to re-input the values.

Program 10.4   Trial run.

```
1000 Y = EXP(X) - 12 + X
RUN
PROGRAM TO FIND ROOTS BY THE METHOD OF BISECTION
======= == ==== ===== == === ====== == =========


TYPE IN LOWER LIMIT & UPPER LIMIT
SEPARATED BY A COMMA, THEN PRESS RETURN
? -5 ", 5
THE APPROXIMATE  ROOT IS 2.27473
END OF PROGRAM


10 PRINT "PROGRAM TO FIND ROOTS BY THE METHOD OF BISECTION"
20 PRINT "======= == ==== ===== == === ====== == ========="
30 PRINT
40 REM NEXT THREE LINES TEST TO SEE IF THE USER HAS SUPPLIED HIS OWN
50 REM FUNCTION & IF NOT, INSTRUCTIONS HOW TO DO THIS ARE PRINTED
60 LET X = 1.2345
70 GOSUB 1000
80 IF ABS(COS(X) - X - Y) > 1.0E - 05 THEN 200
90 PRINT "UNLESS YOU HAVE REPLACED LINE 1000 BY YOUR OWN FUNCTION"
100 PRINT "THE PROGRAM WILL TRY TO FIND A ROOT OF THE FUNCTION"
110 PRINT "    Y = COS(X) - X"
120 PRINT "IE. THE VALUE OF X FOR WHICH COS(X) - X = 0"
130 PRINT "THIS IS BECAUSE LINE 1000 READS:"
140 PRINT "   1000 LET Y = COS(X) - X"
150 PRINT "TO SOLVE YOUR OWN FUNCTION TYPE IN A NEW LINE 1000"
160 PRINT "   1000 LET Y = "
170 PRINT "FOLLOWED BY AN EXPRESSION INVOLVING ONLY X, SUCH AS"
180 PRINT "   1000 LET Y = X^3 - 6*X^2 + 11*X - 6"
190 PRINT "OR 1000 LET Y = EXP(2*X) - 2*X + 3"
200 PRINT
210 PRINT "TYPE IN LOWER LIMIT & UPPER LIMIT"
220 PRINT "SEPARATED BY A COMMA, THEN PRESS RETURN"
230 INPUT L, U
240 IF L < U THEN 270
250 PRINT "THE LOWER LIMIT MUST BE SMALLER THAN THE UPPER LIMIT"
260 GOTO 200
270 LET X = L
280 GOSUB 1000
290 LET Y1 = Y
300 LET X = U
310 GOSUB 1000
320 IF SGN(Y * Y1) = -1 THEN 360
330 PRINT "THE FUNCTION MUST HAVE OPPOSITE SIGNS AT THE UPPER AND"
340 PRINT "LOWER LIMITS.  REFER TO THE PROGRAM WRITE UP"
350 GOTO 200
360 LET M = (L + U) / 2
370 LET X = M
380 REM CALCULATE VALUE OF FUNCTION AT M
390 GOSUB 1000
400 IF Y = 0 THEN 540
410 LET Y1 = Y
420 LET X = L
430 REM CALCULATE VALUE OF FUNCTION AT L
440 GOSUB 1000
450 IF SGN(Y) = SGN(Y1) THEN 480
460 LET U = M
470 GOTO 490
```

```
480 LET L = M
490 IF M <> (L + U) / 2 THEN 360
500 IF ABS (Y) < 1 THEN 530
510 PRINT "DISCONTINUITY IS"; X
520 GOTO 550
530 PRINT "THE APPROXIMATE ";
540 PRINT "ROOT IS"; X
550 PRINT "END OF PROGRAM"
560 GOTO 1020
990 REM SUBROUTINE TO EVALUATE FUNCTION
1000 LET Y = COS (X) - X
1010 RETURN
1020 END
```

For the second test the function is evaluated at L (lines 270–280) and again at U (lines 300–310). These two function values are compared in line 320, and if their signs are both the same then an error message is printed (lines 330–350), and the user is requested to re-type values for L and U. Since the method of bisection works by finding the place where the function changes sign, it cannot work if the function has the same sign at L and U.

Provided the values of the function at L and U have opposite signs, the algorithm in the previous section (a), (b), (c), (d), (e) and (f) is followed. The mid-point M between L and U is calculated at line 360 (step a). The value of the function at M is evaluated in lines 370–390 (step b). If the value is zero then the root has been found, and it is printed in line 540. Otherwise the value of the function at L is then evaluated at lines 420–440 (step c), and the signs of the two function values are compared (lines 450). If the signs are different the sign change lies between L and M and the upper limit U is moved down to M in line 460 (step d). Conversely if the signs are the same then the sign change lies between M and U, and the lower limit L is moved up to M at line 480 (step e). Using the new values of L and U the mid-point is re-calculated and the whole cycle is repeated.

Eventually the exact root should be detected and printed as outlined above. Two other possibilities may occur. Firstly, the exact root may not be found because of computer rounding errors affecting the least significant digit. This remote possibility should be overcome by line 490 which terminates the iteration process if the present M is equal to the average of the new L and U. In this case the new L value is reported as the approximate root (lines 530–540). The second possibility is that the function has a discontinuity between the chosen limits. Discontinuities are fully discussed in the previous section. These will usually cause the computer to fail with an appropriate error message from BASIC, but in some circumstances the discontinuity is detected by the program and the error message at line 510 is printed.

Finally a message (line 550) is printed indicating the end of the program.

Exercises

10.1 Solve the following quadratic equations using the general formula:

(a) $2x^2 - 6x + 4 = 0$

(b) $3x^2 - 6x + 3 = 0$

(c) $4x^2 - 16x + 20 = 0$

10.2 Use the method of bisection to solve the equation
$$x^3 - 6x + 11x - 6 = 0$$

(a) take $L = 0$ and $U = 1.6$

(b) take $L = 1.6$ and $U = 2.5$

(c) take $L = 2.5$ and $U = 4.0$

10.3 Solve $x - \cos x = 0$ using the Newton–Raphson method, starting from $x = 0$.

10.4 Solve $x^4 - x^3 - 2x^2 - 3 = 0$ using the Newton–Raphson method starting from $x = 2$.

11

Integral Approximations

Trapezium Rule

One commonly used technique for finding the integral form of a set of points is called the trapezium rule. This works by taking the first pair of points, joining them by a straight line to form a trapezium, and calculating its area using:

$$\text{Area} = \tfrac{1}{2}\left(\begin{array}{c}\text{Sum of the}\\\text{parallel sides}\end{array}\right)\cdot$$
$$\cdot\left(\begin{array}{c}\text{Perpendicular distance}\\\text{between them}\end{array}\right)$$

Reference to Fig. 11. 1 shows that the area of this trapezium is $\tfrac{1}{2}(y_1+y_2)\cdot\Delta x$. Similarly a trapezium can be formed using the second and third points giving an area $\tfrac{1}{2}(y_2+y_3)\cdot\Delta x$. If the process is repeated for all of the data pairs then an estimate of the total area under the curve is obtained. Thus the estimate for the area under the curve in Fig. 11.1 is:

$$\tfrac{1}{2}(y_1+y_2)\Delta x+\tfrac{1}{2}(y_2+y_3)\Delta x+$$
$$+\tfrac{1}{2}(y_3+y_4)\Delta x+\tfrac{1}{2}(y_4+y_5)\Delta x$$

or

$$(\tfrac{1}{2}y_1+y_2+y_3+y_4+\tfrac{1}{2}y_5)\Delta x$$

More generally this may be expressed:

Estimated area =
$$(\tfrac{1}{2}\text{ First }y+\text{Sum of middle }y\text{ values}+$$
$$+\tfrac{1}{2}\text{ Last }y)\Delta x \qquad (1)$$

Simpson's Rule

A better approximation to the area is generally obtained using Simpson's rule. In this the graph points are taken three at a time, and a quadratic curve is fitted which passes exactly through the points y_1, y_2 and y_3 shown in Fig. 11.2. The area under the quadratic curve is then calculated, and the whole process is repeated using points y_3, y_4 and y_5, etc. A consequence of this method is that it can only be applied when there are an odd number of data values. Comparison of Figs. 11.1 and 11.2 should convince the reader that Simpson's rule (using a curve) is likely to give a better

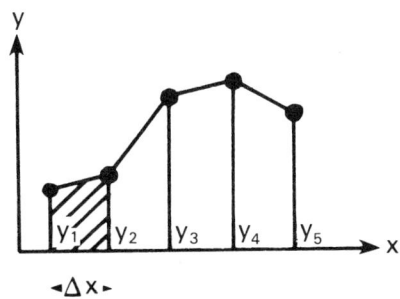

◄Δx►

Fig. 11.1

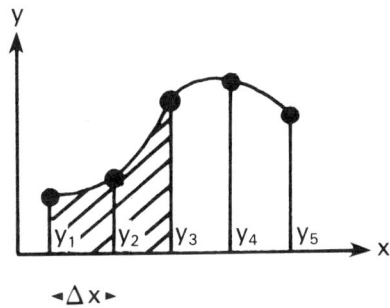

◄Δx►

Fig. 11.2

estimate for the area than the trapezium rule (using a straight line). The accuracy of the result from both methods will always be improved if the magnitude of Δx can be reduced by taking intermediate readings.

The area under the first quadratic is:

$$\text{area} = \tfrac{1}{3}(y_1 + 4y_2 + y_3) \cdot \Delta x \qquad (2)$$

The total area under all of the quadratics is the estimated area under the function and may be expressed:

$$= \tfrac{1}{3}(y_1 + 4y_2 + y_3)\Delta x + \\ + \tfrac{1}{3}(y_3 + 4y_4 + y_5)\Delta x + \ldots$$

$$= \tfrac{1}{3}\left(\begin{array}{l} \text{first } y \\ \text{value} \end{array} + 4 \cdot \begin{array}{l} \text{Sum of even} \\ y \text{ values} \end{array} + \right.$$

$$\left. + 2 \cdot \begin{array}{l} \text{Sum of other} \\ \text{odd } y \text{ values} \end{array} + \begin{array}{l} \text{Last } y \\ \text{value} \end{array} \right) \cdot \Delta x \qquad (3)$$

where the even y values are $y_2, y_4, y_6 \ldots$

and the odd y values are $y_3, y_5, y_7 \ldots$

The derivation of this equation is given in the next section, for completeness. It is important to remember Equation 3 but understanding the derivation is not essential.

Derivation of Simpson's Rule

The objective is to fit a quadratic curve through three points y_1, y_2 and y_3, and integrate this equation to obtain the area under the curve. The working is simplified if the three points are moved along the x axis so that middle point y_2 lies on the y axis as shown in Fig. 11.3. Translation along the x axis does not change the area under the curve.

A quadratic equation has the form

$$y = ax^2 + bx + c \qquad (4)$$

and the constants a, b and c are chosen so that the curve passes through y_1, y_2 and y_3.

The area A under the quadratic may be expressed as an integral

$$A = \int_{-\Delta x}^{+\Delta x} (ax^2 + bx + c) \cdot dx$$

$$= \left(\tfrac{1}{3}ax^3 + \tfrac{1}{2}bx^2 + cx \right)_{-\Delta x}^{+\Delta x}$$

$$= (\tfrac{1}{3}a(\Delta x)^3 + \tfrac{1}{2}b(\Delta x)^2 + c\Delta x) - \\ (-\tfrac{1}{3}a(\Delta x)^3 + \tfrac{1}{2}b(\Delta x)^2 - c\Delta x)$$

$$= \tfrac{1}{3}(2a(\Delta x)^2 + 6c) \cdot \Delta x \qquad (5)$$

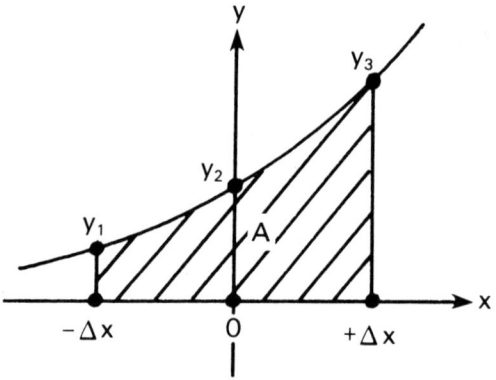

Fig. 11.3

To calculate the terms a and c requires that Equation 4 be solved:

$$\text{at } x = -\Delta x \quad y = y_1 = a(\Delta x)^2 - b\Delta x + c \qquad (6)$$

$$x = 0 \quad y = y_2 = \qquad\qquad c \qquad (7)$$

$$x = +\Delta x \quad y = y_3 = a(\Delta x)^2 + b\Delta x + c \qquad (8)$$

From Equation 7 it can be seen that $c = y_2$. The value of a can be calculated by adding Equations 6 and 8 and then substituting the value for c already obtained.

$$\text{Equations } 6 + 8 \quad y_1 + y_3 = 2a(\Delta x)^2 + 2c$$

substituting for c

$$y_1 + y_3 = 2a(\Delta x)^2 + 2y_2$$

hence

$$a = \frac{y_1 - 2y_2 + y_3}{2(\Delta x)^2} \qquad (9)$$

152

Substituting the values of c and a from Equations 7 and 9 into Equation 5 gives

$$A = \tfrac{1}{3}\left[2\left(\frac{y_1 - 2y_2 + y_3}{2(\Delta x)^2}\right)(\Delta x)^2 + 6y_2\right]\cdot \Delta x$$

$$= \tfrac{1}{3}(y_1 - 2y_2 + y_3 + 6y_2)\cdot \Delta x$$

$$= \tfrac{1}{3}(y_1 + 4y_2 + y_3)\cdot \Delta x$$

This is identical to Equation 2.

A Comparison of the Trapezium Rule, Simpson's Rule and Integration for Calculating the Area Under a Curve

Integration always gives the correct answer, but is often not possible because either the function for the curve is unknown, or the function cannot be integrated analytically. Simpson's rule usually gives a better result than the trapezium rule, as illustrated by evaluating the area under the curve $y = \sin x$ for values of x from 0 to π.

Consider five coordinates:

x	0	$\pi/4$	$\pi/2$	$3\pi/4$	π
y	0	0.7071	1	0.7071	0

Trapezium rule

$$A = \pi/4\,[(\tfrac{1}{2}\times 0) + 0.7071 + 1 +$$
$$+ 0.7071 + (\tfrac{1}{2}\times 0)] = 1.896$$

Simpson's rule

$$A = \tfrac{1}{3}\,\pi/4\,[0 + (4\times 0.7071) +$$
$$+ (2\times 1) + (4\times 0.7071) + 0] = 2.005$$

Integration

$$A = \int_{x=0}^{x=\pi} \sin x\, dx$$

$$= [\cos x]_{x=0}^{x=\pi} = 1 - (-1) = 2$$

The results from the trapezium rule and Simpson's rule can generally be improved by using more coordinates over the same range. Thus with seven coordinates in the above example, the trapezium rule gives an answer of 1.954 and Simpson's rule gives 2.001.

Description of the Program to Calculate Areas by Simpson's Rule (see Program 11.1)

The program prints a heading, and asks if full instructions are required. The reply must be either YES or NO, and this is checked in a subroutine (lines 1830–1920). Detailed or abbreviated instructions are printed out as requested for the first run, but only abbreviated instructions are given on subsequent runs.

The user is then invited to type the interval Δx between readings on the X axis (lines 80–120). The value typed in is checked (lines 140–200) to ensure that it is a positive number. Should a negative value be entered, a message instructs the user to re-type the interval correctly. If a value of zero is entered this is also rejected, and a message explains that this corresponds to a vertical line.

Next the user is requested to type in the data Y values (lines 220–270). The data input loop (lines 300–340) permits up to 200 values to be entered. Usually there will be fewer values than this, in which case the end of data input is signalled by typing the dummy value 999999. A check is performed (lines 380–400) to ensure that some valid data have been typed before the terminator.

A subroutine is then called (lines 930–1820) to check that the data entered are correct. If necessary the current data are listed together with line numbers, and instructions are given explaining how incorrect lines may be replaced or deleted. Additional lines may be inserted at any requested point in the existing data. Great care should be exercised when adding or deleting lines since the order of the data is critical. Except for the coding of the addition section of this subroutine, the remainder is fully described in Chapter 7. The section on adding lines is different from that in other programs described in that the user is asked to type the line number of the line immediately preceding the place where the new value is to be inserted. The value typed is checked to ensure that it is:

(i) an integer,
(ii) in the range one to the number of lines existing, or
(iii) zero—corresponding to inserting before the first line.

When the data are correct, control returns to the main program.

A check is then performed (lines 430–450) to ensure that there are at least three valid data points, since it is impossible to calculate Simpson's rule with fewer points. The number of data points is then checked (lines 470–480) to find if it is odd or even. Simpson's rule requires an odd number of points. If an even number has been provided a warning message is printed (lines 490–540) and the subroutine for checking and editing the data is called, thus providing a final opportunity to change the data. On returning from this subroutine, another check is made (lines 560–570) to establish if the number of points is still even, and a flag T is set to indicate this.

The program then accumulates the sum of the even values, and the sum of the odd values excluding the first and last terms (lines 610–670). The area is then calculated (line 680) by Simpson's rule using Equation 3. Provided that an odd number of data points exist, the area is printed (line 730). If the T flag was set to one above, indicating an even number of data points, the area calculated by Simpson's rule is only that up to the penultimate point, and this is printed (line 700). To

Program 11.1   Trial run.

```
CALCULATION OF THE AREA UNDER A CURVE BY SIMPSONS RULE
=========== == === ==== ===== = ===== == ======== ====

WOULD YOU LIKE FULL INSTRUCTIONS?
 TYPE YES OR NO & PRESS RETURN.

? YES
TYPE IN THE INTERVAL BETWEEN READINGS ON THE X AXIS, AND PRESS RETURN.
? 0.5

TYPE IN FIRST Y VALUE THEN PRESS RETURN,
THEN TYPE IN  NEXT Y VALUE, RETURN, ETC.
THERE MUST BE AN ODD NUMBER OF GENUINE DATA VALUES.
TERMINATE DATA WITH A DUMMY VALUE OF 999999 & PRESS RETURN

? 0.3989
? 0.3521
? 0.2420
? 0.1295
? 0.0540
? 0.0175
? 0.0044
? 999999
ARE THE DATA VALUES ENTERED CORRECT?   TYPE YES OR NO & PRESS RETURN.

? YES
AREA UNDER CURVE = 0.498617

WOULD YOU LIKE ANOTHER RUN
 TYPE YES OR NO & PRESS RETURN.

? NO
JOB COMPLETED
```

```
10 DIM Y(200), Q$(10), I$(3)
20 PRINT "CALCULATION OF THE AREA UNDER A CURVE BY SIMPSONS RULE"
30 PRINT "=========== == === ==== ===== = ===== == ======== ===="
40 PRINT
50 PRINT "WOULD YOU LIKE FULL INSTRUCTIONS?"
60 GOSUB 1850
70 LET I$ = Q$
80 PRINT "TYPE IN THE INTERVAL";
90 IF I$ = "NO" THEN 110
100 PRINT " BETWEEN READINGS ON THE X AXIS, AND PRESS RETURN.";
110 PRINT
120 INPUT X
130 PRINT
140 IF X >= 0 THEN 170
150 PRINT "INTERVAL MUST BE POSITIVE"
160 GOTO 190
170 IF X > 0 THEN 210
180 PRINT "AN INTERVAL OF ZERO MEANS A VERTICAL LINE."
190 PRINT "RETYPE VALUE CORRECTLY."
200 GOTO 110
210 IF I$ = "YES" THEN 240
220 PRINT "TYPE DATA VALUES."
230 GOTO 270
240 PRINT "TYPE IN FIRST Y VALUE THEN PRESS RETURN,"
250 PRINT "THEN TYPE IN  NEXT Y VALUE, RETURN, ETC."
260 PRINT "THERE MUST BE AN ODD NUMBER OF GENUINE DATA VALUES."
270 PRINT "TERMINATE DATA WITH A DUMMY VALUE OF 999999 & PRESS RETURN"
280 PRINT
290 LET N = 0
300 FOR I = 1 TO 200
310    INPUT Y(I)
320    IF Y(I) = 999999 THEN 380
330    LET N = N + 1
340 NEXT I
350 PRINT
360 PRINT "PROGRAM HANDLES A MAXIMUM OF 200 DATA VALUES"
370 PRINT
380 IF N > 0 THEN 420
390 PRINT "PLEASE ENTER SOME DATA"
400 GOTO 300
410 REM ENTER SUBROUTINE TO CHECK & EDIT DATA IF NECESSARY
420 GOSUB 940
430 IF N >= 3 THEN 460
440 PRINT "JOB ABANDONED **** INSUFFICIENT DATA VALUES"
450 GOTO 740
460 LET T = 0
470 REM TEST FOR AN ODD NUMBER OF DATA VALUES
480 IF 2 * INT(N / 2) <> N THEN 600
490 PRINT "AN EVEN NUMBER OF DATA VALUES HAVE BEEN GIVEN."
500 PRINT "SINCE SIMPSONS RULE REQUIRES AN ODD NUMBER OF VALUES,"
510 PRINT "THE PROGRAM WILL CALCULATE THE AREA UNDER THE CURVE FROM"
520 PRINT "TERM 1 TO TERM"; N-1; "USING SIMPSONS RULE, & ADD ON"
530 PRINT "THE AREA OF THE LAST TRAPEZIUM (TERMS"; N-1; "TO"; N;")"
540 PRINT "YOU HAVE ONE LAST CHANCE TO EDIT THE DATA"
550 GOSUB 940
560 REM TEST FOR AN ODD NUMBER OF DATA VALUES
570 IF 2 * INT(N / 2) <> N THEN 600
580 LET T = 1
590 LET N = N - 1
600 LET J = N - 1
610 LET S1 = 0
```

155

```
620 LET S2 = 0
630 FOR I = 2 TO J STEP 2
640    LET S2 = S2 + Y(I)
650    IF I = J THEN 670
660    LET S1 = S1 + Y(I + 1)
670 NEXT I
680 LET A = (1 / 3) * (Y(1) + 4 * S2 + 2 * S1 + Y(N)) * X
690 IF T = 0 THEN 730
700 PRINT "AREA WITHOUT LAST TRAPEZIUM  = "; A
710 LET A = A + 0.5 * (Y(N) + Y(N + 1)) * X
720 PRINT "TOTAL ";
730 PRINT "AREA UNDER CURVE  = "; A
740 PRINT
750 PRINT "WOULD YOU LIKE ANOTHER RUN"
760 GOSUB  1840
770 IF Q$ = "NO" THEN 1940
780 LET I$ = "NO"
790 PRINT "TYPE NEW FOR A RUN WITH COMPLETELY NEW DATA"
800 PRINT "  OR OLD TO EDIT AND RERUN THE EXISTING DATA"
810 INPUT Q$
820 IF Q$ = "NEW" THEN 890
830 IF Q$ = "OLD" THEN 860
840 PRINT "REPLY '"; Q$; " NOT UNDERSTOOD"
850 GOTO 790
860 LET N = N + T
870 GOSUB 990
880 GOTO 430
890 PRINT "NEW SET OF DATA."
900 PRINT "=== === == ====="
910 PRINT
920 GOTO 80
930 REM SUBROUTINE TO CHECK THAT DATA ARE CORRECT AND ALTER IF NECESSARY
940 PRINT "ARE THE DATA VALUES ENTERED CORRECT?";
950 REM A4 SHOULD BE SET TO THE NUMBER OF LINES ON THE VDU
960 LET A4 = 20
970 GOSUB 1840
980 IF Q$ = "YES" THEN 1820
990 PRINT "HERE IS A LIST OF THE CURRENT DATA"
1000 PRINT "LINE NUMBER", "Y"
1010 FOR I = 1 TO N
1020    PRINT I, Y(I)
1030    IF INT(1 / (A4 - 1)) * (A4 - 1) <> I THEN 1070
1040    PRINT "WOULD YOU LIKE TO CONTINUE LISTING";
1050    GOSUB 1840
1060    IF Q$ = "NO" THEN 1080
1070 NEXT I
1080 PRINT "TYPE R TO REPLACE";
1090 IF I$ = "NO" THEN 1110
1100 PRINT " AN EXISTING LINE OF DATA"
1110 IF N = 200 THEN 1160
1120 PRINT TAB(5); " A TO ADD";
1130 IF I$ = "NO" THEN 1150
1140 PRINT " AN EXTRA LINE"
1150 IF N = 1 THEN 1190
1160 PRINT TAB(5); " D TO DELETE";
1170 IF I$ = "NO" THEN 1190
1180 PRINT " AN EXISTING LINE"
1190 PRINT TAB(5); " L TO LIST";
1200 IF I$ = "NO" THEN 1220
1210 PRINT " THE DATA"
1220 PRINT "  OR C TO CONTINUE";
```

156

```
1230 IF I$ = "NO" THEN 1250
1240 PRINT " THE CALCULATION"
1250 INPUT Q$
1260 IF Q$ = "R" THEN 1360
1270 IF N = 200 THEN 1300
1280 IF Q$ = "A" THEN 1490
1290 IF N = 1 THEN 1310
1300 IF Q$ = "D" THEN 1680
1310 IF Q$ = "L" THEN 990
1320 IF Q$ = "C" THEN 1820
1330 PRINT "REPLY '"; Q$; "' NOT UNDERSTOOD."
1340 GOTO 1080
1350 REM REPLACE LINE
1360 PRINT "TYPE THE LINENUMBER OF THE LINE TO BE REPLACED";
1370 INPUT I
1380 IF I <> INT(I) THEN 1400
1390 IF (I - 1) * (I - N) <= 0 THEN 1430
1400 PRINT "LINENUMBER MUST BE AN INTEGER IN THE RANGE 1 -"; N
1410 PRINT "RE-";
1420 GOTO 1360
1430 PRINT "TYPE THE CORRECT LINE TO REPLACE THE ONE WHICH IS WRONG:"
1440 PRINT " Y"
1450 INPUT Y(I)
1460 PRINT "OK"
1470 GOTO 1080
1480 REM ADD A NEW LINE
1490 PRINT "REMEMBER THAT THE ORDER OF THE VALUES IS IMPORTANT"
1500 PRINT "TYPE THE LINENUMBER OF THE LINE IMMEDIATELY BEFORE"
1510 PRINT "THE PLACE WHERE YOU WISH TO INSERT A NEW VALUE"
1520 INPUT N1
1530 IF N1 = INT(N1) THEN 1570
1540 PRINT "LINE NUMBER MUST BE AN INTEGER"
1550 PRINT "RE-";
1560 GOTO 1500
1570 IF N1 * (N1 - N) <= 0 THEN 1600
1580 PRINT "LINE NUMBER MUST BE IN THE RANGE 0 TO"; N
1590 GOTO 1550
1600 FOR I = N + 1 TO N1 + 2 STEP -1
1610    LET Y(I) = Y(I - 1)
1620 NEXT I
1630 PRINT "TYPE IN THE Y VALUE TO BE ADDED"
1640 INPUT Y(N1 + 1)
1650 LET N = N + 1
1660 PRINT "OK"
1670 GOTO 990
1680 REM DELETE A LINE
1690 PRINT "TYPE THE LINENUMBER OF THE LINE TO BE DELETED"
1700 INPUT J
1710 IF (J - 1) * (J - N) > 0 THEN 1730
1720 IF J = INT(J) THEN 1760
1730 PRINT "LINENUMBER MUST BE AN INTEGER IN THE RANGE 1 -"; N
1740 PRINT "RE-";
1750 GOTO 1690
1760 FOR I = J + 1 TO N
1770    LET Y(I - 1) = Y(I)
1780 NEXT I
1790 LET N = N - 1
1800 IF J > N THEN 1460
1810 GOTO 1660
1820 RETURN
1830 REM SUBROUTINE TO CHECK REPLIES
```

```
1840 IF I$ = "NO" THEN 1860
1850 PRINT " TYPE YES OR NO & PRESS RETURN."
1860 PRINT
1870 INPUT Q$
1880 IF Q$ = "YES" THEN 1920
1890 IF Q$ = "NO" THEN 1920
1900 PRINT "REPLY '"; Q$; "' NOT UNDERSTOOD.";
1910 GOTO 1850
1920 RETURN
1930 REM TERMINATE JOB
1940 PRINT "JOB COMPLETED"
1950 END
```

this is added the area of the last trapezium to give the total area which is then printed (lines 720–730).

Finally the user is offered the option of another run (line 750). The answer must be YES or NO and is checked in a subroutine (lines 1830–1920). If another run is required, a choice is offered between typing in completely new data, or editing and re-running the data used for the last run.

Exercises

11.1 Estimate the area under the curve from $x=0$ to $x=6$ using the following data:

x	0	1	2	3	4	5	6
y	0	1	8	27	64	125	216

(a) using the trapezium rule;
(b) using Simpson's rule;
(c) by direct integration of $y=x^3$.

11.2 The five points given below all lie on the circumference of a circle of unit radius

x	-1	$-\frac{1}{2}$	0	$\frac{1}{2}$	1
y	0	$\frac{1}{2}\sqrt{3}$	1	$\frac{1}{2}\sqrt{3}$	0

Calculate the area under the curve

(a) using the trapezium rule;
(b) using Simpson's rule;
(c) from elementary geometry.

11.3 Repeat Question 11.2 including the addition points:

x	$-\frac{3}{4}$	$-\frac{1}{4}$	$\frac{1}{4}$	$\frac{3}{4}$
y	$\frac{1}{4}\sqrt{7}$	$\frac{1}{4}\sqrt{15}$	$\frac{1}{4}\sqrt{15}$	$\frac{1}{4}\sqrt{7}$

Why do these three answers agree more closely?

12

Sorting Techniques

Bubble Sort

Consider a list of n numbers which must be sorted into descending order.

Method

(i) Compare the first two values. If they are the wrong way round, i.e. the first value is smaller than the second value, then the two values are exchanged. Otherwise no action is taken.

(ii) Values two and three in the list are then compared, and exchanged if necessary.

(iii) Similarly values three and four are compared, then values four and five are compared, etc.

(iv) To complete the first pass through the data, the values $(n-1)$ and (n) are compared, and exchanged if necessary.

(v) The position in the list where the last exchange occurred is noted for use in the next pass.

(vi) The above steps are repeated from step (i) up to the point immediately before the place in the list where the last exchange occurred on the previous pass. There is no need to go beyond this point since all later values must be correctly ordered. When a pass is made through the data without any exchanges, then sorting is complete.

Example

Consider sorting the data 3, 2, 4, 5, 1, 2 into descending order.

The terms being compared are underlined:

3 2 4 5 1 2
                   3 is >2 so not exchanged
3 2 4 5 1 2
                   2 is <4 so terms exchanged
3 4 2 5 1 2
                exchanged
3 4 5 2 1 2
                not exchanged
3 4 5 2 1 2
                exchanged
3 4 5 2 2 1

End of first pass through data.
Last exchange was comparison 5 so do four comparisons in next pass.

3 4 5 2 2 1
exchanged
4 3 5 2 2 1
exchanged
4 5 3 2 2 1
not exchanged
4 5 3 2 2 1
not exchanged
4 5 3 2 2 1

End of second pass through data.
Last exchange was comparison 2 so do one comparison in next pass.

4 5 3 2 2 1
              exchanged
5 4 3 2 2 1

End of third pass through data.
Last exchange was comparison 1 so do no comparisons in next pass, i.e. sorting is finished.

Description of Bubble Sort Program (see Program 12.1)

In common with the other BASIC programs for sorting, this program comprises two parts. The first 15 lines input the data to be sorted, call the subroutine to perform the sort, and finally print out the sorted values. This part is provided so that the sorting subroutines may be tried and tested, but it is intended that the second part (the sorting subroutine itself) be included in the users' own programs. For this reason the first part has been kept simple and small rather than longer and student proof!

The subroutine for bubble sorting extends from lines 990 to 1140. The number of comparisons B required in the first pass is evaluated at line 1000, and line 1010 sets the pointer C for the place where the last exchange was made to zero. A loop (lines 1020–1110) performs the B comparisons in each pass. A comparison is made (line 1030) between one term, and the next in the list. If these two terms are in the correct order, the program jumps to the end of the loop, but otherwise the X values are exchanged (lines 1040–1060) and the Y values are exchanged (lines 1070–1090). Furthermore the flag C is set to indicate the place in this list where the exchange occurred. When a complete pass has been made, the value of B the number of comparisons is recalculated (line 1120), and should B be zero (line 1130), the order is correct. Otherwise a new pass is started from line 1010 onwards.

To use the subroutine in other programs, the data values should be stored in arrays X and Y, and the number of data pairs should be stored in N. The values will be ranked into descending order of X. If there are no Y values in a particular application then lines 1070–1090 should be omitted. Finally if the values are required in ascending order, the greater than ($>$) symbol in line 1030 should be replaced by a less than ($<$) symbol.

Program 12.1

```
10  DIM X(100), Y(100)
20  PRINT "TYPE NUMBER OF DATA VALUES"
30  INPUT N
40  PRINT "TYPE PAIRS OF VALUES SEPARATED BY A COMMA"
50  PRINT "AND PRESS RETURN AFTER EACH PAIR"
60  FOR I = 1 TO N
70    INPUT X(I), Y(I)
80  NEXT I
90  REM CALL BUBBLE SORT SUBROUTINE
100 GOSUB 1000
110 PRINT "SORTED VALUES"
120 FOR I = 1 TO N
130   PRINT X(I), Y(I)
140 NEXT I
150 PRINT "FINISHED"
160 STOP
990 REM *** SUBROUTINE FOR BUBBLE SORT
1000 LET B = N - 1
1010 LET C = 0
1020 FOR L = 1 TO B
1030   IF X(L) >= X(L + 1) THEN 1110
1040   LET T = X(L)
1050   LET X(L) = X(L + 1)
1060   LET X(L + 1) = T
1070   LET T = Y(L)
1080   LET Y(L) = Y(L + 1)
1090   LET Y(L + 1) = T
1100   LET C = L
1110 NEXT L
1120 LET B = C - 1
1130 IF B > 0 THEN 1010
1140 RETURN
1150 END
```

Insertion Sort

Consider a list of n numbers which must be sorted into descending order.

Method

The principle of this method is gradually to produce an ordered list of i numbers by taking the ith term and inserting it at the appropriate point in the already ordered section of $i-1$ numbers at the beginning of the list. The process is repeated for all values of i from 2 to n, producing a totally ordered list. This is best explained with an example:

The numbers 3, 2, 5, 4 are to be arranged in descending order.

(i) Initially $i=2$, so the second term (the number 2) is to be inserted into the already ordered list of one term (the number 3).

(ii) This produces an ordered list of two terms 3, 2.

(iii) For $i=3$, the third term (the number 5) is to be inserted into the ordered list of 3, 2.

(iv) This produces the ordered list of three terms 5, 3, 2.

(v) Finally $i=4$, and the fourth term (the number 4) is to be inserted into the ordered list of 5, 3, 2 to give the correctly sorted list of 5, 4, 3, 2. The algorithm used by the program may be illustrated by considering step (v) in detail.

(a) Firstly the ith term in the list is stored temporarily in a variable A.

(b) The ordered list of $i-1$ terms is scanned starting from the end (right-hand side). If A is greater than the current value being examined in the list, then the current value in the list is copied one place further down the list. If A is less than or equal to the current value then the value of A is written into the list in the position immediately to the right of the current value, overwriting the number already there.

In the example:

$A = 4$ and the ordered list is 5, 3, 2.

Since 4 is greater than 2, the value of 2 is copied to produce the list 5, 3, 2, 2.

(c) The scan continues with the next value in the list (the number 3). Since $A=4$ and this is greater than 3, the value of 3 is copied to produce the list 5, 3, 3, 2.

(d) The scan continues with the next value in the list (the number 5). Since A is less than the current value in the list (5), the value of A is copied into the list immediately after the current value to produce the list 5, 4, 3, 2.

Description of the Insert Sort Program (Program 12.2)

The first 15 lines allow the user to input a series of X, Y data pairs into arrays and to print them after being sorted into descending order of X. The remainder of the program comprises two subroutines.

The first subroutine (lines 990–1050) loops through the terms one at a time from $i=2$, 3, 4, ..., n. The X_i and Y_i values are stored temporarily in the variables A and B, and the second subroutine (lines 1060–1190) is called. This finds the appropriate place to insert the values of A and B into the ordered list. Lines 1080–1130 scan back through the ordered list, copying terms one place to the right until the correct place is found to insert A and B. Lines 1170 and 1180 insert the values of A and B into the correct position in the list unless the values are to be inserted into the first position, in which case lines 1140 and 1150 are used.

The following technical points are worthy of note:

161

(i) The two subroutines may be incorporated into the user's own program to sort N data pairs which have been stored in the arrays X and Y.

(ii) Alternatively the second subroutine alone may be used in another program. This is particularly advantageous if the data values are being input from a keyboard, since the terms are ordered as they are typed in. The computer time needed to insert a value in the correct place is small compared with the time taken to type the value. Thus sorting appears to take no time, that is, it is transparent to the user, unless the list is very large. An example of the input loop required to do this is given below:

```
10 DIM X(100), Y(100)
20 FOR I = 1 TO 100
30 INPUT A, B
40 GOSUB 1070
50 NEXT I
```

(iii) The subroutine may be modified to sort numbers into ascending order simply by changing the greater than ($>$) symbol in line 1090 into a less than ($<$) symbol.

(iv) If Y values are not required then lines 1020, 1110, 1150 and 1180 should be

Program 12.2

```
10 DIM X(100), Y(100)
20 PRINT "TYPE NUMBER OF DATA VALUES"
30 INPUT N
40 PRINT "TYPE PAIRS OF VALUES SEPARATED BY A COMMA"
50 PRINT "AND PRESS RETURN AFTER EACH PAIR"
60 FOR I = 1 TO N
70    INPUT X(I), Y(I)
80 NEXT I
90 REM CALL INSERT SORT SUBROUTINE
100 GOSUB 1000
110 PRINT "SORTED VALUES"
120 FOR I = 1 TO N
130    PRINT X(I), Y(I)
140 NEXT I
150 PRINT "FINISHED"
160 STOP
990 REM *** SUBROUTINE TO PERFORM INSERTION SORT
1000 FOR I = 2 TO N
1010    LET A = X(I)
1020    LET B = Y(I)
1030    GOSUB 1070
1040 NEXT I
1050 RETURN
1060 REM *** SUBROUTINE TO INSERT DATA PAIR A, B
1070 IF I = 1 THEN 1140
1080 LET J = I - 1
1090 IF X(J) > A THEN 1170
1100 LET X(J + 1) = X(J)
1110 LET Y(J + 1) = Y(J)
1120 LET J = J - 1
1130 IF J > 0 THEN 1090
1140 LET X(1) = A
1150 LET Y(1) = B
1160 GOTO 1190
1170 LET X(J + 1) = A
1180 LET Y(J + 1) = B
1190 RETURN
1200 END
```

omitted, and the DIMension of Y should be removed from line 10.

(v) It should be noted that the amount of work done, and hence the time taken by this subroutine varies considerably, depending on the order of the original data.

Selection Sort

Consider a list of n numbers which must be sorted into descending order.

Method

(i) A search is made through all the numbers in the list to find the highest value.
(ii) The first value in the list and the highest value are exchanged.
(iii) A search is made starting from the second value in the list, to find the highest remaining value.
(iv) The second value in the list and the highest remaining value are exchanged.
(v) A search is made starting with the third value, values are exchanged, and the process repeated with all subsequent terms in the list.

Example

Sort the numbers 3, 1, 4, 5, 2, into descending order.

Step (i)   5 is the largest
Step (ii)   exchange 5 and 3
            5,| 1, 4, 3, 2
Step (iii) 4 is the largest remaining value
            exchange 4 and 1
            5, 4,| 1, 3, 2
Step (iv)   3 is the largest remaining value
Step (v)   exchange 3 and 1
            5, 4, 3,| 1, 2
Step (vi)   2 is the largest remaining value
Step (vii) exchange 2 and 1
            5, 4, 3, 2, 1
The sort is now completed.

Description of the Selection Sort Program (Program 12.3)

The first 15 lines are written to demonstrate the use of the selection sort subroutine. These lines permit the user to enter N pairs of X and Y values, which are to be sorted into descending order of X. When sorted, the values are printed.

The subroutine extends from lines 990 to 1150, and works in the following manner. The outer loop from lines 1000 to 1140 chooses the position in the list which is to be filled with the highest remaining value in the list. The inner loop (lines 1030–1070) searches all the positions to the right of this point to find the maximum remaining value. The maximum value found is exchanged with the number in the position chosen by the outer loop in lines 1090–1130. The outer loop then selects the next position and the whole process is repeated.

To make the subroutine rank the numbers into ascending order simply change the less than or equal ($< =$) symbol into a greater than or equal ($> =$) symbol in line 1040. Should Y values not be required, omit lines 1110, 1120 and 1130, and remove Y from the DIMension statement.

Finally it should be noted that the time taken by this subroutine depends mainly on the number of data values, and is almost independent of their order.

Address Sort

This is an extremely fast method of sorting one single set of small positive integer numbers in the range 1 to M, or numbers which can be converted into integers in this range.

Method

(i) The integer numbers to be sorted are stored in an array (in this case the X array).

Program 12.3 Selection sort program.

```
10 DIM X(100), Y(100)
20 PRINT "TYPE NUMBER OF DATA VALUES"
30 INPUT N
40 PRINT "TYPE PAIRS OF VALUES SEPARATED BY A COMMA"
50 PRINT "AND PRESS RETURN AFTER EACH PAIR"
60 FOR I = 1 TO N
70    INPUT X(I), Y(I)
80 NEXT I
90 REM CALL SELECTION SORT SUBROUTINE
100 GOSUB 1000
110 PRINT "SORTED VALUES"
120 FOR I = 1 TO N
130    PRINT X(I), Y(I)
140 NEXT I
150 PRINT "FINISHED"
160 STOP
990 REM *** SUBROUTINE TO PERFORM SELECTION SORT
1000 FOR I = 1 TO N - 1
1010    LET M = X(I)
1020    LET P = I
1030    FOR J = I + 1 TO N
1040       IF X(J) <= M THEN 1070
1050       LET M = X(J)
1060       LET P = J
1070    NEXT J
1080    REM *** LARGEST REMAINING VALUE TO POSITION I
1090    LET X(P) = X(I)
1100    LET X(I) = M
1110    LET M = Y(P)
1120    LET Y(P) = Y(I)
1130    LET Y(I) = M
1140 NEXT I
1150 RETURN
1160 END
```

(ii) A second array A is required, of length M, where M is greater than or equal to the largest term in the X array.

(iii) All the elements in the A array must initially be set to zero.

(iv) The first value in the X array is examined and found to have the value V. The value of the element A_V, i.e. $A(V)$ is increased by one. This process is repeated for the second and subsequent values in turn. When this process is complete, the original numbers in the X array have not been changed, but the A array contains the number of occurrences of any particular number. Thus $A(1)$ contains the number of ones, $A(2)$ contains the number of twos, etc.

(v) The ordered list may be produced from the A array in the following way. The array element $A(M)$ is examined, and found to have the value W. The number M is then written into the X array W times. The process is repeated for $A(M-1)$, $A(M-2)$, ..., $A(1)$, and the X array now contains the ordered values.

Certain limitations are imposed by the method and the computer. Firstly, the method does not cater for X, Y pairs of data values. Secondly, the method is restricted to integers. Thirdly, the magnitude of the largest number to be sorted determines the length of the A array. The amount of computer memory available limits the maximum size of the array, and hence the largest number which can be sorted. Fourthly, the method will not handle numbers smaller than one. This is because BASIC does not allow negative subscripts to array elements. (Some but by no means all dialects of BASIC will permit the use of zero as an array subscript.) To handle zero or negative numbers, the data values should be biased by adding a suitable constant to all of them so that they become positive numbers.

Description of the Address Sort Program (see Program 12.4)

The first 15 lines of program allow the user to type in the set of values which are to be sorted, and to print them after sorting.

The address sorting subroutine extends from lines 980 to 1160. A loop (lines 1000–1020) sets the elements of the A array to zero, since this is not done automatically in all implementations of BASIC. A second loop (lines 1030–1060) performs step (iv) outlined above, and a third loop (lines 1080–1150) performs step (v).

To make the subroutine sort into ascending order replace the existing line 1080 with:

1080 FOR I = 1 to M

Some but not all dialects of BASIC permit integer variables and arrays to be declared. This program will run considerably faster if this can be done. It should be noted that the time taken by this subroutine is independent of the initial order of the data values.

Shell Sort

The principle of this method is that pairs of

Program 12.4

```
10 DIM X(100),A(100)
20 LET M = 100
30 PRINT "TYPE THE NUMBER OF DATA VALUES"
40 INPUT N
50 PRINT "TYPE VALUES ONE AT A TIME & PRESS RETURN"
60 FOR I = 1 TO N
70    INPUT X(I)
80 NEXT I
90 REM CALL ADDRESS SORTING SUBROUTINE
100 GOSUB 1000
110 PRINT "SORTED VALUES"
120 FOR I = 1 TO N
130    PRINT X(I)
140 NEXT I
150 PRINT "FINISHED"
160 STOP
980 REM ADDRESS SORTING ROUTINE
990 REM *** ONLY FOR +VE INTEGERS < = M (SIZE OF ARRAY A)
1000 FOR I = 1 TO M
1010    LET A(I) = 0
1020 NEXT I
1030 FOR I = 1 TO N
1040    LET V = X(I)
1050    LET A(V) = A(V) + 1
1060 NEXT I
1070 LET V = 1
1080 FOR I = M TO 1 STEP -1
1090    LET W = A(I)
1100    IF W = 0 THEN 1150
1110    LET X(V) = I
1120    LET W = W - 1
1130    LET V = V + 1
1140    IF W <> 0 THEN 1110
1150 NEXT I
1160 RETURN
1170 END
```

numbers a long way apart in the data list (L places apart), are compared, and exchanged if necessary. Having exchanged a pair of values, the uppermost value is compared with the value L places above it to see if a further exchange is necessary, etc. After a complete pass, the value of L is halved and the process repeated. By these means a data value can 'move' a long way in the list with very few comparisons, making this one of the fastest, simple and general methods for sorting. This program is based on the algorithm by D. L. Shell (*Communications of the ACM*, July 1959).

The method is best illustrated by an example.

Original data 10, 2, 8, 4, 6, 3, 1, 5
Set L the number of places apart to 4.
Compare terms 1 and L+1, i.e. 10 and 6.
These are correctly ordered and are not exchanged.
Next compare terms 2 and L+2, i.e. 2 and 3.
These are the wrong way round and are exchanged.
   10, 3, 8, 4, 6, 2, 1, 5
The number 3 cannot be moved further.
Next compare terms 3 and L+3, i.e. 8 and 1.
These are correctly ordered and are not exchanged.
Next compare terms 4 and L+4, i.e. 4 and 5.
These are the wrong way round and are exchanged.
   10, 3, 8, 5, 6, 2, 1, 4
The number 5 cannot be moved further.
A complete pass has now been performed, and the value of L is halved, i.e. L=2.
10 and 8 are compared but not exchanged.
3 and 5 are compared and exchanged. 5 cannot be moved any further
   10, 5, 8, 3, 6, 2, 1, 4
8 and 6, 3 and 2, and 6 and 1, are compared in turn but not exchanged. 2 and 4 are compared and exchanged:
   10, 5, 8, 3, 6, 4, 1, 2
The 4 just moved is then compared with the

value L places to the left in the list, in this case number 3. Since these are the wrong way round they are exchanged.
   10, 5, 8, 4, 6, 3, 1, 2
Similarly 4 is compared with 5 and no exchange is required.
Since there are no further comparisons on this line, the pass is complete. The value of L is halved, and the process repeated for one further pass.

Description of the Shell Sort Program (see Program 12.5)

The first 15 lines comprise a loop to allow the user to input up to 100 pairs of X, Y values, and after being sorted the values are printed out.

The sorting subroutine extends from lines 990 to 1180. First the step interval L is calculated (line 1010), then a loop from lines 1040–1160 performs one complete pass through the data. The comparison of the two appropriate terms occurs at line 1070, and if necessary values are exchanged (lines 1080–1130). If an exchange has occurred, the possibility of making a second move is checked in lines 1140–1150. After a complete pass through the data, line 1170 jumps back to halve the value of L at line 1010. Provided L is not zero another pass is performed.

To make the algorithm sort into ascending order, it is only necessary to change the greater than or equal ($> =$) symbol in line 1070 to a less than or equal ($< =$) symbol. If Y values are not required, omit lines 1110–1130 in the subroutine, and remove the DIMension for Y from line 10. Finally the time taken to run this subroutine does depend on the order of the data values. However the algorithm quickly moves freak data into place.

Variations on the Shell Sort

The optimum sequence of L values (for the distance between numbers to be compared) has not been determined. In the example

Program 12.5

```
10  DIM X(100), Y(100)
20  PRINT "TYPE NUMBER OF DATA VALUES"
30  INPUT N
40  PRINT "TYPE PAIRS OF VALUES SEPARATED BY A COMMA"
50  PRINT "AND PRESS RETURN AFTER EACH PAIR"
60  FOR I = 1 TO N
70     INPUT X(I), Y(I)
80  NEXT I
90  REM CALL SHELL SORT SUBROUTINE
100 GOSUB 1000
110 PRINT "SORTED VALUES"
120 FOR I = 1 TO N
130    PRINT X(I), Y(I)
140 NEXT I
150 PRINT "FINISHED"
160 STOP
990 REM *** SUBROUTINE TO PERFORM SHELL SORT
1000 LET L = N
1010 LET L = INT(L / 2)
1020 IF L = 0 THEN 1180
1030 LET M = N - L
1040 FOR I = 1 TO M
1050    LET J = I
1060    LET J2 = J + L
1070    IF X(J) >= X(J2) THEN 1160
1080    LET T = X(J)
1090    LET X(J) = X(J2)
1100    LET X(J2) = T
1110    LET T = Y(J)
1120    LET Y(J) = Y(J2)
1130    LET Y(J2) = T
1140    LET J = J - L
1150    IF J > 0 THEN 1060
1160 NEXT I
1170 GOTO 1010
1180 RETURN
1190 END
```

given, there were eight data values to be sorted, and the first value selected for L was $8/2 = 4$. In each subsequent pass the value of L is halved, giving values of 2 and 1 respectively. The sequence of L values may significantly affect the time taken to sort the data.

A pathological case may arise if the number of data values is a power of two. The sample described above has $2^3 = 8$ data points and constitutes such a pathological case. Since all but the last of the values of L are even, it follows that up till the last pass all comparisons are made between either two even positions in the data list or between two odd positions. Immediately prior to the last pass, all of the even positions have been ranked with respect to each other, and similarly all of the odd positions have been ordered with respect

to each other. This is shown by the last line given for the worked example:

Odd position in list

| 10 | 8 | 6 | 1 |

Even position in list

| | 5 | 4 | 3 | 2 |

Plainly this requires a large number of exchanges during the final pass when $L = 1$, and will result in an abnormally large time being taken for this particular case. The position would be even worse if all the odd positions held numbers which are larger than those in even positions or vice versa. This abnormal behaviour can be overcome by selecting odd values for L. Two ways of achieving this are to use values for L of 7, 5, 3 and 1 or alternatively to evaluate L as

2*INT($L/4$)+1 for each successive pass. The coding of the program may be amended as follows:

7, 3, 5, 1

1000 LET $L = 9$

1010 LET $L = L - 2$

delete line 1020

1170 IF $L > 1$ THEN 1010

2*INT(L/4)+1

1010 LET $L = 2*INT(L/4)+1$

delete line 1020

1170 IF $L > 1$ THEN 1010

Ranking an Array of Numbers (see Program 12.6)

For many applications it is not necessary to sort physically a series of numbers into order but it is required to assign ranks to the numbers. This may be needed for ranked correlations (see Chapter 7, Spearman and Kendall) or producing positions from examination marks.

The following program (Program 12.6) first prints a heading (lines 20–30) and then asks how many values are to be ranked (line 50). The value typed is checked to ensure that it is an integer (lines 70–90) and that is is between 2 and 100 inclusive (lines 100–130). The upper limit is imposed by the DIMension of the three arrays in line 10.

The user is then invited to type in the data values (lines 150–160). The data input loop extends from lines 170–190 and stores the values in the X array.

The section from lines 220–300 ranks the X numbers in ascending order, storing the ranks in the A array. This section involves two nested FOR loops. The method of ranking may be explained by considering the first pass through the outer loop. The counter P is set to

Program 12.6   Trial run.

```
PROGRAM TO RANK NUMBERS IN ASCENDING & DESCENDING ORDER
======= == ==== ======= == ========= = ========== =====
TYPE NUMBER OF VALUES TO BE RANKED
? 9
TYPE IN THE FIRST DATA VALUE, AND PRESS RETURN,
THEN TYPE THE SECOND VALUE, RETURN, ETC.
? 1
? 2
? 3
? 25
? 25
? 7
? 8
? 9
? 25
END OF DATA INPUT
```

DATA VALUE	DESCENDING RANKS	ASCENDING RANKS
1	9	1
2	8	2
3	7	3
25	1	7
25	1	7
7	6	4
8	5	5
9	4	6
25	1	7

```
END OF JOB
```

```
10 DIM X(100), A(100), D(100)
20 PRINT "PROGRAM TO RANK NUMBERS IN ASCENDING & DESCENDING ORDER"
30 PRINT "======= == ==== ======= == ========= = ========== ====="
40 PRINT
50 PRINT "TYPE NUMBER OF VALUES TO BE RANKED"
60 INPUT N
70 IF N = INT(N) THEN 100
80 PRINT "NUMBER OF VALUES MUST BE AN INTEGER"
90 GOTO 120
100 IF (N - 2) * (N - 100) <= 0 THEN 140
110 PRINT "NUMBER OF VALUES MUST BE BETWEEN 2 & 100"
120 PRINT "RE-";
130 GOTO 50
140 REM ***START LOOP TO INPUT DATA
150 PRINT "TYPE IN THE FIRST DATA VALUE. AND PRESS RETURN,"
160 PRINT "THEN TYPE THE SECOND VALUE, RETURN, ETC."
170 FOR I = 1 TO N
180    INPUT X(I)
190 NEXT I
200 PRINT "END OF DATA INPUT"
210 PRINT
220 REM ***RANK INTO ASCENDING ORDER
230 FOR I = 1 TO N
240    LET P = 1
250    FOR J = 1 TO N
260      IF X(J) >= X(I) THEN 280
270      LET P = P + 1
280    NEXT J
290    LET A(I) = P
300 NEXT I
310 REM ***RANK INTO DESCENDING ORDER
320 FOR I = 1 TO N
330    LET P = 1
340    FOR J = 1 TO N
350      IF X(J) <= X(I) THEN 370
360      LET P = P + 1
370    NEXT J
380    LET D(I) = P
390 NEXT I
400 REM ***PRINT RESULTS
410 PRINT "DATA", "DESCENDING", "ASCENDING"
420 PRINT "VALUE", "RANKS", "RANKS"
430 FOR I = 1 TO N
440    PRINT X(I), D(I), A(I)
450 NEXT I
460 PRINT "END OF JOB"
470 END
```

MEDIAN, RANGE AND INTERQUARTILE RANGE
====== ===== === ============= =====

WOULD YOU LIKE FULL INSTRUCTIONS
TYPE YES OR NO AND PRESS RETURN.
? YES
THIS PROGRAM CALCULATES THE MEDIAN, RANGE AND INTERQUARTILE
RANGE FROM A SET OF DATA BY FIRST SORTING YOUR VALUES INTO
DESCENDING ORDER. YOU ARE REQUIRED TO SPECIFY HOW MANY
VALUES YOU HAVE AND PRESS RETURN, AND THEN TYPE IN THE
VALUES ONE AT A TIME, PRESSING RETURN AFTER EACH VALUE.

```
TYPE NUMBER OF DATA VALUES
? 9
TYPE THE DATA VALUES, ONE AT A TIME.
PRESS RETURN AFTER EACH VALUE
? 6
? 4
? 3
? 7
? 5
? 8
? 1
? 9
? 2
MEDIAN VALUE = 5
RANGE OF VALUES = 1 TO 9 EQUALS 8
INTERQUARTILE RANGE = 3 TO 7

WOULD YOU LIKE A LIST OF YOUR VALUES IN DESCENDING ORDER.
TYPE YES OR NO AND PRESS RETURN.
? YES
  9
  8
  7
  6
  5
  4
  3
  2
  1

WOULD YOU LIKE ANOTHER RUN
TYPE YES OR NO AND PRESS RETURN.
? NO
```

one and the inner loop compares the first number in the X array with each number in the array in turn. Each time a number is found which is less than the value of $X(1)$ the counter P is incremented. When the inner loop is finished, P holds the rank of $X(1)$ which is stored in array element $A(1)$. The outer loop repeats the procedure for the second, third and subsequent values.

The section from lines 310 to 390 generates the descending order ranks in a similar way and stores the values in the D array.

Finally the original data values and their corresponding descending and ascending ranks are printed out (lines 400–450).

The procedure adopted to resolve ties (if two or more numbers are equal) is to give each number the next available rank. One or more numbers are then omitted before assigning the next rank. This is the same method as is usual for examination results and athletics placings.

Ranks for Spearman's test usually resolve ties in different manner by halving—that is two numbers tie for third place, then both are allocated the rank of $3\frac{1}{2}$.

Description of Program to Calculate the Median (see Program 12.7)

After printing a heading (lines 20–30) the user is asked whether full instructions are required (line 50). The reply, which must be YES or NO is checked in a subroutine (lines 490–560). The instructions given in lines 80–120 are printed only on the first run if the answer is YES.

A message (line 140) requests the number of data values, and the value typed is checked (lines 160–190) to ensure that it is an integer, and between 4 and 100 inclusive. The lower limit is necessary since the inter-quartile range is subsequently calculated, and the upper limit is imposed by the DIMension of the X array in

Program 12.7

```
10 DIM X(100), Q$(9)
20 PRINT TAB(15); "MEDIAN, RANGE AND INTERQUARTILE RANGE"
30 PRINT TAB(15); "======  ===== === ============= ====="
40 PRINT
50 PRINT "WOULD YOU LIKE FULL INSTRUCTIONS"
60 GOSUB 500
70 IF Q$ = "NO" THEN 130
80 PRINT "THIS PROGRAM CALCULATES THE MEDIAN, RANGE AND INTERQUARTILE"
90 PRINT "RANGE FROM A SET OF DATA BY FIRST SORTING YOUR VALUES INTO"
100 PRINT "DESCENDING ORDER.  YOU ARE REQUIRED TO SPECIFY HOW MANY"
110 PRINT "VALUES YOU HAVE AND PRESS RETURN, AND THEN TYPE IN THE"
120 PRINT "VALUES ONE AT A TIME, PRESSING RETURN AFTER EACH VALUE."
130 PRINT
140 PRINT "TYPE NUMBER OF DATA VALUES"
150 INPUT N
160 IF N <> INT(N) THEN 180
170 IF (N - 4) * (N - 100) <= 0 THEN 200
180 PRINT "THE NUMBER OF VALUES MUST BE AN INTEGER BETWEEN 4 & 100"
190 GOTO 140
200 PRINT "TYPE THE DATA VALUES, ONE AT A TIME."
210 PRINT "PRESS RETURN AFTER EACH VALUE"
220 FOR I = 1 TO N
230    INPUT X(I)
240 NEXT I
250 REM CALL SHELL SORT SUBROUTINE
260 GOSUB 1000
270 LET M = INT((N + 1.001) / 2)
280 LET M1 = (N + 1) / 2 - M
290 PRINT "MEDIAN VALUE ="; (1 - M1) * X(M) + M1 * X(M + 1)
300 PRINT "RANGE OF VALUES ="; X(N); "TO"; X(1); "EQUALS"; X(1) - X(N)
310 LET Q = INT((3 * N + 1.001) / 4)
320 LET Q1 = (3 * N + 1) / 4 - Q
330 PRINT "INTERQUARTILE RANGE ="; (1 - Q1) * X(Q) + Q1 * X(Q + 1);
340 LET Q = INT((N + 3.001) / 4)
350 LET Q1 = (N + 3) / 4 - Q
360 PRINT "TO"; (1 - Q1) * X(Q) + Q1 * X(Q + 1)
370 PRINT
380 PRINT "WOULD YOU LIKE A LIST OF YOUR VALUES IN DESCENDING ORDER."
390 GOSUB 500
400 IF Q$ = "NO" THEN 440
410 FOR I = 1 TO N
420 PRINT X(I)
430 NEXT I
440 PRINT
450 PRINT "WOULD YOU LIKE ANOTHER RUN"
460 GOSUB 500
470 IF Q$ = "YES" THEN 130
480 STOP
490 REM *** SUBROUTINE TO CHECK YES/NO ANSWERS
500 PRINT "TYPE YES OR NO AND PRESS RETURN."
510 INPUT Q$
520 IF Q$ = "YES" THEN 560
530 IF Q$ = "NO" THEN 560
540 PRINT "REPLY '"; Q$; "' NOT UNDERSTOOD. RE-";
550 GOTO 500
560 RETURN
990 REM *** SUBROUTINE TO PERFORM SHELL SORT
1000 LET L = N
1010 LET L = INT(L / 2)
1020 IF L = 0 THEN 1180
```

```
1030 LET M = N - L
1040 FOR I = 1 TO M
1050    LET J = I
1060    LET J2 = J + L
1070    IF X(J) >= X(J2) THEN 1160
1080    LET T = X(J)
1090    LET X(J) = X(J2)
1100    LET X(J2) = T
1140    LET J = J - L
1150    IF J > 0 THEN 1060
1160 NEXT I
1170 GOTO 1010
1180 RETURN
1190 END
```

line 10. The requested number of data values are input (lines 220–240).

Next a subroutine is called (line 260) to sort the data values into descending order. The particular method used is the 'Shell sort' described earlier in the chapter, but other sorting methods may be used instead by replacing the subroutine from line 990 onwards. (It should be noted that lines 1110–1130 have been omitted from the general Shell sort subroutine given earlier, since in this application there are no Y values.)

The median value is calculated and printed (lines 270–290). If there is an odd number of data values then the middle value is selected as the median, but if there is an even number of values then the median is taken as the average of the two middle values.

The range of the numbers is printed (line 290) using the first and last of the values in the sorted list.

The inter-quartile range is calculated and printed (lines 310–360) by taking the two values corresponding to values $\frac{1}{4}$ and $\frac{3}{4}$ down the sorted list. The way in which this is done is illustrated by an example:

Values

| 12.5 | 7.9 | 6.3 | 5.5 | 4.3 | 2.8 |

Position in sorted list

| 1 | 2 | 3 | 4 | 5 | 6 |

Middle values

Median $= \frac{1}{2}(6.3 + 5.5) = 5.9$

Range $= 12.5 - 2.8 = 9.7$

Inter-quartile range = 2.25th value and 4.75th value

2.25th value

$$= \frac{(3 \times \text{second value}) + \text{third value}}{4}$$

$$= \frac{3 \times 7.9 + 6.3}{4} = 7.5$$

4.75th value

$$= \frac{\text{fourth value} + (3 \times \text{third value})}{4}$$

$$= \frac{5.5 + 3 \times 4.3}{4} = 4.6$$

Inter-quartile range

$= 4.6$ to 7.5

Following this the user is offered the option of printing an ordered list of the data values (lines 380–430) and finally the option of another run with new data is given (lines 450–470).

Discussion and Comparison of Sorting Methods

Five different methods of sorting data into ascending or descending order have been described. Variations on these and a number of additional methods are described in the literature. For those interested in further details, the following two references are recommended: D. E. Knuth, *The Art of Computer Programming*, Volume III *Sorting and Searching*, Addison Wesley 1971; E. S.

172

Page and L. B. Wilson, *Information Representation and Manipulation in a Computer*, Cambridge University Press 2nd edn 1978.

It would be most convenient if one of the sorting algorithms described out-performed all of the others regardless of the application or the initial arrangement of the data. Unfortunately this is not so, and each of the five methods has its own merits and limitations. These are discussed in the remainder of this chapter.

To provide some basis for comparison, timings were made for each of the five sorting methods using a PRIME 400 minicomputer running a BASIC interpreter under single user conditions. The times given (Table 12.1) are the times clocked by the computer in performing the sort and do *NOT* include the time to input the data, or to print it out after sorting.

The main timing measured was the time taken to order varying numbers of random values. For many situations, this is likely to be the most representative time, and the values given are the mean of several different runs. Since the times for some of the methods are very sensitive to the order of the starting data, the two extreme cases, (i) the 'best' order (starting data already in the correct order), and (ii) the 'worst' order (starting data in the inverse order), are also given. While there is no point in sorting data which are correctly ordered, these timings indicate how well a particular algorithm copes with partially ordered data.

The magnitude of the times taken may be greater by a large factor on less powerful machines. Furthermore variation in the relative times between the different methods may occur on other machines for the following reasons:

(i) The time taken to perform most sorts is largely determined by the number of comparisons made, and the number

Table 12.1

Name of sort	Order of data	Number of terms sorted							
		10	50	100	150	200	250	300	350
Bubble	Best	<0.1	0.1	0.1	0.1	0.2	0.3	0.3	0.4
	Random	0.1	2.6	10.8	23.8	43.0	67.0	95.7	132.4
	Worst	0.2	4.2	16.7	37.8	67.3	105.4	151.2	206.6
Insertion	Best	<0.1	0.2	0.3	0.4	0.6	0.7	0.9	1.0
	Random	0.1	1·5	5.7	12·6	22·9	34·2	49·9	69·9
	Worst	0.1	2.8	11.3	25.2	44.9	69.7	100.4	136.4
Selection	Best	<0.1	1.2	4.4	9.8	17.2	26.7	38.4	52.0
	Random	0.1	1.2	4.5	9.8	17.3	26.9	38.5	52.4
	Worst	0.1	1.3	4.8	10.6	18.6	28.8	41.3	56.1
Address	Best	1.4	1.5	1.5	1.6	1.7	1.8	1.8	1.9
	Random	1.4	1.5	1.5	1.6	1.7	1.8	1.8	1.9
	Worst	1.4	1.5	1.5	1.6	1.7	1.8	1.8	1.9
Shell	Best	<0.1	0.3	0.6	1.1	1.6	1.9	2.7	3.0
	Random	0.1	0.8	1.9	3.2	5.1	6.0	8.1	9.6
	Worst	0.1	0.6	1.5	2.5	3.5	4.9	5.9	7.4

The times given are real time seconds

of exchanges carried out. While the number of comparisons and exchanges required for a particular job will be the same on any computer, the relative times to perform these two operations may differ.

(ii) The time taken to access a particular element in an array varies considerably between different implementations of BASIC.

(iii) A growing number of microcomputer BASICs support a special function SWAP which exchanges two values. This is extremely fast, and correct implementation significantly improves bubble sort and shell sort and slightly improves selection sort.

(iv) Some versions of BASIC allow the user to differentiate between integer and real variables. A saving in time is accomplished by using integer variables for loop counters, etc., and even more time will be saved if the arrays are dimensioned as integers, though this of course requires that the numbers being sorted are also integers.

(v) Faster speeds will always be obtained by using a BASIC compiler rather than an interpreter. In addition it may affect the relative performance of the methods.

Bubble Sort While exchanging pairs of values is perhaps the most obvious method of sorting, the bubble sort has little to recommend it for general use, since the average times for random numbers are bad and the times for the worst case are disastrous! However, the minimum times for the bubble sort are extremely favourable, hence the method may be useful for data which are largely ordered. The average times are slow and increase with the number of terms squared, while the minimum time increases with the number of terms. The execution times will be considerably reduced if the SWAP function can be used.

Insertion Sort The concept of the insertion

sort is the same as a card player arranging his hand of cards by taking each card as it is dealt and inserting it into the correct place among the cards already sorted. The average times for random numbers and maximum execution times are considerably better than for the bubble sort, but are still fairly slow. The average times increase with the number of terms squared, but the best times are fairly fast and are proportional to the number of terms. A particular advantage of this method is that it may be used to order numbers as they are typed in, which makes the sorting time 'invisible'.

Selection Sort In principle the largest term in the list is selected and exchanged with the term in position one. The list is scanned again starting from position two, the largest term selected and exchanged with the term in position two—and so on. If there are *n* terms in the list, there will be only *n* exchanges, but a large number of comparisons are performed. The average timings for random numbers are slightly better than for the insertion-sort. It should be noted that there is hardly any difference between the best and worst times showing that this method is relatively insensitive to the order of the data. The timings will be slightly improved if the SWAP function can be used.

Address Sort The alogrithm described is extremely useful when applied to certain special cases in which the numbers to be sorted must be integers, and the range of the numbers must be sufficiently small. The latter restriction is because an array is required to store the frequency of each integer in the numbers to be sorted. This requires additional computer memory over and above that required for the array to store the original data. The method is analogous to keeping a tally sheet to record the frequencies of each integer in the input data. Reading back from the tally sheet then gives the data in the correct order. The timings shown are not strictly comparable with those from the other methods for the following reasons:

(i) Only one array X is being ranked, whereas the other methods sort both X, Y pairs into order of X.

(ii) The time taken partly depends on the range of the numbers, since the time taken to set the tally array A to zero at the beginning, and the time taken to read back the tally at the end depend on the maximum size M of the array A.

The timings shown permitted data values in the range 1–1000, and to achieve this the DIMension of A (line 10) and the value of M (line 20) were both set to 1000. Three points of interest emerge from the timings: (i) for sorting a moderately large number of terms the timings are spectacular; (ii) there is effectively no difference between the best and worst times; and (iii) for a small number of terms to be sorted the method is slower than the others because of overhead time in zeroing and reading the tally list.

Additional time-saving may be achieved in those implementations of BASIC which support matrix functions. On these, the loop to set the tally array to zero (lines 1000–1020) may be replaced by:

1000 MAT A = ZER

Shell Sort This is sometimes referred to as the diminishing increment sort, and in principle is similar to the bubble sort in that pairs of values are compared and exchanged. The two main differences are that values which are some distance apart in the list are compared, and if an exchange occurs a further comparison is made to determine whether to move the value again.

The times recorded for sorting random numbers are good, but the times for correctly ordered data are slower than for several of the other methods. Readers may find it hard to accept that the times recorded for the 'worst order' (i.e. data in ascending order) are smaller than those for ordering random data. Readers are invited to try the method on their own machine before suspecting a printing error! The Shell sort is particularly suited to sorting badly ordered data, and is the fastest of the general methods described in this chapter. The times can be further improved by the use of the SWAP.

Two common forms of the SWAP command are SWAP X, Y as used in Microsoft BASIC and EXCHANGE X, Y as used in Xitan disc BASIC.

In conclusion it can be seen that for sorting a small number of values there is little to choose between the methods, but for large numbers of values the method should be chosen with care.

Appendix 1

Significance Table for Pearson's Correlation Coefficient r

(Adapted for *Statistical Tables for Biological, Agricultural and Medical Research 6th edition*, by R. A. Fisher and F. Yates, Longman, 1974, by permission.)

Two-tailed	Probability of r occurring by chance				
	10%	5%	2%	1%	0·1%

No. of degrees of freedom (= number of x, y pairs minus two)

	10%	5%	2%	1%	0·1%
1	.987 69	.996 92	.999 507	.999 877	.999 998 8
2	.900 00	.950 00	.980 00	.990 000	.999 00
3	.805 4	.878 3	.934 33	.958 73	.991 16
4	.729 3	.811 4	.882 2	.917 20	.974 06
5	.669 4	.754 5	.832 9	.874 5	.950 74
6	.621 5	.706 7	.788 7	.834 3	.924 93
7	.582 2	.666 4	.749 8	.797 7	.898 2
8	.549 4	.631 9	.715 5	.764 6	.872 1
9	.521 4	.602 1	.685 1	.734 8	.847 1
10	.497 3	.576 0	.658 1	.707 9	.823 3
11	.476 2	.552 9	.633 9	.683 5	.801 0
12	.457 5	.532 4	.612 0	.661 4	.780 0
13	.440 9	.513 9	.592 3	.641 1	.760 3
14	.425 9	.497 3	.574 2	.622 6	.742 0
15	.412 4	.482 1	.557 7	.605 5	.724 6
16	.400 0	.468 3	.542 5	.589 7	.708 4
17	.388 7	.455 5	.528 5	.575 1	.693 2
18	.378 3	.443 8	.515 5	.561 4	.678 7
19	.368 7	.432 9	.503 4	.548 7	.665 2
20	.359 8	.422 7	.492 1	.536 8	.652 4
25	.323 3	.380 9	.445 1	.486 9	.597 4
30	.296 0	.349 4	.409 3	.448 7	.554 1
35	.274 6	.324 6	.381 0	.418 2	.518 9
40	.257 3	.304 4	.357 8	.393 2	.489 6
45	.242 8	.287 5	.338 4	.372 1	.464 8
50	.230 6	.273 2	.321 8	.354 1	.443 3
60	.210 8	.250 0	.294 8	.324 8	.407 8
70	.195 4	.231 9	.273 7	.301 7	.379 9
80	.182 9	.217 2	.256 5	.283 0	.356 8
90	.172 6	.205 0	.242 2	.267 3	.337 5
100	.163 8	.194 6	.230 1	.254 0	.321 1
One-tailed	5%	2·5%	1%	0·5%	0·05%

Appendix 2

Significance Table for Spearman's Rank Correlation Coefficient

		Probability of rho occurring by chance					
Two-tailed		20%	10%	5%	2%	1%	0.2%
Number of (x,y) pairs n	4	.8000	.8000				
	5	.7000	.8000	.9000	.9000		
	6	.6000	.7714	.8286	.8857	.9429	
	7	.5357	.6786	.7450	.8571	.8929	.9643
	8	.5000	.6190	.7143	.8095	.8571	.9286
	9	.4667	.5833	.6833	.7667	.8167	.9000
	10	.4424	.5515	.6364	.7333	.7818	.8667
	11	.4182	.5273	.6091	.7000	.7455	.8364
	12	.3986	.4965	.5804	.6713	.7273	.8182
	13	.3791	.4780	.5549	.6429	.6978	.7912
	14	.3626	.4593	.5341	.6220	.6747	.7670
	15	.3500	.4429	.5179	.6000	.6536	.7464
	16	.3382	.4265	.5000	.5824	.6324	.7265
	17	.3260	.4118	.4853	.5637	.6152	.7083
	18	.3148	.3994	.4716	.5480	.5975	.6904
	19	.3070	.3895	.4579	.5333	.5825	.6737
	20	.2977	.3789	.4451	.5203	.5684	.6586
	21	.2909	.3688	.4351	.5078	.5545	.6455
	22	.2829	.3597	.4241	.4963	.5426	.6318
	23	.2767	.3518	.4150	.4852	.5306	.6186
	24	.2704	.3435	.4061	.4748	.5200	.6070
	25	.2646	.3362	.3977	.4654	.5100	.5962
	26	.2588	.3299	.3894	.4564	.5002	.5856
	27	.2540	.3236	.3822	.4481	.4915	.5757
	28	.2490	.3175	.3749	.4401	.4828	.5660
	29	.2443	.3113	.3685	.4320	.4744	.5567
	30	.2400	.3059	.3620	.4251	.4665	.5479
	35	.2198	.2821	.3361	.3990	.4417	.5300
	40	.2052	.2634	.3139	.3725	.4125	.4948
	45	.1932	.2480	.2955	.3507	.3883	.4659
	50	.1831	.2350	.2800	.3323	.3680	.4415
	55	.1744	.2238	.2667	.3166	.3505	.4205
	60	.1669	.2141	.2552	.3029	.3353	.4023
	65	.1602	.2056	.2450	.2908	.3220	.3863
	70	.1543	.1980	.2360	.2801	.3101	.3720
	75	.1490	.1912	.2278	.2704	.2994	.3592
	80	.1442	.1851	.2205	.2617	.2898	.3477
	85	.1398	.1795	.2139	.2538	.2810	.3372
	90	.1358	.1744	.2078	.2466	.2730	.3276
	95	.1322	.1697	.2022	.2399	.2657	.3187
	100	.1288	.1653	.1970	.2338	.2589	.3106
One-tailed		10%	5%	2.5%	1%	0.5%	0.1%

The top of the table has been calculated exactly, whereas a slight approximation that the distribution of rho is normal with variance (n-1) has been used for n > 30.

Appendix 3

Significance Levels of Kendall's Rank Correlation Coefficient τ

Kendall's rank correlation coefficient τ between two different orders of n objects is given by

$$\tau = \frac{\text{No. of agreements in order} - \text{No. of disagreements}}{\frac{1}{2}n\,(n-1)}$$

all pairs being compared.

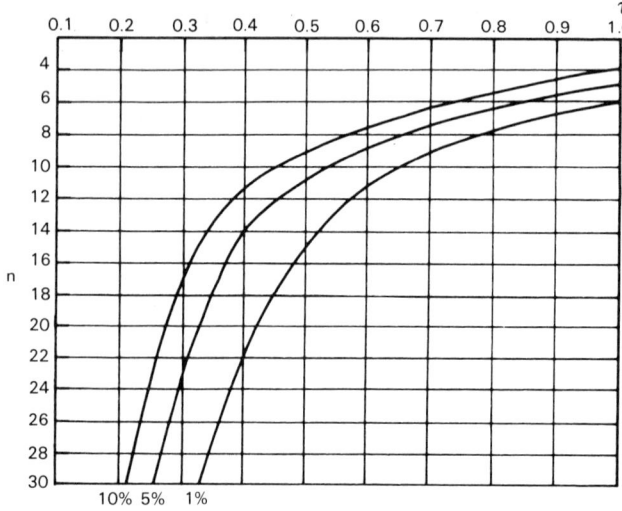

Appendix 4

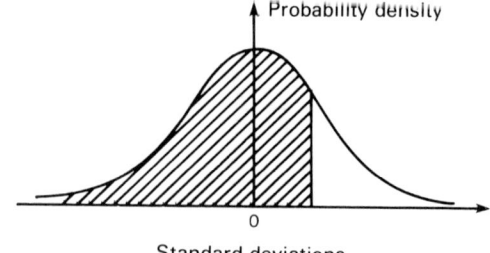

Probability density

0

Standard deviations

AREA UNDER NORMAL CURVE TABLE
==== ===== ====== ===== =====

NUMBER OF STANDARD DEVIATIONS	0.00	0.01	0.02	0.03	0.04	0.05	0.06	0.07	0.08	0.09
0.0	.5000	.5040	.5080	.5120	.5160	.5199	.5239	.5279	.5319	.5359
0.1	.5398	.5438	.5478	.5517	.5557	.5596	.5636	.5675	.5714	.5753
0.2	.5793	.5832	.5871	.5910	.5948	.5987	.6026	.6064	.6103	.6141
0.3	.6179	.6217	.6255	.6293	.6331	.6368	.6406	.6443	.6480	.6517
0.4	.6554	.6591	.6628	.6664	.6700	.6736	.6772	.6808	.6844	.6879
0.5	.6915	.6950	.6985	.7019	.7054	.7088	.7123	.7157	.7190	.7224
0.6	.7257	.7291	.7324	.7357	.7389	.7422	.7454	.7486	.7517	.7549
0.7	.7580	.7611	.7642	.7673	.7704	.7734	.7764	.7794	.7823	.7852
0.8	.7881	.7910	.7939	.7967	.7995	.8023	.8051	.8078	.8106	.8133
0.9	.8159	.8186	.8212	.8238	.8264	.8289	.8315	.8340	.8365	.8389
1.0	.8413	.8438	.8461	.8485	.8508	.8531	.8554	.8577	.8599	.8621
1.1	.8643	.8665	.8686	.8708	.8729	.8749	.8770	.8790	.8810	.8830
1.2	.8849	.8869	.8888	.8907	.8925	.8944	.8962	.8980	.8997	.9015
1.3	.9032	.9049	.9066	.9082	.9099	.9115	.9131	.9147	.9162	.9177
1.4	.9192	.9207	.9222	.9236	.9251	.9265	.9279	.9292	.9306	.9319
1.5	.9332	.9345	.9357	.9370	.9382	.9394	.9406	.9418	.9429	.9441
1.6	.9452	.9463	.9474	.9484	.9495	.9505	.9515	.9525	.9535	.9545
1.7	.9554	.9564	.9573	.9582	.9591	.9599	.9608	.9616	.9625	.9633
1.8	.9641	.9649	.9656	.9664	.9671	.9678	.9686	.9693	.9699	.9706
1.9	.9713	.9719	.9726	.9732	.9738	.9744	.9750	.9756	.9761	.9767
2.0	.9772	.9778	.9783	.9788	.9793	.9798	.9803	.9808	.9812	.9817
2.1	.9821	.9826	.9830	.9834	.9838	.9842	.9846	.9850	.9854	.9857
2.2	.9861	.9864	.9868	.9871	.9875	.9878	.9881	.9884	.9887	.9890
2.3	.9893	.9896	.9898	.9901	.9904	.9906	.9909	.9911	.9913	.9916
2.4	.9918	.9920	.9922	.9925	.9927	.9929	.9931	.9932	.9934	.9936
2.5	.9938	.9940	.9941	.9943	.9945	.9946	.9948	.9949	.9951	.9952
2.6	.9953	.9955	.9956	.9957	.9959	.9960	.9961	.9962	.9963	.9964
2.7	.9965	.9966	.9967	.9968	.9969	.9970	.9971	.9972	.9973	.9974
2.8	.9974	.9975	.9976	.9977	.9977	.9978	.9979	.9979	.9980	.9981
2.9	.9981	.9982	.9982	.9983	.9984	.9984	.9985	.9985	.9986	.9986
3.0	.9987	.9987	.9987	.9988	.9988	.9989	.9989	.9989	.9990	.9990
3.1	.9990	.9991	.9991	.9991	.9992	.9992	.9992	.9992	.9993	.9993
3.2	.9993	.9993	.9994	.9994	.9994	.9994	.9994	.9995	.9995	.9995
3.3	.9995	.9995	.9995	.9996	.9996	.9996	.9996	.9996	.9996	.9997
3.4	.9997	.9997	.9997	.9997	.9997	.9997	.9997	.9997	.9997	.9998
3.5	.9998	.9998	.9998	.9998	.9998	.9998	.9998	.9998	.9998	.9998

Area Under Normal Curve Table and Program to Produce it

```
10  PRINT TAB(26); "AREA UNDER NORMAL CURVE TABLE"
20  PRINT TAB(26); "==== ===== ====== ===== ====="
30  PRINT
40  PRINT "NUMBER OF"
50  PRINT "STANDARD"
60  PRINT "DEVIATIONS 0.00   0.01   0.02   0.03   0.04";
70  PRINT TAB(42); "0.05   0.06   0.07   0.08   0.09"
80  PRINT
90  FOR I = 0 TO 35
100   PRINT TAB(5); I / 10;
110   FOR J = 0 TO 9
120     LET X = I / 10 + J / 100
130     GOSUB 270
140     PRINT TAB(12 + 6 * J); INT((1 - F) * 10000 + .5) / 10000;
150   NEXT J
160   PRINT
170   IF INT(I / 5) * 5 <> I THEN 190
180     PRINT
190 NEXT I
200 PRINT
210 PRINT
220 PRINT "TABLE FINISHED"
230 GOTO 420
240 REM CALC CUMULATIVE AREA UNDER NORMAL CURVE
250 REM CONSTANTS SET FOR 8 FIGURE ACCURACY
260 REM USE ONLY FOR -4.5 TO 9 STANDARD DEVIATIONS
270 LET X9 = -X * .707107
280 LET T = 1 - 7.5 / (ABS(X9) + 3.75)
290 LET Y = 0
300 FOR I1 = 1 TO 12
310   READ C
320   LET Y = Y * T + C
330 NEXT I1
340 RESTORE
350 DATA 3.14753E-05, -.000138746, -6.41279E-06, .00178663
360 DATA -.00823169, .0241519, -.0547992, .102602
370 DATA -.163572, .226008, -.273422, .14559
380 LET F = 0.5 * EXP(-X9 * X9) * Y
390 IF X9 <= 0 THEN 410
400 LET F = 1 - F
410 RETURN
420 END
```

Appendix 5
Chi-Squared Significance Table

For larger v, $\sqrt{(2\chi^2)}$ is approximately normally distributed with mean $\sqrt{(2v-1)}$ and $\sigma^2 = 1$. (Reprinted from *Statistical Tables for Biological, Agricultural and Medical Research 6th edition*, by R. A. Fisher and F. Yates, Longman, 1974, by permission.)

No. of degrees of freedom v	Probability of chi-squared χ^2 occurring by chance													
	99%	98%	95%	90%	80%	70%	50%	30%	20%	10%	5%	2%	1%	0.1%
1	$.0^3157$	$.0^3628$	.00393	.0158	.0642	.148	.455	1.074	1.642	2.706	3.841	5.412	6.635	10.827
2	.0201	.0404	.103	.211	.446	.713	1.386	2.408	3.219	4.605	5.991	7.824	9.210	13.815
3	.115	.185	.352	.584	1.005	1.424	2.366	3.665	4.642	6.251	7.815	9.837	11.345	16.266
4	.297	.429	.711	1.064	1.649	2.195	3.357	4.878	5.989	7.779	9.488	11.668	13.277	18.467
5	.554	.752	1.145	1.610	2.343	3.000	4.351	6.064	7.289	9.236	11.070	13.388	15.086	20.515
6	.872	1.134	1.635	2.204	3.070	3.828	5.348	7.231	8.558	10.645	12.592	15.033	16.812	22.457
7	1.239	1.564	2.167	2.833	3.822	4.671	6.346	8.383	9.803	12.017	14.067	16.622	18.475	24.322
8	1.646	2.032	2.733	3.490	4.594	5.527	7.344	9.524	11.030	13.362	15.507	18.168	20.090	26.125
9	2.088	2.532	3.325	4.168	5.380	6.393	8.343	10.656	12.242	14.684	16.919	19.679	21.666	27.877
10	2.558	3.059	3.940	4.865	6.179	7.267	9.342	11.781	13.442	15.987	18.307	21.161	23.209	29.588
11	3.053	3.609	4.575	5.578	6.989	8.148	10.341	12.899	14.631	17.275	19.675	22.618	24.725	31.264
12	3.571	4.178	5.226	6.304	7.807	9.034	11.340	14.011	15.812	18.549	21.026	24.054	26.217	32.909
13	4.107	4.765	5.892	7.042	8.634	9.926	12.340	15.119	16.985	19.812	22.362	25.472	27.688	34.528
14	4.660	5.368	6.571	7.790	9.467	10.821	13.339	16.222	18.151	21.064	23.685	26.873	29.141	36.123
15	5.229	5.985	7.261	8.547	10.307	11.721	14.339	17.322	19.311	22.307	24.996	28.259	30.578	37.697
16	5.812	6.614	7.962	9.312	11.152	12.624	15.338	18.418	20.465	23.542	26.296	29.633	32.000	39.252
17	6.408	7.255	8.672	10.085	12.002	13.531	16.338	19.511	21.615	24.769	27.587	30.995	33.409	40.790
18	7.015	7.906	9.390	10.865	12.857	14.440	17.338	20.601	22.760	25.989	28.869	32.346	34.805	42.312
19	7.633	8.567	10.117	11.651	13.716	15.352	18.338	21.689	23.900	27.204	30.144	33.687	36.191	43.820
20	8.260	9.237	10.851	12.443	14.578	16.266	19.337	22.775	25.038	28.412	31.410	35.020	37.566	45.315
21	8.897	9.915	11.591	13.240	15.445	17.182	20.337	23.858	26.171	29.615	32.671	36.343	38.932	46.797
22	9.542	10.600	12.338	14.041	16.314	18.101	21.337	24.939	27.301	30.813	33.924	37.659	40.289	48.268
23	10.196	11.293	13.091	14.848	17.187	19.021	22.337	26.018	28.429	32.007	35.172	38.968	41.638	49.728
24	10.856	11.992	13.848	15.659	18.062	19.943	23.337	27.096	29.553	33.196	36.415	40.270	42.980	51.179
25	11.524	12.697	14.611	16.473	18.940	20.867	24.337	28.172	30.675	34.382	37.652	41.566	44.314	52.620
26	12.198	13.409	15.379	17.292	19.820	21.792	25.336	29.246	31.795	35.563	38.885	42.856	45.642	54.052
27	12.879	14.125	16.151	18.114	20.703	22.719	26.336	30.319	32.912	36.741	40.113	44.140	46.963	55.476
28	13.565	14.847	16.928	18.939	21.588	23.647	27.336	31.391	34.027	37.916	41.337	45.419	48.278	56.893
29	14.256	15.574	17.708	19.768	22.475	24.577	28.336	32.461	35.139	39.087	42.557	46.693	49.588	58.302
30	14.953	16.306	18.493	20.599	23.364	25.508	29.336	33.530	36.250	40.256	43.773	47.962	50.892	59.703
32	16.362	17.783	20.072	22.271	25.148	27.373	31.336	35.665	38.466	42.585	46.194	50.487	53.486	62.487
34	17.789	19.275	21.664	23.952	26.938	29.242	33.336	37.795	40.676	44.903	48.602	52.995	56.061	65.247
36	19.233	20.783	23.269	25.643	28.735	31.115	35.336	39.922	42.879	47.212	50.999	55.489	58.619	67.985
38	20.691	22.304	24.884	27.343	30.537	32.992	37.335	42.045	45.076	49.513	53.384	57.969	61.162	70.703
40	22.164	23.838	26.509	29.051	32.345	34.872	39.335	44.165	47.269	51.805	55.759	60.436	63.691	73.402
42	23.650	25.383	28.144	30.765	34.157	36.755	41.335	46.282	49.456	54.090	58.124	62.892	66.206	76.084
44	25.148	26.939	29.787	32.487	35.974	38.641	43.335	48.396	51.639	56.369	60.481	65.337	68.710	78.750
46	26.657	28.504	31.439	34.215	37.795	40.529	45.335	50.507	53.818	58.641	62.830	67.771	71.201	81.400
48	28.177	30.080	33.098	35.949	39.621	42.420	47.335	52.616	55.993	60.907	65.171	70.197	73.683	84.037
50	29.707	31.664	34.764	37.689	41.449	44.313	49.335	54.723	58.164	63.167	67.505	72.613	76.154	86.661
52	31.246	33.256	36.437	39.433	43.281	46.209	51.335	56.827	60.332	65.422	69.832	75.021	78.616	89.272
54	32.793	34.856	38.116	41.183	45.117	48.106	53.335	58.930	62.496	67.673	72.153	77.422	81.069	91.872
56	34.350	36.464	39.801	42.937	46.955	50.005	55.335	61.031	64.658	69.919	74.468	79.815	83.513	94.461
58	35.913	38.078	41.492	44.696	48.797	51.906	57.335	63.129	66.816	72.160	76.778	82.201	85.950	97.039
60	37.485	39.699	43.188	46.459	50.641	53.809	59.335	65.227	68.972	74.397	79.082	84.580	88.379	99.607
62	39.063	41.327	44.889	48.226	52.487	55.714	61.335	67.322	71.125	76.630	81.381	86.953	90.802	102.166
64	40.649	42.960	46.595	49.996	54.336	57.620	63.335	69.416	73.276	78.860	83.675	89.320	93.217	104.716
66	42.240	44.599	48.305	51.770	56.188	59.527	65.335	71.508	75.424	81.085	85.965	91.681	94.626	107.258
68	43.838	46.244	50.020	53.548	58.042	61.436	67.335	73.600	77.571	83.308	88.250	94.037	98.028	109.791
70	45.442	47.893	51.739	55.329	59.898	63.346	69.334	75.689	79.715	85.527	90.531	96.388	100.425	112.317

Appendix 6
t-Distribution Table

(Reprinted from *Statistical Tables for Biological, Agricultural and Medical Research 6th edition*, by R. A. Fisher, and F. Yates, Longman, 1974, by permission.)

Two-tailed	Probability of *t* occurring by chance												
	90%	80%	70%	60%	50%	40%	30%	20%	10%	5%	2%	1%	0.1%
No of degrees of freedom *v*													
1	.158	.325	.510	.727	1.000	1.376	1.963	3.078	6.314	12.706	31.821	63.657	636.619
2	.142	.289	.445	.617	.816	1.061	1.386	1.886	2.920	4.303	6.965	9.925	31.598
3	.137	.277	.424	.584	.765	.978	1.250	1.638	2.353	3.182	4.541	5.841	12.924
4	.134	.271	.414	.569	.741	.941	1.190	1.533	2.132	2.776	3.747	4.604	8.610
5	.132	.267	.408	.559	.727	.920	1.156	1.476	2.015	2.571	3.365	4.032	6.869
6	.131	.265	.404	.553	.718	.906	1.134	1.440	1.943	2.447	3.143	3.707	5.959
7	.130	.263	.402	.549	.711	.896	1.119	1.415	1.895	2.365	2.998	3.499	5.408
8	.130	.262	.399	.546	.706	.889	1.108	1.397	1.860	2.306	2.896	3.355	5.041
9	.129	.261	.398	.543	.703	.883	1.100	1.383	1.833	2.262	2.821	3.250	4.781
10	.129	.260	.397	.542	.700	.879	1.093	1.372	1.812	2.228	2.764	3.169	4.587
11	.129	.260	.396	.540	.697	.876	1.088	1.363	1.796	2.201	2.718	3.106	4.437
12	.128	.259	.395	.539	.695	.873	1.083	1.356	1.782	2.179	2.681	3.055	4.318
13	.128	.259	.394	.538	.694	.870	1.079	1.350	1.771	2.160	2.650	3.012	4.221
14	.128	.258	.393	.537	.692	.868	1.076	1.345	1.761	2.145	2.624	2.977	4.140
15	.128	.258	.393	.536	.691	.866	1.074	1.341	1.753	2.131	2.602	2.947	4.073
16	.128	.258	.392	.535	.690	.865	1.071	1.337	1.746	2.120	2.583	2.921	4.015
17	.128	.257	.392	.534	.689	.863	1.069	1.333	1.740	2.110	2.567	2.898	3.965
18	.127	.257	.392	.534	.688	.862	1.067	1.330	1.734	2.101	2.552	2.878	3.922
19	.127	.257	.391	.533	.688	.861	1.066	1.328	1.729	2.093	2.539	2.861	3.883
20	.127	.257	.391	.533	.687	.860	1.064	1.325	1.725	2.086	2.528	2.845	3.850
21	.127	.257	.391	.532	.686	.859	1.063	1.323	1.721	2.080	2.518	2.831	3.819
22	.127	.256	.390	.532	.686	.858	1.061	1.321	1.717	2.074	2.508	2.819	3.792
23	.127	.256	.390	.532	.685	.858	1.060	1.319	1.714	2.069	2.500	2.807	3.767
24	.127	.256	.390	.531	.685	.857	1.059	1.318	1.711	2.064	2.492	2.797	3.745
25	.127	.256	.390	.531	.684	.856	1.058	1.316	1.708	2.060	2.485	2.787	3.725
26	.127	.256	.390	.531	.684	.856	1.058	1.315	1.706	2.056	2.479	2.779	3.707
27	.127	.256	.389	.531	.684	.855	1.057	1.314	1.703	2.052	2.473	2.771	3.690
28	.127	.256	.389	.530	.683	.855	1.056	1.313	1.701	2.048	2.467	2.763	3.674
29	.127	.256	.389	.530	.683	.854	1.055	1.311	1.699	2.045	2.462	2.756	3.659
30	.127	.256	.389	.530	.683	.854	1.055	1.310	1.697	2.042	2.457	2.750	3.646
40	.126	.255	.388	.529	.681	.851	1.050	1.303	1.684	2.021	2.423	2.704	3.551
60	.126	.254	.387	.527	.679	.848	1.046	1.296	1.671	2.000	2.390	2.660	3.460
120	.126	.254	.386	.526	.677	.845	1.041	1.289	1.658	1.980	2.358	2.617	3.373
Normal = ∞	.126	.253	.385	.524	.674	.842	1.036	1.282	1.645	1.960	2.326	2.576	3.291
One-tailed	45%	40%	35%	30%	25%	20%	15%	10%	5%	2.5%	1%	0.5%	0.05%

Appendix 7

Significance Table for *F*-Test

(Reprinted from *Statistical Tables for Biological, Agricultural and Medical Research 6th edition*, by R. A. Fisher and F. Yates, Longman, 1974, by permission.)

Research by R.A. Fisher and F. Yates, Oliver and Boyd, Edinburgh 1963.)

No. of degrees of freedom v_1	1	2	3	4	5	6	8	12	24	∞
No. of degrees of freedom v_2										
1	39.86	49.50	53.59	55.83	57.24	58.20	59.44	60.70	62.00	63.33
2	8.53	9.00	9.16	9.24	9.29	9.33	9.37	9.41	9.45	9.49
3	5.54	5.46	5.39	5.34	5.31	5.28	5.25	5.22	5.18	5.13
4	4.54	4.32	4.19	4.11	4.05	4.01	3.95	3.90	3.83	3.76
5	4.06	3.78	3.62	3.52	3.45	3.40	3.34	3.27	3.19	3.10
6	3.78	3.46	3.29	3.18	3.11	3.05	2.98	2.90	2.82	2.72
7	3.59	3.26	3.07	2.96	2.88	2.83	2.75	2.67	2.58	2.47
8	3.46	3.11	2.92	2.81	2.73	2.67	2.59	2.50	2.40	2.29
9	3.36	3.01	2.81	2.69	2.61	2.55	2.47	2.38	2.28	2.16
10	3.28	2.92	2.73	2.61	2.52	2.46	2.38	2.28	2.18	2.06
11	3.23	2.86	2.66	2.54	2.45	2.39	2.30	2.21	2.10	1.97
12	3.18	2.81	2.61	2.48	2.39	2.33	2.24	2.15	2.04	1.90
13	3.14	2.76	2.56	2.43	2.35	2.28	2.20	2.10	1.98	1.85
14	3.10	2.73	2.52	2.39	2.31	2.24	2.15	2.05	1.94	1.80
15	3.07	2.70	2.49	2.36	2.27	2.21	2.12	2.02	1.90	1.76
16	3.05	2.67	2.46	2.33	2.24	2.18	2.09	1.99	1.87	1.72
17	3.03	2.64	2.44	2.31	2.22	2.15	2.06	1.96	1.84	1.69
18	3.01	2.62	2.42	2.29	2.20	2.13	2.04	1.93	1.81	1.66
19	2.99	2.61	2.40	2.27	2.18	2.11	2.02	1.91	1.79	1.63
20	2.97	2.59	2.38	2.25	2.16	2.09	2.00	1.89	1.77	1.61
21	2.96	2.57	2.36	2.23	2.14	2.08	1.98	1.88	1.75	1.59
22	2.95	2.56	2.35	2.22	2.13	2.06	1.97	1.86	1.73	1.57
23	2.94	2.55	2.34	2.21	2.11	2.05	1.95	1.84	1.72	1.55
24	2.93	2.54	2.33	2.19	2.10	2.04	1.94	1.83	1.70	1.53
25	2.92	2.53	2.32	2.18	2.09	2.02	1.93	1.82	1.69	1.52
26	2.91	2.52	2.31	2.17	2.08	2.01	1.92	1.81	1.68	1.50
27	2.90	2.51	2.30	2.17	2.07	2.00	1.91	1.80	1.67	1.49
28	2.89	2.50	2.29	2.16	2.06	2.00	1.90	1.79	1.66	1.48
29	2.89	2.50	2.28	2.15	2.06	1.99	1.89	1.78	1.65	1.47
30	2.88	2.49	2.28	2.14	2.05	1.98	1.88	1.77	1.64	1.46
40	2.84	2.44	2.23	2.09	2.00	1.93	1.83	1.71	1.57	1.38
60	2.79	2.39	2.18	2.04	1.95	1.87	1.77	1.66	1.51	1.29
120	2.75	2.35	2.13	1.99	1.90	1.82	1.72	1.60	1.45	1.19
∞	2.71	2.30	2.08	1.94	1.85	1.77	1.67	1.55	1.38	1.00

Probability 5%

No. of degrees of freedom v_1	1	2	3	4	5	6	8	12	24	∞
No. of degrees of freedom v_2										
1	161.4	199.5	215.7	224.6	230.2	234.0	238.9	243.9	249.0	254.3
2	18.51	19.00	19.16	19.25	19.30	19.33	19.37	19.41	19.45	19.50
3	10.13	9.55	9.28	9.12	9.01	8.94	8.84	8.74	8.64	8.53
4	7.71	6.94	6.59	6.39	6.26	6.16	6.04	5.91	5.77	5.63
5	6.61	5.79	5.41	5.19	5.05	4.95	4.82	4.68	4.53	4.36
6	5.99	5.14	4.76	4.53	4.39	4.28	4.15	4.00	3.84	3.67
7	5.59	4.74	4.35	4.12	3.97	3.87	3.73	3.57	3.41	3.23
8	5.32	4.46	4.07	3.84	3.69	3.58	3.44	3.28	3.12	2.93
9	5.12	4.26	3.86	3.63	3.48	3.37	3.23	3.07	2.90	2.71
10	4.96	4.10	3.71	3.48	3.33	3.22	3.07	2.91	2.74	2.54
11	4.84	3.98	3.59	3.36	3.20	3.09	2.95	2.79	2.61	2.40
12	4.75	3.88	3.49	3.26	3.11	3.00	2.85	2.69	2.50	2.30
13	4.67	3.80	3.41	3.18	3.02	2.92	2.77	2.60	2.42	2.21
14	4.60	3.74	3.34	3.11	2.96	2.85	2.70	2.53	2.35	2.13
15	4.54	3.68	3.29	3.06	2.90	2.79	2.64	2.48	2.29	2.07
16	4.49	3.63	3.24	3.01	2.85	2.74	2.59	2.42	2.24	2.01
17	4.45	3.59	3.20	2.96	2.81	2.70	2.55	2.38	2.19	1.96
18	4.41	3.55	3.16	2.93	2.77	2.66	2.51	2.34	2.15	1.92
19	4.38	3.52	3.13	2.90	2.74	2.63	2.48	2.31	2.11	1.88
20	4.35	3.49	3.10	2.87	2.71	2.60	2.45	2.28	2.08	1.84
21	4.32	3.47	3.07	2.84	2.68	2.57	2.42	2.25	2.05	1.81
22	4.30	3.44	3.05	2.82	2.66	2.55	2.40	2.23	2.03	1.78
23	4.28	3.42	3.03	2.80	2.64	2.53	2.38	2.20	2.00	1.76
24	4.26	3.40	3.01	2.78	2.62	2.51	2.36	2.18	1.98	1.73
25	4.24	3.38	2.99	2.76	2.60	2.49	2.34	2.16	1.96	1.71
26	4.22	3.37	2.98	2.74	2.59	2.47	2.32	2.15	1.95	1.69
27	4.21	3.35	2.96	2.73	2.57	2.46	2.30	2.13	1.93	1.67
28	4.20	3.34	2.95	2.71	2.56	2.44	2.29	2.12	1.91	1.65
29	4.18	3.33	2.93	2.70	2.54	2.43	2.28	2.10	1.90	1.64
30	4.17	3.32	2.92	2.69	2.53	2.42	2.27	2.09	1.89	1.62
40	4.08	3.23	2.84	2.61	2.45	2.34	2.18	2.00	2.79	1.51
60	4.00	3.15	2.76	2.52	2.37	2.25	2.10	1.92	1.70	2.39
120	3.92	3.07	2.68	2.45	2.29	2.17	2.02	1.83	1.61	1.25
∞	3.84	2.99	2.60	2.37	2.21	2.10	1.94	1.75	1.52	1.00

Probability 1%

No. of degrees of freedom v_1	1	2	3	4	5	6	8	12	24	∞
No. of degrees of freedom v_2										
1	4052.	4999.	5403.	5625.	5764.	5859.	5982.	6106.	6234.	6366.
2	98.50	99.00	99.17	99.25	99.30	99.33	99.37	99.42	99.46	99.50
3	34.12	30.82	29.46	28.71	28.24	27.91	27.49	27.05	26.60	26.12
4	21.20	18.00	16.69	15.98	15.52	15.21	14.80	14.37	13.93	13.46
5	16.26	13.27	12.06	11.39	10.97	10.67	10.29	9.89	9.47	9.02
6	13.74	10.92	9.78	9.15	8.75	8.47	8.10	7.72	7.31	6.88
7	12.25	9.55	8.45	7.85	7.46	7.19	6.84	6.47	6.07	5.65
8	11.26	8.65	7.59	7.01	6.63	6.37	6.03	5.67	5.28	4.86
9	10.56	8.02	6.99	6.42	6.06	5.80	5.47	5.11	4.73	4.31
10	10.04	7.56	6.55	5.99	5.64	5.39	5.06	4.71	4.33	3.91
11	9.65	7.20	6.22	5.67	5.32	5.07	4.74	4.40	4.02	3.60
12	9.33	6.93	5.95	5.41	5.06	4.82	4.50	4.16	3.78	3.36
13	9.07	6.70	5.74	5.20	4.86	4.62	4.30	3.96	3.59	3.16
14	8.86	6.51	5.56	5.03	4.69	4.46	4.14	3.80	3.43	3.00
15	8.68	6.36	5.42	4.89	4.56	4.32	4.00	3.67	3.29	2.87
16	8.53	6.23	5.29	4.77	4.44	4.20	3.89	3.55	3.18	2.75
17	8.40	6.11	5.18	4.67	4.34	4.10	3.79	3.45	3.08	2.65
18	8.28	6.01	5.09	4.58	4.25	4.01	3.71	3.37	3.00	2.57
19	8.18	5.93	5.01	4.50	4.17	3.94	3.63	3.30	2.92	2.49
20	8.10	5.85	4.94	4.43	4.10	3.87	3.56	3.23	2.86	2.42
21	8.02	5.78	4.87	4.37	4.04	3.81	3.51	3.17	2.80	2.36
22	7.94	5.72	4.82	4.31	3.99	3.76	3.45	3.12	2.75	2.31
23	7.88	5.66	4.76	4.26	3.94	3.71	3.41	3.07	2.70	2.26
24	7.82	5.61	4.72	4.22	3.90	3.67	3.36	3.03	2.66	2.21
25	7.77	5.57	4.68	4.18	3.86	3.63	3.32	2.99	2.62	2.17
26	7.72	5.53	4.64	4.14	3.82	3.59	3.29	2.96	2.58	2.13
27	7.68	5.49	4.60	4.11	3.78	3.56	3.26	2.93	2.55	2.10
28	7.64	5.45	4.57	4.07	3.75	3.53	3.23	2.90	2.52	2.06
29	7.60	5.42	4.54	4.04	3.73	3.50	3.20	2.87	2.49	2.03
30	7.56	5.39	4.51	4.02	3.70	3.47	3.17	2.84	2.47	2.01
40	7.31	5.18	4.31	3.83	3.51	3.29	2.99	2.66	2.29	1.80
60	7.08	4.98	4.13	3.65	3.34	3.12	2.82	2.50	2.12	1.60
120	6.85	4.79	3.95	3.48	3.17	2.96	2.66	2.34	1.95	1.38
∞	6.64	4.60	3.78	3.32	3.02	2.80	2.51	2.18	1.79	1.00

No. of degrees of freedom v_1	1	2	3	4	5	6	8	12	24	∞
No. of degrees of freedom v_2										
1	405284	500000	540379	562500	576405	585937	598144	610667	623497	636619
2	998.5	999.0	999.2	999.2	999.3	999.3	999.4	999.4	999.5	999.5
3	167.0	148.5	141.1	137.1	134.6	132.8	130.6	128.3	125.9	123.5
4	74.14	61.25	56.18	53.44	51.71	50.53	49.00	47.41	45.77	44.05
5	47.18	37.12	33.20	31.09	29.75	28.84	27.64	26.42	25.14	23.78
6	35.51	27.00	23.70	21.92	20.81	20.03	19.03	17.99	16.89	15.75
7	29.25	21.69	18.77	17.19	16.21	15.52	14.63	13.71	12.73	11.69
8	25.42	18.49	15.83	14.39	13.49	12.86	12.04	11.19	10.30	9.34
9	22.86	16.39	13.90	12.56	11.71	11.13	10.37	9.57	8.72	7.81
10	21.04	14.91	12.55	11.28	10.48	9.92	9.20	8.45	7.64	6.76
11	19.69	13.81	11.56	10.35	9.58	9.05	8.35	7.63	6.85	6.00
12	18.64	12.97	10.80	9.63	8.89	8.38	7.71	7.00	6.25	5.42
13	17.81	12.31	10.21	9.07	8.35	7.86	7.21	6.52	5.78	4.97
14	17.14	11.78	9.73	8.62	7.92	7.43	6.80	6.13	5.41	4.60
15	16.59	11.34	9.34	8.25	7.57	7.09	6.47	5.81	5.10	4.31
16	16.12	10.97	9.00	7.94	7.27	6.81	6.19	5.55	4.85	4.06
17	15.72	10.66	8.73	7.68	7.02	6.56	5.96	5.32	4.63	3.85
18	15.38	10.39	8.49	7.46	6.81	6.35	5.76	5.13	4.45	3.67
19	15.08	10.16	8.28	7.26	6.62	6.18	5.59	4.97	4.29	3.52
20	14.82	9.95	8.10	7.10	6.46	6.02	5.44	4.82	4.15	3.38
21	14.59	9.77	7.94	6.95	6.32	5.88	5.31	4.70	4.03	3.26
22	14.38	9.61	7.80	6.81	6.19	5.76	5.19	4.58	3.92	3.15
23	14.19	9.47	7.67	6.69	6.08	5.65	5.09	4.48	3.82	3.05
24	14.03	9.34	7.55	6.59	5.98	5.55	4.99	4.39	3.74	2.97
25	13.88	9.22	7.45	6.49	5.88	5.46	4.91	4.31	3.66	2.89
26	13.74	9.12	7.36	6.41	5.80	5.38	4.83	4.24	3.59	2.82
27	13.61	9.02	7.27	6.33	5.73	5.31	4.76	4.17	3.52	2.75
28	13.50	8.93	7.19	6.25	5.66	5.24	4.69	4.11	3.46	2.70
29	13.39	8.85	7.12	6.19	5.59	5.18	4.64	4.05	3.41	2.64
30	13.29	8.77	7.05	6.12	5.53	5.12	4.58	4.00	3.36	2.59
40	12.61	8.25	6.60	5.70	5.13	4.73	4.21	3.64	3.01	2.23
60	11.97	7.76	6.17	5.31	4.76	4.37	3.87	3.31	2.69	1.90
120	11.38	7.32	5.79	4.95	4.42	4.04	3.55	3.02	2.40	1.54
∞	10.83	6.91	5.42	4.62	4.10	3.74	3.27	2.74	2.13	1.00

Appendix 8

Derivation of Formulae for Combining Variances

Consider two variables x and y and let z be a known function of x and y

$$\bar{z} = f(\bar{x}, \bar{y})$$

the mean values of x and y are $\bar{x}$ and $\bar{y}$, thus,

$$\bar{z} = f(\bar{x}, \bar{y})$$

provided that x and y are independent (unrelated).

Take a pair of x, y values where x is an amount Δx from $\bar{x}$ and y is an amount Δy from $\bar{y}$. The difference Δz between z and $\bar{z}$ may be estimated:

$$\Delta z \simeq \frac{\partial z}{\partial x} \Delta x + \frac{\partial z}{\partial y} \Delta y \qquad (1)$$

If a large number n of x, y pairs is taken then the variance of z may be calculated as:

$$\text{Variance of } z = \sigma_z^2 = \Sigma(\Delta z)^2/n \qquad (2)$$

$$= \left(\frac{\partial z}{\partial x}\right)^2 \frac{(\Delta x)^2}{n} + \left(\frac{\partial z}{\partial y}\right)^2 \frac{(\Delta y)^2}{n} +$$

$$+ 2\frac{\partial z}{\partial x}\frac{\partial z}{\partial y}\frac{\Delta x \, \Delta y}{n}$$

but

$(\Delta x)^2/n$ is the variance of $x = \sigma_x^2$

$(\Delta y)^2/n$ is the variance of $y = \sigma_y^2$

and

$\Delta x \, \Delta y/n$ is the covariance of x and y which equals σ_{xy}^2. (This is the same as s_{xy} used in Chapter 2.)

If x and y are independent (that is unrelated) then the covariance of x and y is zero, and hence the variance of z becomes:

$$\sigma_z^2 = \left(\frac{\partial z}{\partial x}\right)^2 \sigma_x^2 + \left(\frac{\partial z}{\partial y}\right)^2 \sigma_y^2 \qquad (3)$$

Four functions of x and y are now considered, namely addition, subtraction, multiplication and division.

(i) *Addition* $z = x + y$
   Partially differentiating
   $$\frac{\partial z}{\partial x} = 1 \text{ and } \frac{\partial z}{\partial y} = 1$$
   Substituting into Equation 3,
   $$\sigma_z^2 = \sigma_x^2 + \sigma_y^2 \qquad (4)$$

(ii) *Subtraction* $z = x - y$
   Partially differentiating
   $$\frac{\partial z}{\partial x} = 1 \text{ and } \frac{\partial z}{\partial y} = -1$$
   Substituting into Equation 3
   $$\sigma_z^2 = \sigma_x^2 + \sigma_y^2 \qquad (5)$$

(iii) *Multiplication* $z = xy$
   Partially differentiating
   $$\frac{\partial z}{\partial x} = y \text{ and } \frac{\partial z}{\partial y} = x$$
   Substituting into Equation 3
   $$\sigma_z^2 = y^2 \sigma_x^2 + x^2 \sigma_y^2$$
   this is sometimes expressed as
   $$\frac{\sigma_z^2}{x^2 y^2} = \frac{\sigma_x^2}{x^2} + \frac{\sigma_y^2}{y^2}$$
   or
   $$\frac{\sigma_z^2}{z^2} = \frac{\sigma_x^2}{x^2} + \frac{\sigma_y^2}{y^2} \qquad (6)$$

(iv) *Division* $z = x/y$
   Partially differentiating

$$\frac{\partial z}{\partial x} = \frac{1}{y} \text{ and } \frac{\partial z}{\partial y} = \frac{-x}{y^2}$$

Substituting into Equation 3

$$\sigma_z{}^2 = \frac{1}{y^2} \sigma_x{}^2 + \frac{x^2}{y^4} \sigma_y{}^2$$

$$\frac{\sigma_z{}^2}{x^2/y^2} = \frac{1}{x^2} \sigma_x{}^2 + \frac{1}{y^2} \sigma_y{}^2$$

Hence

$$\frac{\sigma_z{}^2}{z^2} = \frac{\sigma_x{}^2}{x^2} + \frac{\sigma_y{}^2}{y^2} \tag{7}$$

The final equations for combining variances or standard deviations are the same regardless of whether n or $(n-1)$ is used in the denominator.

Appendix 9

List of Symbols

A	area under curve	$\bar{x}$	mean value of x_i
a, b, c, d	coefficients for quadratic and cubic equations	X_i	$(x_i - \bar{x})$
c	intercept on y axis	y_i	set of y values
D	difference in ranks	$\bar{y}$	mean value of y_i
E	expected frequency (theoretical frequency)	Y_i	$(y_i - \bar{y})$
		Δ	large difference
F	variance ratio (F-test)	∂	partial derivative
$f(\ )$	frequency of	μ	mean of parent population
m	slope of straight line or mean of sample	ν	number of degrees of freedom
m_1, m_2	means of samples 1 and 2	π	3.141 592 65
$n!$	factorial n, i.e. $n \cdot (n-1) \cdot (n-2) \ldots 3.2.1$	ρ	Spearman's rank correlation coefficient
n	number of values	Σ	sum of
O	observed frequency	σ	standard deviation of parent population
r	Pearson's correlation coefficient	σ^2	variance of parent populatition
s, s_1, s_2, s_x, s_y	standard deviations	τ	Kendall's rank correlation coefficient
s_{xy}	covariance of x and y		
t	Student's t value	χ^2	chi-squared
x_i	set of x values	$\int$	integral of

Answers and Solutions

1.1 (b) 0.5 matches, 7.0 cm

1.2 Density = mass/volume
$$= 3.8251/(4/3 \times 3.1416 \times 0.563^3)$$
$$= 5.117 \text{ g cm}^{-3}$$

Relative error in answer
$$= \frac{0.0001}{3.8251} + \frac{0.0005}{1.126} \times 3 = 0.001\ 36$$

Absolute error
$$= 0.001\ 36 \times 5.117 = 0.0070$$
Hence result is 5.117 ± 0.007 g cm^{-3}

1.3 Refer to Fig. 1.1
(a) 15.87% below mean corresponds to one standard deviation, hence machine should be set to 255 g.
(b) 260 g
(c) 265 g

2.1 Sample mean = 60 m.p.h.; standard deviation of sample = 7 m.p.h.
Estimated mean for all cars = 60 m.p.h.; estimated standard deviation for all cars = 7.15 m.p.h. (For the last result the divisor was $(n-1) = 23$ rather than $n = 24$.)

2.2 Mean = 160 cm; standard deviation = 6.63 cm with Yates's correction

2.3 (a) Mean = 2μ; standard deviation
$$= \sqrt{(\sigma^2 + \sigma^2)} = \sqrt{(2 \cdot \sigma)}$$
(b) Mean = 0; standard deviation
$$= \sqrt{(2 \cdot \sigma)}$$
(c) Mean = μ; standard deviation
$$= \tfrac{1}{2}\sqrt{(2 \cdot \sigma)} = \sigma/\sqrt{2}$$
(d) Mean = 0; standard deviation
$$= \sigma/\sqrt{2}$$

2.4 (a) Mean = 110; standard deviation
= 14.1
(b) Mean = 0; standard deviation = 0
(c) mean = 55, standard deviation
= 7.07

2.5 Mean = £75. Median is in the range £65–75. 104 people have wages < £65 and 168 have wages < £75. Assuming that the wages of the 64 people in this group are evenly distributed, the wage of the 150.5th. person (median wage) is estimated as £72.3.
Mean-mode approximately equals (mean-median) × 3, hence mode approximately equals £66.9.
Standard deviation = £20.1 hence skewness = +0.403

3.1 Mean catch on one day = 650 lbs
Mean weight in one box = 26 lbs
Estimated standard deviation for catch on one day = 112 lbs
Estimated standard deviation for one box = 22.4 lbs

3.2 The sample of 13 people will have a mean weight of $13 \times 70 = 910$ kg and a standard deviation of $\sqrt{13} \times 10 = 36.1$ kg. To overload the lift requires a weight of 90 kg above the mean which is 2.5 standard deviations. Since by central limit theorem the sample means are approximately normally distributed, the chance of this occurring is $1 - 0.9938 = 0.0062 = 1/161$. Thus there is a 1/161 chance of overloading the lift with 13 people. Without being superstitious, this is not very safe!

3.3 $4925 - (75 \times 64) = 125$ kg

$125/(8 \times \sqrt{64}) = 1.953$ standard deviations

From normal distribution table (Appendix 4) probability of a weight less than 1.953 standard deviations is 97.46% hence probability of being overweight $= 2.54\%$

3.4 Mean thickness of 100 washers
$= 249.82$ mm

Standard deviation of 100 washers
$= 2.42$

Estimated value for mean thickness of 1 washer $= 2.50$ mm

Estimated value for standard deviation of 1 washer $= 2.42/\sqrt{100} = 0.242$ mm

4.1 15 apples $= 10\%$. From normal table $= 1.282\sigma$

30 apples $= 20\%$. From normal table $= 0.842\sigma$.

Mean $- 1.282\sigma = 71$

Mean $+ 0.842\sigma = 103$

Hence mean $= 90.3$ g and $\sigma = 15.1$ g.

53 apples above 96 g

4.2 Hint! How many standard deviations are needed for 25% and 75% of a normal population?

4.3 See Table S1. Probability of being in range 100–110 is $0.7340 - 0.5000 = 0.2340$ (since the curve is symmetrical, this is also the value for the range 90–100).

Table S1

Value	Number of standard deviations from mean	Area under normal curve up to this point
100	0	0.5000
110	0.625	0.7340
120	1.25	0.8944
130	1.875	0.9696

Similarly for 110–120 and 80–90 probability $= 0.1604$

Similarly for 120–130 and 70–80 probability $= 0.0752$

Similarly for > 130 and < 70 probability $= 0.0304$.

4.4 Mean $= 1.01$, variance $= 0.93$, Poisson distribution:

Number of houses struck			
0	1	2	3 or more
Number of years			
36.4	36.8	18.6	8.2

The data appear to fit a Poisson distribution. This is suggested by the fact that the mean and variance are approximately equal. (A chi-squared test could be used to confirm that the data do not differ significantly from Poisson. Chi-squared $= 0.54$.)

5.1 (a) Chi-squared $= 8.88$, probability of worst chi-squared from a fair die $= 11\%$, hence there are no grounds to suspect the die.

(b) Chi-squared $= 8.21$, probability of worst chi-squared from a fair die $= 0.4\%$, hence die almost certainly unfair.

These results are not contradictory! The die is unfair if one tests the frequency of 3's specifically, but not sufficiently unfair to show in a general test.

5.2 Frequency of digits

7	9	14	8	12	8	12	9	12	9
Digits									
0	1	2	3	4	5	6	7	8	9

chi-squared $= 4.8$, probability of larger chi-squared from random digits $= 85\%$.

5.3 Chi-squared $= 15.36$, probability of worse results $= 3.2\%$ which suggests either that the theory is wrong or that the data are inaccurate or fabricated.

5.4 If there is no preference then the number of people on each beach will be as follows:

	A	B	C
No. males	72	72	96
No. females	78	78	104

Chi-squared = 4.32, 2 degrees of freedom, probability of a larger discrepancy arising by chance is 12%, hence there is no evidence that the proportion of females differs significantly.

5.5 Chi-squared = 10.4, probability of worse results by chance if the wheel is fair is 0.1%. It is highly likely that the wheel is biased. With 35 zeros, chi-squared = 2.14 and the probability of worse results by chance is 14%, hence there is no evidence for a biased wheel.

5.6 Chi-squared = 2·54, probability of worse results by chance is 11%. There is no evidence that the proportions of animals suffering vitamin deficiency differ between the two diets.

5.7 Expected Poisson distribution

Number of deaths					
0	1	2	3	4	5 or more
Number of days					
203.4	251.4	155.3	64.0	19.8	6.1

Chi-squared = 3.06, probability of more different results arising by chance = 55%, hence the data do not differ significantly from a Poisson distribution.

5.8 Chi-squared = 0.05 (remember the Yates's correction). Probability of worse results = 82%. The data agree with the theory, and are not so good that their authenticity is questioned.

6.1 Difference in means = 24 hours
Standard error of difference in means = 11.8 hours.

Difference in means = 2.03 standard errors.
Using a normal table the probability of A appearing better than B by this amount is $1 - 0.9788 = 0.0212 = 2.12\%$ if the bulbs are both as good. This provides moderately strong evidence that bulbs A last longer than bulbs B.

6.2 Difference in means = 24 hours
Standard error of difference in means = 12.3 hours
Difference in means = 1.95 standard errors which is insignificant at the 5% level.

6.3 Difference in means = 2.76 standard errors, which is significant at the 1% level, hence there is strong evidence for an increase in mean height.

6.4 Estimated standard deviation for the combined sample =

$$\sqrt{\left[\frac{(11-1)\times 1.2^2 + (8-1)\times 1.4^2}{(11-1) + (8-1)}\right]}$$
$$= 1.29 \text{ metres}$$

Standard error of difference in means $= 1.29 \sqrt{(1/11 + 1/8)} = 0.598$ metres.
Difference in means $= 5.3 - 4.2 = 1.1$ metres = 1.84 standard errors. Using a t-table (Appendix 6) with $(11-1) + (8-1) = 17$ degrees of freedom, the probability of a t-value of 1.84 occurring by chance is between 5% and $2\frac{1}{2}\%$ (one tailed). If the missiles are equally good/bad then there is more than a $2\frac{1}{2}\%$ chance of getting results which show B to be better by so much, and a $2\frac{1}{2}\%$ chance of getting results which show A to be better by the same amount. There is no statistical evidence that the missiles differ significantly.

6.5 Road A mean = 30.0 m.p.h.; estimated standard deviation = 0.616 m.p.h.

Road B mean = 31.0 m.p.h.; estimated standard deviation = 0.990 m.p.h.
Estimated standard deviation for the combined group = 0.798 m.p.h.
Difference in means = 1 m.p.h.
Standard error of difference in means = 0.402 m.p.h.
Difference in means = 2.49 standard errors
Using a t-table (Appendix 6) with $(9-1)+(7-1) = 14$ degrees of freedom, the probability of a t-value of 2.49 arising by chance if the mean speed of all cars (rather than the small samples) is the same is between 5% and 2% (two tailed). Since there is less than a 5% probability of the observed result occurring by chance if the mean speed of all cars is the same, it is reasonable to conclude that the mean speeds of cars on the two roads are significantly different.
$F = 2.58$
Using the F-tables (Appendix 7) with $v_1 = (7-1)$ and $v_2 = (9-1)$ it is found that the calculated F value is less than the 10% significance value of 2.67, hence there is more than a 10% probability of standard deviations as different arising by chance if the standard deviation of all cars (as opposed to the samples) is the same. There is no statistical evidence that the standard deviations of speeds of cars on the two roads are different, thus the result of the t-test is valid.

7.1 (a) $r = 0$ (no linear correlation)
(b) $r = 0.996$ (high degree of linear correlation)

7.2 $r = 0.831$. Using the table in Appendix 1 with 8 degrees of freedom the 1% significance value is 0.765 hence the correlation is very significant.

7.3 $r = 0.742$. 5% significance value = 0.707 hence result is significant at this level.

7.4 Observer 1 $\rho = 0.6$, Observer 2 $\rho = 0.7$

hence Observer 2 was the most self consistent.

7.5 $\rho = 0.9$. Using the table in Appendix 2 with $n = 5$ the result is significant at the 5% level.

7.6 $\tau = 0.714$. Using Appendix 3 with $n = 8$ shows that agreement is significant at the 5% level.

8.1 x on y $x = -0.5y + 12.75$
     y on x $y = -0.125x + 6.75$

8.2 (b) 41.25, 52.5, 56.25, 68.75, 98.75, 106.25
(c) age (x), pocket money (y), slope 13.61, intercept -113.1.

8.3 Slope -0.0163, intercept 53.4, cost £45.20

8.4 Slope 2.3, intercept 4.3, bill £11.20

8.5 x on y slope 0.696, intercept 4.42, age of wife 21.8 years
     y on x slope 0.814, intercept 8.49, age of husband 28.8 years

8.6 Population (x), Civil Servants (y), slope 1.34, intercept 1.85, Civil Servants 22.

10.1 (a) $x = 1$ or $x = 2$
(b) $x = 1$ (two coincident roots)
(c) $x = (2+i)$ or $x = (2-i)$

10.2 (a) $L = 0$, $U = 1.6$ $L = 0.8$, $U = 1.6$, then $L = 0.8$, $U = 1.2$, then solution at $x = 1$.
(b) $x = 2$
(c) $x = 3$

10.3 Derivative of $x = 1$, derivative of cos $x = -\sin x$.

$$x_{i+1} = x_i - \frac{x_i - \cos x_i}{1 + \sin x_i}$$

$x_0 = 0$
$x_1 = 1$
$x_2 = 0.7504$
$x_3 = 0.7391$ (this is the solution to 4 significant figures)

10.4 $x = 2.195$

11.1   (a) 333; (b) 324; (c) 324

11.2
(a) $\frac{1}{2}(1+\sqrt{3}) = 1.367$

(b) $\frac{1}{3}(1+2\sqrt{3}) = 1.488$

(c) $\pi r^2/2 = \frac{1}{2}\pi = 1.571$

11.3
(a) $\frac{1}{4}(\frac{1}{2}\sqrt{7}+\sqrt{3}+\frac{1}{2}\sqrt{15}+1) = 1.498$

(b) $\frac{1}{6}(\sqrt{7}+\sqrt{3}+\sqrt{15}+1) = 1.542$

(c) 1.571

Index